ROMAN DRAMA

STUDIES IN LATIN LITERATURE
AND ITS INFLUENCE

Editors

D. R. Dudley and T. A. Dorey

CICERO

Chapters by J. P. V. D. Balsdon, M. L. Clarke, T. A. Dorey, A. E. Douglas, R. G. M. Nisbet, H. H. Scullard, G. B. Townend

LUCRETIUS

Chapters by D. R. Dudley, B. Farrington, O. E. Lowenstein, W. S. Maguinness, T. J. B. Spencer, G. B. Townend, D. E. W. Wormell

ROMAN DRAMA

Chapters by W. R. Chalmers, C. D. N. Costa, G. L. Evans, J. A. Hanson, A. Steegman, T. B. L. Webster, T. L. Zinn

ROMAN DRAMA

C. D. N. Costa   T. L. Zinn
John Arthur Hanson   Gareth Lloyd-Evans
T. B. L. Webster   Andre Steegman
Walter R. Chalmers

Edited by
T. A. DOREY
and
DONALD R. DUDLEY

BASIC BOOKS, INC., PUBLISHERS
NEW YORK

Contents

Illustrations

Introduction

DONALD R. DUDLEY

SHAKESPEARE has set the influence of Roman drama at its highest in the words with which Polonius commends the players at Elsinore:

> The best actors in the world either for tragedy, comedy, history, pastoral, pastoral-comical, historical-pastoral, tragical-historical, tragical-comical-historical-pastoral, scene individible, or poem unlimited: Seneca cannot be too heavy nor Plautus too light.

Here is the full range of drama (real and imaginary) as known to the Renaissance world, and it exists under the joint consulship, so to say, of Seneca and Plautus. In a sense the compliment is more than they deserve. It is by an accident of history that the playwrights of the Renaissance traced their ancestry back to Plautus, Terence, and Seneca, rather than to the Greek authors from whom the Romans derive. One might fairly say that, if the plays of Seneca are indeed the ancestors of *Lear* and *Hamlet* and *Macbeth*, it is in the same way that the pterodactyl is the ancestor of the bird— it is not the ancestry of genius, as in the sequence Homer-Virgil-Dante-Milton. As for Plautus and Terence, other factors were in their favour in sixteenth- and seventeenth-century Europe. Boys had to learn Latin, and they like to act: there was room for the rollicking fun of Plautus and the pure Latin and refined sentiments of Terence. Hence the vogue for Latin plays, original or imitative, in the schools, universities, and courts of Europe. And when the Jesuits felt the need for something better attuned to the Christian ethos, the result was the Jesuit college drama, a true derivative of the Roman theatre. *Habent sua fata libelli*. If the Roman playwrights for so long commanded greater attention than perhaps their intrinsic merits allow, in modern times they have certainly had to make do with less. In the schoolroom, as in the theatre, the Greeks have put them into eclipse. In tragedy there is no cause for regret: Seneca could not contend in any case with Aeschylus, Sophocles, and Euripides, still less when they have been reinforced by Shaw and Gilbert Murray, by the Greek National Theatre, and by the fine translations of Greek tragedy which have appeared in recent years. In comedy, the case is rather different. We must concede the greater claims of Aristophanes, especially in an age when his brilliantly imaginative bawdiness is a recommendation rather than an impediment. But Plautus and Terence have their merits. It is wrong that a classics master should, in the words of a contributor (p. 194) 'know' 'that Latin plays are dull, derivative, badly constructed, lacking in imagination, artificial, banal, and humourless: and what is more that if you know one you know them all'. It is wrong because it is untrue, as our contributor found out in the best of all possible ways, by putting them on the stage. For that, of course, is what the Roman comedians demand—and deserve. Yet, though school and university performances of Latin plays occur sporadically in Britain and the United States, the Westminster Latin Play alone, so far as we know, has an established tradition.

On the professional stage, neglect was for long absolute. Professor Allardyce Nicoll informs us that he can trace no professional production of a Roman comedy anywhere in the world between 1900 and 1930. In recent years there has been a welcome change. Three plays of Plautus have been staged in Warsaw. The Milan Little Theatre has presented *Il Vantatore*, a version of the *Miles Gloriosus*, in the language and setting of Trastevere. *The Comedy of Errors*, a Shakespearean derivative from Plautus, was for two seasons the most popular comedy at Stratford: modern derivatives in *The Boys from Syracuse* and *A Funny Thing Happened on the Way to the Forum* have had successful runs in London and New York. The illustrations we present of *A Funny Thing* show in spirited fashion some of the reasons for its appeal. Surveying the concurrence of these three plays, a *Times* editorial declared Plautus the leading dramatist on the London stage. Terence, as yet, has had no share in the revival, but may do so if the vogue is sustained. (Even Seneca may not be beyond the sympathies of an age that has seen the possibility of undiluted evil, and conceived a taste for the Theatre of Cruelty.) The time may now be ripe, we feel, to plead for a step which would firmly establish Plautus and Terence in the dramatic experience of the modern world. By this we mean the regular presentation of their plays by a professional company, the only way to build up a theatrical tradition which could compare (*mutatis mutandis*) with the Comédie Française or the Greek National Theatre. In these days of theatre festivals it is surely not an impracticable suggestion —especially if it could be realized in one of the great Roman theatres, at Orange perhaps, or Vaison, or Taormina? Or, best of all, at Ostia; an enrichment, truly, of the Roman summer, if to the opera in the Baths of Caracalla could be added a season of Plautus and Terence in the theatre at Ostia Antica! It would be more than a tourist attraction, for there can be no doubt that Plautus, now as of old, would appeal to an Italian audience.

In accordance with the plan of the series, contributions to the present volume deal not only with Roman drama, but also with its Greek background and its influence on later literature. The recent discoveries of substantial portions of the work of Menander make possible a critical estimate of a poet whose stature we have had to take on trust from the judgment of antiquity. Plautus provides the theme for three contributions, one of which deals with his audience and what the plays tell us about their taste, the others, on the *Amphitryo* theme and the *Miles Gloriosus*, are concerned with the long literary tradition fostered by these two plays, which show no sign of being exhausted. A most welcome contribution from France evaluates the influence of Seneca on Corneille and, incidentally, on other writers of the French baroque theatre. Seneca's influence on Shakespeare is discussed in the light of the new understanding of the world of melodrama we have gained from the successful performance of the plays which—as with *Titus Andronicus*—earlier generations had discarded as unsuitable for the stage. The article on the Westminster Latin Play shows the part this time-honoured tradition has played in the life of a great school, and how it has been possible to revive it in the austerities of the post-war world.

Two great gaps, in dramatist and contributor, will at once strike the reader. No article has Terence as its main theme, though he has his place as the comedian most in vogue at Westminster. No Latin author, perhaps, has known such violent fluctuations between popularity and disfavour over the last four centuries. The important subject of 'The Reputation of Terence' was to have been undertaken by Professor Walter Beare, of Bristol, who has done more than any other British scholar in our day to foster an intelligent and discriminating interest in Roman drama. His sudden death means that this project—like so much else—must remain unfulfilled. He is well described in the lines of Ennius:

> doctus, fidelis,
> suavis homo, facundus, suo contentus, beatus,
> scitus, secunda loquens in tempore, commodus, verbum
> paucum, multa tenens antiqua sepulta, vetustas
> maiorum veterum leges divomque hominumque,
> quae faciunt mores veteresque novosque tenentem.

This book is dedicated to his memory.

I

The Comedy of Menander

T. B. L. WEBSTER

THE long line of writers of social comedy from Shakespeare and Goldoni to Galsworthy, A. A. Milne, and their present-day successors have, partly consciously and partly unconsciously, been writing in a tradition which goes back to Plautus and Terence. But Plautus and Terence themselves were adapting and translating Greek New Comedy, which has only recently become known to us from considerable stretches of original text. The approach of the two Roman writers to their Greek originals was very different. Terence translated texts accurately but often flattened out the colour of the original and twice at least combined scenes from two different Greek plays; certainly also he sometimes converted monologues of the original into dialogues. Plautus seems to have been an actor himself and it is a reasonable conjecture that he translated actors' texts rather than library texts; such texts probably preserved the original much less carefully than the library texts which Terence used, and it is at least possible that some of the elements which we regard as Plautine, particularly the expansion of the slave parts, may have been due to Greek actors during the century or so which separates Plautus from his originals. As long as our knowledge of Menander and his contemporaries depended on the adaptations of Plautus and Terence and the numerous short fragments preserved in quotations, we could not appreciate the flavour of Menander's comedy. At the very end of the last century large portions of a papyrus roll were discovered giving two-thirds of Menander's *Arbitrants*, about half of his *Rape of the Locks*, about a third of his *Samian Woman*, and the first scene of his *Hero*. The succeeding years have added considerable fragments from a number of plays, but we only gained a complete play, when in 1959 Professor

V. Martin published the first edition of the papyrus of the *Dyskolos* (or *Grumpy*, to borrow the title of an early twentieth-century comedy).

Let us review some of the general characteristics of this kind of social comedy. Aristotle would have said that the characters were people 'like ourselves', and if he had lived to express himself about the earliest productions of Menander, would have so distinguished them from the characters of mid-fourth century and earlier comedy, whom he calls 'worse than ourselves' in the *Poetics*. The heroes and their families belong to the upper middle class. They move in the same sort of world as we do, even if they have rather more leisure and are more lavishly equipped with butlers, nurses, and housemaids. Comparison with fourth-century Athenians as they appear in the speeches of the Attic orators suggests that Menander probably exaggerates their wealth just about as much as the modern writers of social comedy. The characters are clearly divided into old and young: parents and grandparents are lumped together as old, and the young consist of grown up children. (Young children do not have speaking parts in Menander, although his babies may exercise, as Gilbert Murray said, a devilish ingenuity.) There is also a clear division between masters and servants; it is curious that in the original texts of Menander slaves are not particularly efficient, and it looks as if the really masterful slaves of Roman comedy were developed on hints given in Menander's text by actors who played his comedies between his death and the time of Plautus. Neither action nor language strays far outside the conventions of middle-class life. It is true that Menander writes in verse, because this is the tradition of Greek drama. His spoken iambics are stricter than those of Aristophanes, and though he uses a considerable range from the earthy utterances of slaves to the almost tragic solemnity of love-sick young men and deceived fathers, he does not proceed nearly so far outside the possibilities of conventional speech as Aristophanes. When Menander changes from spoken iambic trimeters to intoned trochaic tetrameters for the scene which contains Knemon's self-defence in the *Dyskolos*, he is probably following a tragic rather than a comic model. The final ballet-like scene in iambic tetrameters is a survival from a more boisterous form of comedy.

No one undertakes anything very adventerous or fantastic or

villainous; no one has any very wild political or anti-social dreams. In Aristophanes Dikaiopolis makes his private peace with Sparta and Peisthetairos builds Cloudcuckoo land to escape from Athenian politics; Menander's soldier who cuts off his mistress's hair because he believes her unfaithful and the kindly uncle who pretends to die so that his property may form a dowry for a penniless girl are pale remnants of such fantastic actions, and their relevance is private not political. The world proceeds on a fairly even and predictable course, but an unexpected event like the shipwreck which lost Pataikos the means to support his orphaned twin-babies in the *Rape of the Locks* or Knemon's disaster of falling down the well in the *Dyskolos* may be introduced to throw a character off balance so that he can gradually recover equilibrium; more often the characters of Menander are thrown off balance by the gossip of their slaves. The only emotion to which one may devote oneself wholeheartedly is the emotion of love, and conjugal felicity is the normal end of this kind of play: its plot consists therefore of the gradual overcoming of the obstacles in the way of conjugal felicity.

The standard obstacle is the disapproval of parent or guardian on either or both sides. Knemon in the *Dyskolos* is the obstacle to his daughter's marriage to the young townsman Sostratos who has fallen in love with her. Knemon so hates the commercial motives which govern the world that he works his considerable farm with no one to help him: 'he likes it best if he can see nobody. He works with his daughter beside him for the most part; he only speaks to her; he finds it difficult to say anything to anybody else; and he says he will only marry her off when he finds a young man exactly like himself '. Sostratos' slave who has tried to make a date for his master is chased off the farm; his helpful friend deserts him; he himself wilts before the torrent of fury which Knemon pours upon him. He has the good luck to help the girl draw water from the spring of the Nymphs, but this action is reported to the girl's half-brother Gorgias as an attempt by the corrupt rich to exploit the honest poor. He convinces Gorgias of his honest intentions and works a day on the farm in the hope that Knemon may accept him as a working man. But Knemon dare not leave his house when he sees a procession approaching the shrine of the Nymphs: Sostratos' mother wishing to sacrifice to avert a bad dream about Sostratos, her daughter, and several slaves; the cook had arrived just before with the sheep for the sacrifice. The cook tries to borrow pots from Knemon but is driven off with contumely. Sostratos returns frustrated and joins his family in the sacrifice. Knemon falls down his well in the attempt to get out the bucket and the mattock which his old slave-woman has dropped in earlier in the play. Gorgias and Sostratos rescue him. He is so shattered that he tells Gorgias to provide for his daughter. Gorgias introduces Sostratos, and Knemon accepts him as a sun-tanned labourer and therefore a suitable son-in-law. Arrangements are made for Sostratos to marry Knemon's daughter and Gorgias to marry Sostratos' sister. The play ends with the cook and a fellow slave taking vengeance on Knemon for his meanness.

The obstacle need not be parental disapproval. In the *Rape of the Locks* the first obstacle is the soldier's jealousy of a supposed rival, which makes him treat the girl like a slave, cutting off her hair, and the second obstacle is the girl's pride, which makes her refuse to be reconciled until her own status as a citizen is established. In the *Arbitrants* the pair are already married but the young husband has deserted his wife because a slave has told him that she has borne a child which he thinks cannot be his; her father tries to persuade her to leave her husband on the ground that he is spending her dowry on a prostitute.

A great many variations can be played on this general theme, and the emphasis can be laid on the plot or the characters, on the lovers themselves, or on the nature of the obstacles, or on the ingenuity with which the obstacles are overcome. Such comedy is optimistic because we see people we like achieving an end which we desire for them; in addition to our satisfaction with their happiness we may also, if the author is skilful and the acting is good, feel some sympathy for the obstacle which has been overcome, for Hornblower in the *Skin Game*, for Shylock in the *Merchant of Venice*, and for Knemon in Menander's *Dyskolos*. The essence of this kind of comedy is that it shows us a world like our own, which in the modern theatre we view across the footlights, separated from us but moving on a course like our own.

The ancient dramatist lacked the obvious resources of the modern dramatist for making drama realistic in this way. Menander had three different sorts of experience which helped him when he started producing in 322 B.C. at the age of 18 (he was only 24 when he produced the *Dyskolos*): comedy, tragedy, and philosophy. Several elements in the *Dyskolos* show Menander's debt to earlier comedy, particularly the ragging of Knemon with its descriptions of eating and drinking in the last act, but also the breathless arrival of Sostratos' slave in the first act and the arrival of the cook with the sheep on his shoulders in the second act. We can only reconstruct the kind of comedy which intervened between Aristophanes and Menander from the fragments of plays quoted by later authors and with the help of terracotta statuettes of comic actors and representations of comic scenes on vases.[1] It is possible that young lovers, who are the essential element in social comedy, were first introduced in mythological comedy, which parodied tragedy and was very popular in the first half of the fourth century. The fragments make it certain that the love affairs of imaginary contemporaries occurred in comedy soon after 350 B.C. and well before the earliest plays of Menander; but the actors still wore the old obscene costume that they wore in the plays of Aristophanes.

Tragedy, by which I mean largely but not exclusively the tragedy of Euripides, was a classic for Menander in the same sense that Shakespeare is a classic for us, a classic constantly performed in the theatre and used for illustrations in lectures on ethics and as the basis of literary criticism. The transformation of *Romeo and Juliet* into *West Side Story* would have won Menander's approval, even if he himself preferred to transpose the single tragic scene or situation into terms of contemporary life rather than a complete play. He could also count on his audience taking an allusion to tragedy, whether the allusion was employed by a slave adding verisimilitude to the deception of his master, by a young man in a solemn moment of self-discovery, or by a father when he reached a tragic agony of self-deception.

Menander was a pupil of Theophrastus, the philosopher who succeeded Aristotle as the head of the Peripatetic school when Aristotle died in 322 B.C. We do not know what he learnt from Theophrastos, but it is a reasonable guess that he learnt literary criticism and ethics. Aristotle had laid down that the tragic poet should construct his plot in general terms as a sequence of necessary or probable incidents with a beginning and middle and end, and he meant, partly at least, by necessary or probable incidents, incidents which resulted from the mental qualities of the characters. This is exactly the kind of play which Menander wrote; he adapted the Aristotelian rules for tragedy to the comic stage. It is easy to see this already in the youthful *Dyskolos*. The main events occur because Knemon is grumpy and mean (he would not have fallen down the well if he had not been too mean to provide an extra bucket, a special hook to recapture a lost bucket, and a well-head to make the top of the well safe), because Sostratos is too much in love to bother about propriety, because Gorgias has a charity which can charm Knemon out of his grumpiness for a moment, because the slave Daos realistically sees that Sostratos is good for a free day's work on the farm, and because the pompous cook cannot forgive Knemon's refusal to lend him a cooking-pot. Menander's plays are good drama in Aristotle's sense and he is also aware of Peripatetic ethics. In the *Rape of the Locks* he adopts a form of opening which he used in several other plays: instead of starting with a prologue speech to give the audience the essentials of the situation (like the speech of Pan at the beginning of the *Dyskolos*) he starts with a scene of action: the soldier in fury at his slave's mistaken report of his mistress's unfaithfulness cuts off her hair. Then personified Ignorance (or perhaps Misunderstanding would be a better translation for this situation) explains that she is responsible for his action, besides giving the audience an outline of the preceding story. The conception that a crime committed in ignorance of facts relevant to the situation is less heinous than a premeditated crime is elaborated in Aristotle's *Ethics* and quoted in his *Poetics*. The introduction of Ignorance to speak the prologue is therefore an indication that the poet knew Peripatetic Ethics and that the audience would do well to remember them. Two other early plays were called *Anger* and *Drunkenness*: Aristotle links them with Ignorance as causes of unpremeditated crime, and it seems likely that Menander personified them too as prologue speakers in the plays named after them and there too made explicit reference to Peripatetic Ethics.

I shall return later to Polemon, the soldier hero of the *Rape of the Locks*. The bare outline given of the *Dyskolos* must suffice to show the efficient mechanics of Menander's plot-construction. A good verse translation like J. H. Quincey's[2] gets something of the felicity of his language (at least the difference between the iambic trimeters of the dialogue, the trochaic tetrameters of Knemon's self-defence, and the iambic tetrameters of the final

6

ragging scene stand out clearly). Here I want to consider how Menander used the modest scenic resources at his disposal to achieve a realism which was far greater than that of his predecessors and comparable, when due allowances are made, with the realism of modern social comedy.

The modern dramatist gives his audience a programme which tells them the names, status, and sometimes the relative ages of the characters; status and relative ages Menander could show to some extent by his masks (and this I shall consider further later) and convention seems to have established separate sets of names for old men, young men, soldiers, parasites, slaves, wives, daughters, and prostitutes.

The modern dramatist also uses the programme to give the time, date, and place of every scene; moreover, he can change the scene as often as he likes and rely on having a realistic setting for any place that he likes to imagine. Menander's possibilities were much more restricted. Conventionally the prologue speech only summarized events up to the beginning of the action and only gave the most general intimation as to the future: Ignorance in the *Rape of the Locks* prophesies that the exposed children will find their father, but Pan makes no prophecy in the *Dyskolos*. Menander seems to have accepted Aristotle's dictum that the events of tragedy should be confined within a single day and to have applied it to comedy. The glaring unrealities of Aristophanes, who makes Amphitheos get from Athens to Sparta and back in the space of forty lines of dialogue, have been abandoned; time experienced in the *Dyskolos* is a single long day. Within this single long day the time-table has no regard for geographical distances.[3] The action takes place at the shrine of the Nymphs and Pan, which (in defiance of the terrain) is between the house of Knemon and the house of Gorgias. Athens is in fact fifteen miles away, but Getas has time to leave home in the morning walk to Athens, hire the cook in the agora, walk back with him, pick up the picnic gear and the sheep and arrive at the shrine before the end of the second act, during most of which time Knemon, who is said to spend the maximum of time on his farm, is doing nothing in his house. But Menander can disregard geography because already by the time of the *Dyskolos* the convention is established that town, country (and in other plays the harbout) are too far from each other to be visited between scenes but near enough to be visited between acts, and this convention overrides the audience's knowledge of the actual distances.

Realistic lighting and realistic scenery were also impossible for the ancient dramatist. Menander does occasionally want to make a young man pass a sleepless night because he cannot get hold of his beloved. The words and a lamp in the hands of his slave create the illusion; but here we can trace the convention back to the time of Aristophanes.[4] For scenery all the evidence suggests that at any one time a Greek theatre only possessed three sets: one for tragedy, one for satyr play, one for comedy.[5] Menander produced his early plays in the theatre as rebuilt by the statesman Lycurgus soon after 330 B.C. In this reconstruction the theatre had a stone stage-building with projecting wings, between which was a façade containing three doors: only the large central door was used for tragedy: comedy could use either the two smaller side doors or all three doors; the intervening panels were painted with the scenery. (Early in the third century and probably before Menander's death the action was moved on to the roof of the stage-building, but essentially the same background was then repeated at that level.) The set for tragedy gave buildings in perspective; the set for satyr play gave rocks and caves; the set for comedy was decorated with garlands, libation bowls, and other symposion equipment, the kind of decoration that would be found on the walls of a men's dining-room in a rich house. There is a little evidence that for a tragedy (like the *Philoctetes*) or for a comedy with a country scene (like the *Dyskolos*) the set for the satyr play could be used. The dramatist had to create in words the particular locality which he wanted his audience to imagine, but he also knew that they had before their eyes a real locality of three doors in a row, which he could exploit when he needed it.

In the *Dyskolos* the action is put in Phyle, an area which Menander and many of his audience would know from their period of military service. The 'famous shrine' with the hard country, 'the rocks that bear only thyme and sage-apples', and the richer land below which is farmed by Sostratos' father, the road along the bottom of Knemon's farm, the pear trees, the fig tree and the olive trees, the scrub which Knemon shares with Gorgias, are all verbal aids to the audience's imagination. What they saw was a façade with a large central door and two smaller side doors and intervening panels decorated with rocks, and altar, and perhaps also a statue of Pan (since wooden statues were easily obtainable and easily brought on between one play and the next). The central door belongs to the 'famous shrine' of the Nymphs and Pan, and the two side doors to the houses of Knemon and Gorgias. In fact the 'famous shrine' was much too inaccessible to have any houses near it and much too small to accommodate a large picnic party. But once Menander had translated the shrine and the two houses into terms of conventional stage setting, the central door was obviously capable of admitting any number of people and the contiguity of the three doors made it possible to interweave the actions in the two houses and the shrine. When Knemon's daughter comes out of his house to fetch water, Sostratos can take her pitcher to the shrine and the slave Daos, coming out of Gorgias' house, can overhear what is going on. When Knemon falls down the well inside his own house, his old slave-woman can fetch Gorgias from his house and Gorgias can fetch Sostratos from the shrine in a moment, and the cook outside the shrine can hear and comment on what is going on in Knemon's house. Both are good dramatic moments which are made possible by the setting.

The normal Greek house had its rooms grouped round a courtyard into which the front door opened.[6] The stage doors would therefore naturally open into the courtyards of the houses to which they belong and this house-plan is described in some detail by Demeas, who owns one of the stage-houses in the *Samian Woman*. Moreover, Menander establishes the stage doors as front doors by sometimes making characters knock on them when they are going in and slide the bolts back noisily when they are coming out. He has therefore no easy way, like the modern dramatist, of playing interior scenes. Yet he cannot do without interior scenes. There are, however, two mitigations of the improbability of intimate conversations between members of the family taking place in the street. One is that, although the stage doors are established as front doors, the traditional decoration of the panels with libation bowls, etc., is an interior decoration and suggests the walls of the dining-room, so that the comic set is itself a mixture of outside and inside. The other mitigation is to arrange the interior scene so that one of the participants is a visitor; thus the intimate conversation becomes a protracted greeting or farewell, which is not so unnaturally performed on the doorstep.

In the *Dyskolos* most of the action can take place outside quite naturally because all three doors are in action and people come and go between them, Knemon's farm, Gorgia's farm, and Sostratos' family farm. But it is extremely unnatural that, when Knemon has been rescued from the well, he should be carried outside his front door to make his final dispositions. The arrangement is made a little easier by the fact that his wife has to be fetched from Gorgias' house to hear him (698).

Given the convention Menander exploits it. In the *Arbitrants* (510) Smikrines and his daughter discuss the infidelities of her husband Charisios on her doorstep; he is going back to fetch her old nurse in the hope of persuading her to return home, and so the scene can be played as a protracted farewell. But Charisios, who has deserted her and is supposedly enjoying a prostitute in his friend's house next door, puts his head out of that front door and listens to the conversation. In real life the conversation between father and daughter would take place in the women's quarters of her house, and Charisios would be endeavouring to drown his sorrows in the men's quarters of the next house. But given the stage-necessity of a conversation on the doorstep, Menander takes advantage of it to allow Charisios to overhear it.

Menander shows himself a master in using the conventions of the Greek stage, but there is no reason to suppose that he invented them: tragedy had long established the convention of intimate conversations outside the palace door in the presence of the chorus. But the decisive change in costume which made comic actors look like contemporary Athenians was either due to him or was carried through in the early years of his production. At the same time (and perhaps at his instigation) the stock masks of New Comedy were systematized so that he could predict the faces of his characters far more accurately than the modern dramatist who has to use unmasked actors. It is worth while trying to sketch the history of this change in costume and masks, so as to have the material to ask a final question: how far did Menander's characters run true to the form predictable by the audience from their masks?

Aristotle in the *Poetics* (1449*a* 32) describes the characters of comedy as 'worse than the average' and says that 'the mask which excites laughter is something ugly and distorted without causing pain'. A glance at Athenian comic terracottas and South Italian comic vases of the second quarter of the fourth century, when this passage was written, explains Aristotle's judgment and shows that 'worse than the average' applies even more to costume than masks.[7] But about the time that Aristotle was writing, the new intrigue comedy was coming in and included new characters as well as new situations, the lover, the parasite, the young hetaira (or prostitute), the free girl, the procurer and procuress, and the heavy father. In the new young masks there is little distortion, and some of them can be shown to be derived from contemporary fashions. Some of the young women's masks which on the monumental evidence were introduced rather before or rather after the middle of the fourth century, the girl with a peek of hair over the forehead, the girl with a scarf round her hair, the girl with a pony-tail, and the girl with melon hair, can be paralleled in everyday life as represented by Attic vases and terracottas dating from the same period[8]: the mask-maker evidently copied the hair styles of contemporary hetairai (and because hetairai are servants of Aphrodite some of these hairstyles are also found on contemporary figures of Aphrodite). All of these continue into the New Comedy period. The mask of a young man with hair waving up from his forehead appears late in the Middle Comedy period and is a favourite in the New Comedy period; the style must have appeared in the earliest portraits of Alexander and from that time became extremely popular.

But although from the middle of the fourth century or even a little earlier the masks of young women and slightly later the masks of young and old men might reasonably be termed 'like the average' rather than 'worse than the average', Aristotle's judgment was still valid as long as men normally showed a large phallus and both men and women were grotesquely padded. The photographs of Middle Comedy terracottas are often taken from the front view and do not show the padding clearly, but in side view it can at once be seen on figures of old men, young men, slaves, old women, and young women alike. In New Comedy only slaves are fat, and they are neither abnormally fat nor are they always fat. Unfortunately the evidence is weakest for the last quarter of the fourth century, and we cannot tell whether the reduction of padding for free men and women was gradual or sudden. It must, however, have been a sudden decision to give men a chiton which reached half-way down the thighs or nearly to the ankles instead of stopping at the hips. Two preliminary changes are significant. From the middle of the fourth century the phallus worn by slaves becomes much less obtrusive, and about the middle of the fourth century clean-shaven men, who are presumably the lovers of intrigue comedy, sometimes (as old men earlier) wear a long himation which conceals the phallus. The exuberant obscenity of Old Comedy evidently decreased in Middle Comedy as the interest shifted to plot and characters. In the third century there is plenty of evidence for the long chiton; and a rough terracotta group from the small Boeotian town of Halai, dated between 335 and 280 B.C., surely implies an Attic original of the fourth century—both the young man and the slave have chitons which cover the thighs. The plays of Menander show no trace of obscenity, though the scene at the end of the *Dyskolos* gave opportunities which Aristophanes would not have missed. It is therefore a reasonable assumption that the longer chitons for male characters were introduced early in the New Comedy period, but we do not know whether one poet introduced longer chitons and the others followed or whether some reformer such as Demetrios of Phaleron gave instructions to the costume makers.

With the new costumes and naturalistic masks, either inherited from Middle Comedy or newly introduced, Menander's characters looked like the Athenians of his day. For the masks the likeness to real life has been sufficiently demonstrated already and we shall have more to say about them later. The costumes can in some cases be compared with contemporary and later terracottas and other monuments. The man about town, young and old, wore long chiton and himation. On Attic grave reliefs and statues the himation is shown but the chiton is often omitted by convention; occasionally, however, it can be seen.[9] The *chlanis*, worn by an older man in the *Orge* (fr. 303) and by Sostratos in the *Dyskolos* (257), was a particularly fine and fashionable kind of himation. The *tribon* or *tribonion* was a much coarser and smaller himation worn by poor men, usually without a chiton, and by philosophers who affected to be poor. Gorgias in the *Georgos* (132) is said 'to belong to the class of *tribon* wearers'; on this evidence his namesake in the *Dyskolos* and Knemon would also wear it, and we can form a good idea of Knemon from a terracotta in Boston[10] of the earliest third century, probably a philosopher.

Sostratos wore the fashionable *chlanis* but with it a thigh-length chiton because he was an energetic young man. The thigh-length chiton is the dress of the soldier, but he wears over it a *chlamys* or military cloak; when Polemon changes into civilian clothing in the *Perikeiromene*, he sends Sosias to fetch him a *himation* (58) to put on instead of his military *chlamys*, which he has been wearing with his sword (164). A very fine terracotta mould[11] of the last quarter of the fourth century from the Agora represents a soldier wearing the *chlamys* pinned on the right shoulder and hanging diagonally across the body, and the chiton shows beneath the breastplate.

It is much more difficult to find representations of slaves in real life to match the slaves of comedy. The very fine third-century terracotta from the Agora of an actor playing the part of a running slave in short chiton and fringed himation gives us a good idea of Pyrrhias' first entry in the *Dyskolos* (81) and there is no reason to suppose that slaves in real life looked any different. Country slaves, like Daos in the *Dyskolos*, wore the *diphthera*: 'you with the diphtherai, have you time for law suits?' says Smikrines in the *Epitrepontes* (53, cf. 124). This is a chiton made of skin. A short form was worn by Middle Comedy actors. A Roman marble figure[12] of a fisherman wears a short skin-chiton girt round the waist and pinned on the right shoulder. This, but probably less exiguous, is the kind of garment which would be worn by the rustic slave of comedy.

The characters looked like ordinary Athenians and their clothes told the audience their sex, their age, and in some cases their social position. The masks confirmed all these points and added rather more. Beyond that the poet had to rely on gestures and words. We can say nothing useful of gestures, but we can ask what expectations the masks aroused and whether Menander fulfilled or contradicted them, what in this sphere was the interplay between production and imagination. The list in the late lexicographer Pollux gives the common stock of New Comedy masks in the third century B.C. The forty-four masks are partly new additions, partly known already in the Middle Comedy archaeological material. Here it will suffice to state the principles which can be observed in the changes. It looks very much as if families could be recognized by the hair-style of their male members. Thus we find a neat-haired old man, four neat-haired young men (in a descending sequence of age), an older and a younger neat-haired slave; a wavy-haired old man, two wavy-haired young men (the older a soldier), an older and a younger wavy-haired slave; a curly-haired old man (who is also characterized by Pollux as 'interfering'), a curly-haired young man, and a curly-haired slave. Wavy hair (derived from Alexander) suggested impetuosity; curly hair suggests energy. Further characterization is given by colour of hair and of complexion, forehead (wrinkled or smooth), brows (raised or level), nose (aquiline, straight, or snub). New Comedy families are mostly better off than their predecessors and therefore the scrubbier masks of old men and women have been dropped. New Comedy adds a curly-haired wife and a grey-haired wife, but takes over the types of young women which had been developed in Middle Comedy. The great increase is in young men, largely because of the great interest in the various types of male lover.

On the evidence of the archaeological material the stock masks of New Comedy seem to have been established by the middle of the third century B.C. What part Menander himself played in this and whether he invented the hypothetical grouping of families by hair-style we cannot say. Such a prolific poet, so concerned with differentiation of character, is unlikely to have left the invention to others. In any case the new masks passed quickly into stock.

Occasionally a character in Menander is described by another character and the description includes or implies a judgment. Raised brows are the mark of a person who regards himself as superior, often a philosopher (fr. 34, 395): so in the *Arbitrants* (18 f) Smikrines, the father-in-law of the young husband Charisios, 'has a scowl on his face like a miserable philosopher'—Smikrines as an interferer should wear the old curly-haired mask, which has raised brows; the cook in the *Dyskolos* (423) tells Sostratos' slave Getas to relax his brows at last because he is going to have a good feed: as the leading wavy-haired slave he has raised brows and lives up to them in his anger at the women, his fury that Sostratos should invite the yokels to the sacrifice, and his readiness to join the cook in ragging Knemon at the end of the play. Knemon also looks 'not very beneficent' to Sostratos as he appears shouting his soliloquy (147); again brows are part of the reason. If the division of families by hair-styles is accepted, Gorgias must be the rustic youth, who has neat hair; Sostratos, his father, and their slaves, Pyrrhias and Getas, will form the wavy-haired group and this suits Sostratos as the wild young man about town; but Knemon cannot wear the old curly-haired mask, which Pollux characterizes as interfering. This is right for Smikrines in the *Epitrepontes* but entirely wrong for Knemon; on the other hand Knemon could very well wear the wedge-beard mask of Middle Comedy, which survives into the New Comedy period: 'raised eyebrows, pointed beard, rather bad tempered'. This would give him an old-fashioned as well as an angry air. But how can Gorgias decide immediately that Sostratos is 'a scoundrel to judge by his looks' (258)? Sostratos should be the second young man with wavy hair, and the wavy hair on the top of the fine *chlanis* and of Daos' insinuations awake Georgias' prejudices against the rich.

These descriptions, which are preserved with their contexts, show that Menander did expect other characters, and therefore the audience, to make the obvious predictions from the masks. Mask and costume give the audience a good general idea of the age, sex, social position of the character, and tell them something about how the character may be expected to behave. Many characters run true to type but are individual because they take part in individual events: these individual events are part of the plot, and this is what Plutarch's story (*Moralia* 347F) means when Menander says that he has made the comedy because he has finished the plot. The younger man with wavy hair may be expected to fall helplessly in love and to flout conventions in getting what he wants: Chaireas in the *Eunuch* seizes the chance of changing clothes with the eunuch so as to be introduced into his girl's house, and Sostratos in the *Dyskolos* seizes the chance of working as an agricultural labourer so as to make himself acceptable to his future father-in-law. The events are completely individual and beautifully realized, but both young men run true to predictable form.

There are, however, three young men who do not run true to form: Gorgias in the *Dyskolos*, Charisios in the *Arbitrants*, and Polemon in the *Perikeiromene*. Gorgias is an incredibly virtuous young man, who supports his mother on a tiny farm, who works so hard that he has no knowledge of love, who construes the report of Sostratos' approach to his half sister as the exploitation of the hard-working poor by the idle rich, but immediately accepts Sostratos' self-defence as genuine, if also misguided, and immediately leaps into the well to rescue Knemon without a thought for cavalier treatment in the past. At the end his pride flares up again when a marriage with Sostratos' sister is proposed, and he is naturally embarrassed at joining the rich man's party in the shrine of the Nymphs. Yet the rustic mask has a snub nose and thick lips, which should betoken sensuality and cowardice. The mask is well attested early (and is carried by the skeleton of Menander on a silver cup from Boscoreale). Menander here contrasts appearance and reality.

Charisios in the *Arbitrants* is a different case. Robert[13] assigned him the mask of the dark young man, who is studious rather than athletic. Perhaps the studious young man in comedy was always liable to forsake philosophy at least temporarily for love. What however is individual in Charisios is his whole course of action after he finds out that his wife Pamphile has been, as he thinks, unfaithful to him and has borne a child. He tries to drown his sorrows in drink and women, and fails. He then receives the shattering piece of news that he is himself the father of the baby, which he believes to be the child of the prostitute Habrotobon. Then by the convenient arrangement of the three-door stage he overhears his wife telling her father that she refuses to leave him in spite of this. The slave Onesimos thinks he has gone mad and describes him groaning, tearing his hair, changing colour, and abusing himself as a hypocrite. Then at last the audience sees him and hears him express his conclusion, perhaps as startling to a Greek as to a Victorian audience, that he should judge his wife's act by the same standard as his own and accept her willingness to stay with him. Perhaps we should say not so much that he does not run true to form as that two shattering experiences made him aware of a new truth on which he acts. But Menander has given something more than the label on the mask 'studious rather than athletic' predicts.

In the *Rape of the Locks* Menander himself almost tells us not to trust the label. Polemon wears the mask of the first wavy-haired young man, 'soldier and braggart', and we expect arrogance and irascibility. Our expectations are fulfilled in the first scene when Polemon immediately believes the report that his mistress has been unfaithful, cuts off her hair with his sword, and leaves her to drown his sorrows in drink. But then personified Ignorance tells the audience that this 'all flared up because of the future, that Polemon might fly into a rage—for I led him, though this was not his true character' (42 ff). The rest of the play shows his repentance and ends with reconciliation. The pride and irascibility which the mask proclaims is short-lived, and his true character is to be a faithful husband.

Slaves in Menander are mostly individualized by their situations, but two stand out as individual people: Daos in the *Hero* and Syriskos in the *Arbitrants*. In the first scene of the *Hero*, Daos is described by his fellow-slave Getas rather as Charisios is described by Onesimos in the *Arbitrants*: 'Why do you keep beating your head? Why do you stop and tear out your hair? Why do you groan?' The realistic Getas supposes that Daos has committed some major misdemeanour for which he expects to be punished. But Daos has fallen in love with a poor girl, who is working wool in the house. He has made no attempt to seduce her but has told his master, and his master has promised that she shall live with him but at present he has gone to Lemnos. A slave not only in love but prepared to wait for his girl is startling; and in the sequel, which we only know from the brief summary preserved at the beginning of the papyrus, Daos, discovering that the girl is pregnant, claims that he is responsible, to the fury of his mistress; a fragment of his speech is preserved: 'Mistress, nothing is stronger than Eros, not even Zeus himself, Lord of the Gods in Heaven; even he does all that Eros commands.' This beginning is strongly reminiscent of a fragment of Euripides' *First Hippolytus* (431 N). Like Syriskos in the *Arbitrants* (and other slaves in Menander) Daos has seen tragedy, but nothing in the mask distinguishes this educated highly individual slave from his earthy friend Getas. In the *Arbitrants* the charcoal burner Syriskos is similarly contrasted with the realistic shepherd Daos. Syriskos is a slave, but he is out on his own as a charcoal burner and has come in to pay what is due from his takings to his master. His wife had lost her baby, and so he gladly accepted the foundling from Daos, but he also demands the trinkets with which the child had been exposed, because they are the baby's property and may prove his birth, as indeed they do. Syriskos is entirely disinterested and in fact acts against his own interest, because the baby is immediately recognized by its trinkets as Charisios' child and is therefore taken from him. He pleads his case with considerable skill and idealism. Again the contrast between appearance and reality is clear.

Of the older men only Demeas in the *Samian Woman* and Knemon in the *Dyskolos* need discussion. Both are contrasted with more ordinary old men, Demeas with the straightforward Nikeratos (who would wear the leading old man's mask) and Knemon with the rich, hasty, complacent Kallippides, the father of Sostratos (who would wear the wavy-haired old man's mask). Demeas is drawn in much more detail than Nikeratos and stands out as a completely individual figure. His two big preserved speeches are brilliantly written. The first is a detailed narrative of what he saw, ending with the horrible suspicion that his son Moschion and not he is the father of the baby, which he wrongly believes his mistress Chrysis to have borne. He tries to interrogate the slave Parmenon, but when he threatens him with a whip Parmenon escapes. By his second speech he tries to convince himself that Moschion was the innocent victim of his mistress Chrysis, and at the end he rushes into the house to turn her out; 'Demeas, now you must be a man. Forget your desire for her, be through with love, and hide the disaster, as far as possible, for your son's sake'. The cook thinks he is mad and fears for his pots. Demeas drives Chrysis out of the door with the old nurse and the baby: she did not know how to behave herself when he gave her a comfortable home; now she can go on the streets and drink herself to death or starve. Like Charisios, Demeas does not speak out of character; we should rather say that Menander has exposed his character to unexpected depths.

Knemon has his own ancestry in a line of Comedies which go back to the *Hermit* of Phrynichos, produced in 414 B.C. Nothing suggests that the heroes of these plays were anything more than bad-tempered men who objected to extravagance and human society. This then was the obvious forecast for the audience to make of Knemon, and if we are right in supposing that he wore an old-fashioned, bad-tempered looking mask, the mask would confirm their views. In the first three acts this forecast seems to be confirmed again and again, not least when it appears that Knemon is not a poor man at all but insists on living as a poor man although he is quite well off. But when he makes his, as he supposes, death-bed speech to his family, he justifies his conduct; he had withdrawn into solitude because he saw that all men were governed by purely mercenary motives. Gorgias' disinterested action in saving him has charmed him out of his isolation far enough to make his dispositions for his wife and daughter and to make his final proclamation of faith: 'if all men were like me, there would not be law courts nor would they hale each other to prison nor would there be war, but each would have his modicum and be content'. This is true, unpractical perhaps but undeniably true; it restamps Knemon as an idealist and suggests that the comparison which we made earlier with the statuette of a philosopher was not wholly unjustified.

Masks and costumes can give a much closer approximation to reality than the stage-building and its modest possibilities of scenery. But the reality to which they approximate is only external appearance. Imagination has to supplement production in creating a detailed picture of the characters themselves as well as of the world in which they live, and may succeed in giving them a reality which not only completes but also transcends their external appearance. This is a subtle and civilized form of comedy. The wedding-bells ring at the end and the young lovers at least are happy. But they have not achieved their happiness without a considerable struggle, and in the course of the struggle a depth and complexity of character is revealed, either in them or in those who help them or hinder them, which goes beyond what could be predicted even from the diversified and ingenious masks of New Comedy, and in the revelation a truly humane ideal is asserted. Menander's fertility of invention and the complexity of his plots survive translation into Latin. Plautus has heightened the colours and altered the emphases so much that the original outlines of the characters can only be perceived with difficulty. Terence is at best like a Roman copy of a Greek statue; the outlines are well preserved but the bloom and life is largely lost. To appreciate them we must turn to what survives in the original Greek.

NOTES

[1] My *Studies in Later Greek Comedy* (Manchester, 1952), pp. 62 ff, 77.
[2] *The Old Curmudgeon of Menander* (Sydney, 1962).
[3] On the details cf. my article in *Bulletin of the John Rylands Library* 45 (1962-3), pp. 237 ff.
[4] Cf. *op. cit.*, p. 236.
[5] Cf. *op. cit.*, pp. 241 ff.

⁶ Cf. *op. cit.*, pp. 253 ff.

⁷ For illustrations of Middle Comedy, cf. my *Greek Theatre Production* (London, 1956), pp. 55 ff; *Hesperia* 29 (1960), pp. 261 ff. For illustrations of New Comedy, cf. my *Greek Theatre Production*, pp. 73 ff; *Hesperia* 29 (1960), pp. 273 ff.

⁸ Cf. the hetairai on the Attic bell-krater, Naples 2202, H. Metzger, *Representations* (Paris, 1951), pl. 48/2, and the Attic terracottas Agora T 1680 and 1736, D. B. Thompson, *Hesperia*, 21 (1952), pp. 131 ff, nos. 19 and 26.

⁹ E.g. Athens, National Museum 244. Winter, *Kunstgeschichte in Bildern* (Leipzig, 1924), p. 318/3.

¹⁰ Boston 13.155, D. B. Thompson, *Hesperia* 26 (1957), p. 118, pl. 35.

¹¹ Agora T 295, D. B. Thompson, *op. cit.*, p. 114, pl. 34, no. 5.

¹² British Museum 1766, M. Bieber, *Hellenistic Sculpture*² (Princeton, 1962), fig. 592.

¹³ *Masken der neueren attischen Komödie* (Berlin, 1911), p. 65.

II

Plautus and his Audience

WALTER R. CHALMERS

THE plays of Plautus are of considerable importance for a variety of reasons. They are the earliest substantial works of Latin literature which we possess, and they are still our most extensive evidence about Greek New Comedy. Although they are essentially derivative, they reveal throughout the touch of a real master in the art of writing Comedy. Can they do more than this? Is it possible for us to derive from them information about the audiences who first saw them performed; the ordinary inhabitants of Rome during one of the most important periods of her historical development? Many scholars would deny this possibility, but in view of the dearth of other evidence, it may be worth while to consider what information can be extracted from the plays.

Comedy is a form of literature which often reflects the life and interests of the members of its audience fairly clearly. Since people can usually be moved to laughter by the incongruous and the unexpected, the Comic writer has to take into account what his audience will be likely to consider normal. The comedies of Aristophanes, Shakespeare, Molière, and Shaw, to name but a few, all supply valuable information about the social life and cultural attitudes of their contemporaries. In the case of Aristophanes, we may learn not only about the day-to-day life of fifth-century Athenians, but also about their political ideas. Even his most preposterous flights of fantasy help to reveal what their deepest aspirations were. Of course, we cannot expect to learn quite so much from New Comedy, since for the most part it avoids political comment. Nevertheless, it purports to depict ordinary characters and, to judge from the famous epigram of Aristophanes of Byzantium, 'Menander and life, which of you imitated the other?', it did so with considerable success. This, of course, does not mean that the plots of New Comedy depicted happenings which were commonplace.[1] Nevertheless, the settings are taken from life, and it may fairly be claimed that the recent discovery of Menander's *Dyskolos* has given us a much better picture than we could otherwise have formed of what life in a country-deme of Attica must have been like in the fourth century B.C.

It may, however, be objected that this is irrelevant to a discussion of Plautus; that since all his plays are based on Greek originals, they may perhaps add to our knowledge of Greek life, but not significantly to our knowledge of the life of Plautus's Roman audiences. This would be a very valid objection if Plautus had contented himself with merely translating his Greek models, but quite manifestly he did much more than this. Although we do not possess any of the original Greek plays which he used, or even any sizeable fragment of any of them, as, thanks to Aulus Gellius (II, 23), we do in the case of Caecilius, it is quite clear that Plautus felt free to make considerable adaptations. Opinions may vary about the actual extent of these adaptations, but their existence is undeniable. We must also remember that Plautus was a very popular writer. His plays were revived after his death (cf. the prologue to the *Casina*, 11 ff), and even during his own lifetime, if we accept that *Bacch.* 214 f,

> *etiam Epidicum, quam ego fabulam aeque ac me ipsum amo,*
> *nullam aeque invitus specto si agit Pellio,*

comes from his own pen, and not from that of someone who was producing a revival of the *Bacchides* after Plautus's death.[2] Moreover, his plays were written down and treasured for posterity, and his authorship was claimed for many more plays than he could conceivably have written himself. This implies that Plautus knew how to appeal to the taste of his audience. The work of playwrights who were near-contemporaries and who championed close adherence to the original, such as Luscius Lanuvinus, does not seem to have been equally popular, and so it seems reasonable to infer that Plautus owed his popularity to the fact that the methods he adopted made his plays come alive. We must not forget that his audiences came to the theatre to enjoy themselves, not to study the theatrical remains of a foreign writer. Plautus was a man of the theatre. He had served his apprenticeship *in operis artificum scaenicorum* (Aulus Gellius, III. 3, 14), and had most probably appeared himself as an actor in Atellane farces.[3] It is unlikely that, with this kind of professional background, he would frequently have indulged in the luxury of making esoteric jokes which could be understood only by a very select minority. It is much more reasonable to assume that he intended what he wrote to be understood and appreciated by at least a considerable proportion of his audience. Moreover in the theatrical conditions of his time, his whole career depended on pleasing the aediles and other magistrates responsible for the presentation of dramatic entertainments, and they, through an understandable desire to influence the electorate, would scarcely have fostered the work of a dramatist who consistently wrote plays which were not adequately comprehensible to his audience. If these considerations are borne in mind, we may feel that we can reasonably expect to learn something about Plautus's audiences from his plays.

The fact that all Plautus's plays were based on Greek originals is in itself informative. It implies that the Romans of his day were no longer satisfied with the rather more crude dramatic performances to which they had previously been accustomed—the mime, the Atellane farce, the Fescennine verses, and the dramatic *satura*, if this last really existed as a separate *genre*.[4] Plautus was, of course, writing during the later years of the Second Punic War and immediately afterwards, and many, perhaps even the majority, of the members of his audience must have served in the army. This we could easily infer, even if other evidence were lacking, from the frequency with which he uses military terms such as *legio, centuriare, subcenturiare, velitatio*,[5] etc. Many of these soldiers must, like their fathers before them in the First Punic War, have campaigned in South Italy and Sicily, and so have come into contact with the more refined and cultured life of the Greek cities of Magna Graecia, and, in particular, with the more sophisticated dramatic entertainment which was popular in these cities.[6] This is not, of course, in itself an adequate explanation for the popularity of the *fabula palliata*. The dissatisfaction with the older native dramatic forms which was engendered by acquaintance with Greek Comedy might easily have encouraged the development of plays about Roman life, such as were later written by the writers of the *fabula togata*. Probably it did have this effect to some extent, as we know that the *Ariolus* of Naevius was set in Italy,[7] and there may have been other plays of this nature produced by contemporaries of Plautus. Plautus himself, however, wrote only *fabulae palliatae*. His preference may be partially due to a desire to avoid any accusation that he had libelled prominent Romans. It may be that there is no truth in the old story about Naevius' imprisonment as a result of his strictures on the Metelli,[8] to which it was claimed by Verrius Flaccus[9] that Plautus alluded in *Mil. Glor.* 211-12:

> *nam os columnatum poetae esse indaudivi barbaro,*
> *quoi bini custodes semper totis horis occubant.*

But it is important to note that whether it is true or not, it was considered plausible by Latin writers who, although writing at a later date, nevertheless presumably had more evidence to work on than we now possess. The Roman laws of libel[10] may well have had an inhibiting effect on Plautus. More generally it is highly probable that the choice of a Roman setting would limit the scope for plot and character development. Even if objectionable personalities were avoided, some activities were seemingly regarded as un-Roman and not therefore to be ascribed even in jest to Roman characters on the stage. For example, Donatus tells us that no Roman master could be shown being outwitted by a slave.[11]

There were no such limitations imposed in plays taken from the Greek. Plautus's own pejorative use of such words as *pergraecari*, *congraecari*, etc., while adding to the general amusement by their pleasing incongruity in a play with a Greek setting, would also appear to reflect a popular attitude not unlike that adopted by Cato. The Greeks were looked on as dissolute and unstable, fit only to be the objects of public scorn, though also possibly of private envy. In view of this attitude, comedies about the Greeks were assured of favourable attention.

By choosing to write *fabulae palliatae*, Plautus did not preclude himself from making allusions to the contemporary Roman scene. Indeed, since he was using a safer medium, he could allude to contemporary events and conditions with less inhibitions than he might have felt had the scene of his plays been set in Italy. Thus he feels free, for example, to make frequent allusions to the Bacchanals who were causing a scandal at Rome during his period of composition; to the ease by which triumphs might be obtained (*Bacch.* 1073); and even to bribery at elections (*Amph.* 74), if this part of the prologue belongs to the first production, and not to some later revival.[12] Plautus here uses a comic device for which there are many parallels. Shakespeare has no qualms about caricaturing a contemporary jealous Puritan or a dissolute country knight in the setting of a story-book Illyria, and Beaumarchais' criticisms of pre-Revolutionary French society are not rendered any less effective because his barber operates in Seville and not in Paris. The Romans of later days seem to have been quick to recognize topical allusions,[13] and it would be unwise to assume that their ancestors were necessarily more slow-witted.

By making use of plays with a Greek setting, Plautus is able to adopt a comic device which shows us his audience in a rather favourable light. He is able to show, or to pretend to show, his fellow-countrymen how they appeared to other people. The frequency of his jocular references to the Romans as *barbari* or *pultiphagi* indicates that this was a popular jest and that his audiences had enough sense of humour to appreciate a joke directed against themselves.

But the popularity of the *fabula palliata* shows, perhaps most of all, that in Plautus's time there were plenty of people in Rome whose taste was sensitive enough to appreciate the merits of Greek New Comedy. One may concede that they preferred it to be presented to them with certain adaptations, some of which had the tendency to broaden the comic effect, and that, quite probably, they may have found the more boisterous humour of Diphilus and Philemon more to their taste than the quieter, more reflective comedies of Menander. Nevertheless, the mere fact that Greek comedies were produced on such a scale may in itself be taken as an indication of discrimination on the part of the Roman audience.

In adapting the Greek originals to suit Roman taste, Plautus greatly increased the musical element. It is difficult to say to what extent music featured in the original plays, It would certainly be tempting to assume that in the *Dyskolos*, where the note *XOPOY* indicates a change of Act, that there may have been an entr'acte of music and possibly of dancing. Such an interlude would be particularly appropriate after line 232, where reference is made to the arrival of some rather drunken worshippers of Pan. We cannot, however, assume that much of the dialogue was accompanied by music. In the Latin plays, as Beare pointed out,[14] the manuscripts supply the note C (for *canticum*) against all passages in metres other than the Iambic Senarius, while passages in the Senarius are marked DV (for *diverbium*). This implies that all passages in metres other than the Senarius were originally sung, and Beare supports this theory by pointing out that in *Stichus* 762-8, when the flute-player is invited to have a drink and is thereby unable to accompany song, the metre changes from the Trochaic Septenarius to the Iambic Senarius. The word *canticum* is now generally applied in a more restricted sense to the passages of complex and varying metre which Plautus so frequently inserts into his plays. According to Sedgwick,[15] Plautus used *cantica* more frequently as he developed his professional technique. Only one play, the *Miles Gloriosus*, lacks this feature, and it is one which has generally been assigned on other grounds to an early period in Plautus's career.[16] Plautus probably realized that he possessed considerable talent in the handling of metre and therefore enjoyed writing *cantica* into his plays, but it is doubtful whether he would have done so if he had not been able to count on his skill receiving appreciative criticism. This, too, is an important piece of evidence about his audiences. It would appear that, not long after the time when, as Horace puts it (*Ep.* II. i, 157-8), *horridus ille defluxit numerus Saturnius*, they were already becoming connoisseurs in the complexities of the very different quantitative metres employed by Plautus in the *cantica*. Although there is some evidence that Caecilius may have written *cantica* of the Plautine type,[17] Terence did not do so, probably in deference to the feeling prevalent in his time that Roman playwrights should adhere closely to their originals. Yet, even in the plays of Terence, to judge from the *didascaliae*, the musical element was important.

It is impossible now to establish exactly in every case whether, in the *cantica*, Plautus altered material which already existed in the Greek original, or whether he inserted a fair amount of his own composition. It is clear that, on occasion, Plautus did insert passages, often of considerable length—and not only in the *cantica*. Fraenkel has shown[18] that quite often there are passages in the plays containing Roman allusions which begin and end with almost the same phrase. In such cases, Plautus has inserted a 'cadenza' of his own and then, usually quite neatly, carried on with the original material at the point where he had left it. Fraenkel also suggests[19] that besides these Plautus inserted passages which are introduced by certain recurring formulae. One such formula is to be found in *Persa* 1 f:

> *qui amans egens ingressus est princeps in Amoris vias*
> *superavit aerumnis suis aerumnas Herculei.*

Here a particular state of affairs is compared with a similar well-known and often mythological situation. Another such formula is, Fraenkel suggests,[20] to be found e.g. in *Amph*. 305; *Quintus fiam e Sosia*, where reference is made to a transformation. Fraenkel also argues[21] that many of the passages which contain mythological allusions are Plautus's own handiwork. Prescott's criticisms[22] suggest that Fraenkel may have over-stated his case and that the formulae mentioned may sometimes merely be a characteristic method adopted by Plautus to translate material which was in the Greek but which may not necessarily have appeared there in this form. Fraenkel's general point about the Plautine origin of most of the mythological passages seems to be largely substantiated by the fact that such passages are much more frequent in Plautus than in the plays and fragments of Greek New Comedy which we now possess. This does not, however, affect our discussion greatly. If Plautus is himself the author of these passages, that certainly is a strong indication that they were intended to be understood by his audiences, but even if he is not himself their originator, he is certainly responsible for their presence in his plays. Where excision would have been so easy, and where presumably it would have passed un-noticed except perhaps by a very few, it is almost impossible to imagine that he would deliberately have retained passages of some length if he had reason to believe that they would be incomprehensible.

Fraenkel also suggested[23] that in many plays Plautus increased the importance of the part played by slaves, and it has been generally agreed that many of the passages which gloatingly describe punishment inflicted on slaves are Plautine insertions. 'Slaves were', to quote Webster,[24] 'beaten up through the whole history of comedy', and even Menander has in the *Perinthia* (393K) a passage as brutal as anything in Plautus .The Plautine epithet *mastigia* may often be taken over direct from the Greek as it is used also by Menander (*Perikeir*. 204, and *Dyskolos*,140 and 473). Outside the field of Comedy proper, the fifth Mime of Herondas contains lurid details of slave punishments. Nevertheless, as

Westaway has shown,[25] many of the descriptions in Plautus, particularly for example the references to crucifixion, are Roman and must be Plautine insertions. In writing such passages in which human suffering is treated for comic purposes either with callous indifference or with sadistic *Schadenfreude*, Plautus is probably doing two things. He is catering for a fondness for abuse which had been formed by the Fescennine verses and the Atellane farces, and, secondly, he is, rather regrettably we may feel, pandering to the rather cruel streak in his audience which accounted for the later popularity of the bloody sports of the Amphitheatre. This may, of course, be an over-statement. After all, enjoyment of the rather cruel humour of a Punch and Judy show, or of the physical discomfiture of a circus clown, is not necessarily taken as a sign of a reprehensible enjoyment of the infliction of pain.

Some of the alterations of the Greek originals seem to be concessions to a popular taste which had been nurtured on rather different dramatic fare. Many, and in particular the allusions to Roman customs or topicalities, were probably intended to make the exotic setting of the plays appear more familiar, and so to produce a greater degree of 'audience-participation'. A similar device is adopted by Shakespeare when, for instance, he introduces his Elizabethan 'base mechanicals' in the court of 'Duke' Theseus, or when he stations Dogberry and Verges in the Court at Messina.

It is perhaps important to remember that in many ways, a Roman comic dramatist had to cope with conditions which were rather different from those with which his Greek predecessors were familiar. They, in the main, were writing plays for production in a well-built theatre with admirable acoustics, at dramatic festivals hallowed by long tradition, before audiences who looked on attendance at the dramatic festivals as an important part of their way of life. In Rome, the dramatic festivals which existed before the time of Plautus were few,[26] and traditionally it was only in 240 B.C. that the first translation from the Greek by Livius Andronicus was produced. There was as yet no permanent theatre, and indeed the building of such a theatre was destined to be postponed till 55 B.C. through the activities of the puritanical opposition in the Senate.[27] A playwright who cannot count on good acoustics in the theatre is quite justified in repeating points which are dramatically important, as Plautus frequently does. If we bear in mind the lack of amenities with which he had to contend, we may well commend Plautus for the efforts which he makes to hold the attention of his audience, but at the same time we need not dismiss that audience as being composed of uncultured boors because these efforts were necessary.

One of the devices which Plautus employs to heighten the degree of 'audience-participation' is what one might term the 'speech out of character', in which, in the course of the action, a character briefly apostrophises the audience.[28] For examples one may cite *Men.* 128-9:

> *ubi sunt amatores mariti? dona quid cessant mihi*
> *conferre omnes congratulantes quia pugnavi fortiter?*

and *Most.* 356 ff:

> *ubi sunt isti plagipatidae, ferritribaces viri,*
> *vel isti qui hosticas trium nummum caussa subeunt sub falas*, etc.

Hence the references (most probably) to legionary pay (357), and certainly to crucifixion (359) mark the whole passage as a Plautine insertion.

The most frequent remarks addressed to the audience are, naturally enough, to be found in the prologues, and these supply some useful information about the actual composition of the audience and about theatrical conditions. The prologue to the *Poenulus* is especially valuable, but its obviously exaggerated tone indicates that we should not accept its data without considerable reservations. Its jocular nature is immediately apparent when we note that the first edict of the *imperator histricus* (a phrase which is in itself a joke) is a prohibition against *scorta exoleta* taking a seat on the *proscaenium*. There is no other evidence that spectators actually occupied the stage as happened occasionally in the Elizabethan theatre, to judge from the 'Induction' of Beaumont and Fletcher's 'Knight of the Burning Pestle'. The other remarks, requesting *matronae* not to laugh in an annoying fashion (32-5), and nursing mothers not to bring young children whose wailing may distract the rest of the audience (28-31), and, in particular, the instructions forbidding ushers to show people to their places after the show has begun (19-20), all have a ring of truth about them. We gather from lines 23-4 that slaves might attend the theatre, although it is implied that strictly they were not entitled to do so. The prologue to the *Amphitruo* (64 ff) contains references to an organized *claque*, but there are grounds for thinking that this passage may be from a revival.[29] We might perhaps try to supplement the information given us by the Plautine prologues by reference to the prologues of Terence. Terence tells us in the prologue to the *Hecyra* (4) that his audiences might be wooed away from the performance by the rival attraction of a rope-dancer, or (39 f) by the rumour that a gladiatorial show was about to be given. We must however remember that Terence was writing some twenty years after the death of Plautus, and his own prologues tell us explicitly that the playwrights who were his contemporaries had adopted a different style of composition from that of Plautus.[30] It is highly probable that audiences too may have changed. They may have become more *blasé* about theatre-going, or else they may quite simply not have liked this particular play of Terence, which, after all, lacks those features which Plautus included to gratify Roman taste. It would therefore be unwise to rely too much on the evidence supplied by Terence in attempting to form a picture of Plautus's audiences.

The general impression which Plautus himself gives us is that his audiences came to the theatre in a relaxed, holiday mood, and in consequence were delighted by entertainment which might nowadays seem more appropriate to the music-hall or to revue than to the legitimate theatre. This need not, however, be taken as indicating a low standard of intellectual attainment, and in fact some of the evidence which I shall put forward suggests that they were more cultured than we might have expected to be the case.

It may be useful at this point to consider the names which Plautus gives to his plays and to the characters who appear in them. In general Plautus seems to have aimed at giving his plays short titles, which could be understood, or at least easily remembered, by those whose knowledge of Greek was limited or non-existent. Seven of the plays (*Amphitruo*, *Bacchides*, *Casina*, *Epidicus*, *Menaechmi*, *Pseudolus*, and *Stichus*) have Greek names derived from those of characters in the plays. The other fourteen have Latinized names—the number would be fifteen if we include *Sortientes*, which, we gather from the *Casina* prologue (32) was the title originally given to that play. *Sortientes* is a literal translation of the Greek title of the original, and we are told in the *Asinaria* (10) and in the *Mercator* (9) that these titles too are translated from the Greek original. Plautus, however, obviously did not feel bound in every case to translate the Greek literally. We know from *Rudens* (32) that this play was translated from a play of Diphilus, but the name is not an exact translation of any title which we now possess for a play of Diphilus. Plautus himself gave the name *Patruos* to the play later known as the *Poenulus* (54), and in the case of the *Trinummus*, he appears to have 'coined' a completely new title. In five cases (*Asinaria, Aulularia, Cistellaria, Mostellaria*, and *Vidularia*) he has used a Latin adjectival ending—*aria* which had apparently also been used by Naevius, who wrote a *Carbonaria* and a *Nervolaria*. Caecilius, Luscius Lanuvinus, and Terence seem to have preferred to use the titles of the Greek originals, though Terence does substitute the name *Phormio* for the original *Epidicazomenos* (*Phorm.* 25-6). Terence refers to a *Colax* of both Naevius and Plautus, and grammarians quote from an *Agroecus* and a *Dyskolos* by Plautus. It is, however, possible that Plautus himself gave these plays other titles. We know that Verrius Flaccus referred to the *Cistellaria* as the *Synaristosae*,[31] and so it seems possible that in later times it may have been usual to refer to his plays by the title of the Greek original, without regard to the title which he had himself given to them.

In his choice of titles, Plautus seems to have been making concessions to those whose knowledge of Greek was limited, but he makes no such concessions in the choice of names for his characters. One might be tempted to assume that the character-names in his plays would be the same as those employed in the Greek originals, but there are strong grounds for believing that this is not the case. The researches of Schmidt[32] and Ullman[33] indicate that Plautus, to quote Ullman, 'handled his sources rather freely in the matter of names, using *contaminatio*, if the word may be thus employed, or else going outside the field of New Comedy altogether'. Schmidt argues that when he did go outside the field of New Comedy, he borrowed names from life and from Greco-Italian folk-humour. To these sources Leo[34] would add Old Comedy. Schmidt also points out that the double names such as we find in *Miles* 14, *Bumbomachides Clutomestoridy-sarchides*, are not paralleled at all in Greek, and he suggests that these must be Plautine inventions. In the instance quoted the name is almost intrinsically funny, through the onomatopoeic effect of *Bumbo*—, and because of its all but sesquipedalian length, but, if Plautus invented it, he clearly took pains to invent a name

31

which made sense in Greek. A large number of Plautus's names are, in fact, jocular, but the jokes are in Greek. Very occasionally a note of explanation is added, as in the case of Harpax (*Pseud.* 655), and also of Phronesium (*Truc.* 78a) if the text is sound. It would perhaps be as rash to claim that all these jokes would be appreciated by all his audience as it would be to argue that all the original 'Twelfth Night' audience could appreciate the etymological significance of the name *Malvolio*, but it seems reasonable to assume that neither Plautus nor Shakespeare would make such jokes purely for their own amusement, and that they both felt that they could count on being understood by at least some sections of their audiences.

Some of the Greek names have clearly been chosen on account of their Latin connotations, e.g. Saturio in the *Persa*, Sceledrus in the *Miles*, and Simia, the *sycophanta* in the *Pseudolus*, but there are remarkably few wholly Latin names. Five of these are divine characters who appear as speakers of the prologue; Mercurius in the *Amphitruo*, the Lar in the *Aulularia*, Auxilium in the *Cistellaria*, and Luxuria and Inopia in the *Trinummus*. This is in accordance with Plautus's general practice of translating the names of Greek deities by their Latin equivalents. Apart from these there are two *parasiti*, Curculio in the play of the same name and Peniculus in the *Menaechmi*, and the slave Truculentus in the play of which he is the eponymous hero. In the case of Curculio and Truculentus, it is possible that Plautus first named the play, and then adjusted the character-names to suit. Peniculus makes it clear that his name is in fact a nick-name (*Men.* 77), and another parasite, Ergasilus in the *Captivi* states that he also bears a Latin nick-name— 'Scortum' (69). In each case the information is given when the characters make their first appearance, and we are told that the nick-name has been bestowed by the *iuventus*, the young men about town. Both these characters are described by the Greek term *parasitus*, and it looks as if Plautus had given them these soubriquets in order to help an audience which was unfamiliar with the role of the Greek *parasitus* to understand what sort of men they were. *Sycophanta* is another character-description which is not translated, and the inference is that *parasiti* and *sycophantae* were people of a sort to be expected in Greece but not in Rome. They are thus clearly differentiated from the *clientes* with which the Romans of Plautus's time were familiar and to whom reference

is made in *Men.* 574 ff. (The feminine, *clienta*, is to be found in
Miles 789 and *Rud.* 893.) The term *rex*, which is sometimes used to
refer to Roman *patroni* is, however, applied to the patrons of
parasiti on occasion, e.g. at *Asin.* 919, *Capt.* 92, and *Stich.* 455.

Plautus's audiences did not, of course, have programmes with
cast-lists, but since we have mentioned two character-descriptions,
it may be convenient to discuss some others which are not
translated into Latin. Two of these, *trapezita* in the *Curculio*,
and *danista* in the *Epidicus* and *Mostellaria*, relate to the world of
business, and exist alongside the Latin *argentarius* which is used
quite frequently. The scansion of some of the lines in which it
occurs indicates that *trapezita* had been turned by metathesis into
tarpezita,[35] which suggests that it was already a familiar word in
Latin. Probably Plautus used these words because they were at
least as common as the nearest Latin equivalents. The reason for
this may be, as Tenney Frank suggests,[36] that they were 'canteen'
words, learned by Roman soldiers on service in Greek-speaking
areas on pay-day. This may well be true, but one must not forget
that at this period much of Rome's foreign trade was passing
through the Bay of Naples area at Puteoli, and that, for instance,
Naples and Paestum both felt sufficiently friendly towards Rome
to make voluntary contributions to the Roman war-effort (Livy,
xxii. 32, 4-9, and 36, 9). Plautus obviously expects his hearers to be
familiar with the Greek monetary system, and often uses terms
taken from the sphere of Greek business relations, e.g. *emporium*,
exagoga, *syngraphus*, etc. One of the most interesting of these
'business' words is *arrhabo*. The payment of an *arrhabo* or deposit
was apparently not customary in Rome at this time,[37] but Plautus
quite clearly expects his audience to understand what the word
means, as he does not feel obliged to introduce any explanation of
it. On the whole the evidence suggests that his audience was
quite familiar with Greek business practice.

The description *paedagogus* is another which is not translated
from the Greek. If Plutarch is right and the soldiers of Fabius
Cunctator did actually call him Hannibal's *paedagogus*,[38] the term
must already have been familiar in Rome during Plautus's life-time.
It is, however, worth noting that when the *paedagogus* Lydus
appears in the *Bacchides* (109 ff), the dialogue makes it clear what
his functions are, and an explanatory note is provided at *Merc.*
90 f, where the term is used; *paedagogus fuerat, quasi uti mihi foret*

custos. This suggests that Plautus was doubtful whether the word would be readily understood.

It is interesting to note that the word *hetaera* is not used as a character-description. Leo argued on the evidence of Polybius (xxxii. 11, 4) that *hetaerae* only became 'fashionable' in Rome some fifteen years after the death of Plautus.[39] But the word *meretrix* is frequently used by Plautus, alongside the more pejorative *scortum* and *prostibulum*. (*Cist.* 331 shows that the *meretrix* was expected to behave more modestly than the *prostibulum*.) One must infer that a kind of class-distinction among women of easy virtue was already recognised at Rome. This is borne out by Livy (xxxix. 9, 5-7) in his account of the suppression of the Bacchanals in 186 B.C. In that account, Hispala Faecenia, who is classified as a *scortum*, is described as a *meretricula* after her enfranchisement. *Cist.* 562 f obliquely describes a *meretrix* as 'one who shamefully earns her dowry in the Tuscan manner'. This suggests that there were *meretrices* at Rome who were connected in the popular mind with Etruria—unless perhaps the reference is to the *vicus Tuscus*, which appears from *Curc.* 482 to have been a notorious 'red-light' district. Consequently Plautus is able to describe the courtesans who feature so frequently in his plays by a Latin word which corresponds fairly closely to the *hetaera* of the original. If, as Fraenkel suggests,[40] the brothel-scene in the *Pseudolus* (I. ii) is really Roman in its setting, the Roman *meretrices* may not generally have enjoyed the same social freedom as the Greek *hetaerae*. The Latin word with its mercenary connotations implies a more disapproving attitude on the part of the Romans than the more euphemistic Greek term.

The setting of the plays is not of great importance. In twelve of them, the scene is set in Athens, and when the action is set elsewhere, some local colour is often given, such as the reference to the temple of Aesculapius in Epidaurus, the scene of the *Curculio* (14); to the temple of Diana in Ephesus in the *Miles* (411); and to the shrine of Venus in Cyrene in the *Rudens* (61). These details, as well as the general settings, were presumably taken over by Plautus from the Greek originals. The reference to the *Magalia*, a suburb of Carthage, in *Poen.* 86 may, however, come from the pen of Plautus himself. The topography of Thebes in the *Amphitruo* is rather odd, as it has a harbour, the *portus Persicus* (404), apparently within easy reach of the city, but we cannot hold

Plautus responsible for this peculiar error until we can establish more certainly what original play or plays he was using.[41] Presumably in any case his audience was as little perturbed by this slip as an Elizabethan audience would have been by Shakespeare's allusion to the sea-coast of Bohemia. It is of more interest to note that Plautus, like the writers of pantomime today, assumed that his audience would be amused by references to familiar places in a foreign context. The Capitolium, which is to be found both in Athens (*Trin.* 84) and in Epidaurus (*Curc.* 269), may have been considered almost as a common noun, and so as an appropriate name for a citadel. But when, in the *Captivi*, a parasite in Aetolia speaks with familiarity of such Roman landmarks as the Porta Trigemina (90) and the Velabrum (489), we may be justified in concluding that Plautus is catering for an unsophisticated fondness for the incongruous. The speech of the Choragus in the *Curculio* (462-86) gives us a most interesting picture of the Rome of Plautus's time, unless it comes from a revival, but as it is not spoken by one of the characters, its function was perhaps mainly to help 'audience-participation'.

Many of the details which we have just discussed would nowadays be found in a printed programme. The audience was, of course, uninformed about the entertainment which was about to be presented until the first actor appeared on the stage. Plautus was therefore obliged to give his audience essential information as quickly as possible. This he did either by an expository first scene, of which one of the best examples is the opening scene of the *Mostellaria*, or by a prologue, or, on occasion as in the *Miles*, by a 'prologue' delivered after the action has begun. This last may seem rather strange, but we know of at least one precedent for it in Greek New Comedy, in Menander's *Perikeiromene*. Recently valuable light has been cast on Plautus's technique in writing the prologues by Lloyd's comparison of the prologue to the *Dyskolos* with lines 31-82 of the prologue to the *Rudens*.[42] He points out that both these prologues give, in the same order and with very similar general treatment, (*a*) a general identification of the locale of the play, perhaps necessitated by the fact that both are set outside Athens, (*b*) a revelation of the opening situation, (*c*) an announcement of the god's general intentions—both are 'divine' prologues—and (*d*) an introduction to the first scene. Since the original of the *Rudens* was by Diphilus, not Menander, this comparison would suggest that expository prologues of this type may have been fairly common in New Comedy. In the *Rudens* prologue there are some thirty lines before the expository part proper begins, and similar passages are to be found at the beginning of other Plautine prologues. This part, apparently described by the effective hybrid term *antelogium* (*Men.* 13), was almost certainly not in the Greek original. In these *antelogia* Plautus endeavours to win the favour of his audience at the outset and to allow them time to settle down. They thus to a certain extent perform the function of the modern overture. In consequence he frequently makes jokes with a definitely Roman flavour, such as puns, and also, as we have seen, sometimes directs bantering remarks at the audience. In the *Rudens antelogium*, for example, we probably have a near-pun in line 2 *civitate caelitum* (perhaps a play on *civitate Caeritum*),[43] and the jingles *inter deos* and *interdiu* (6-7) and *inveniet veniam* (27). The *antelogium* also often provides an opportunity to name the Greek original.

Leo maintained[44] that expository prologues spoken by a character who does not take part in the action of the play were only used when the plot involved a 'recognition' scene. As Lloyd has pointed out, this view is no longer tenable now that we possess the *Dyskolos* prologue, as the action of that play does not involve 'recognition'. Nevertheless, Leo is right to a certain extent in that many of the plays whose plots hinge on 'recognition' do have expository prologues of this type. The reason for this is very probably that adduced by Tenney Frank.[45] Ancient audiences were interested less in what happened than in how it happened, and they enjoyed dramatic irony—knowing more about the real state of affairs than the characters involved in the action. Therefore, when a prologue seems to give the game away too early, we should not conclude from this that Plautus felt that his audience lacked the intelligence to grasp what was happening unless they had it clearly explained to them beforehand. At the same time, it must be noted that in the action of many of the plays Plautus seems to prepare the audience almost too repetitiously for some deception or other change in the course of the plot. Hough,[46] after analysing Plautus's practice in this connexion concludes that he is most repetitious in the earlier plays, and in his later works trusted more and more in the capacity of his audience to follow the action of the play without undue preparation. 'Therefore', Hough says, 'it is suggested that the Roman audience, in spite of the slurs which scholars have so often cast upon it, became, during the literary activity of Plautus, sufficiently familiar with the Romanized Hellenistic comedy not to need so much help and explanation in 184 B.C. as it had needed twenty or thirty years earlier.'

It is difficult to generalize about the Plautine prologues. We know, in the case of the *Casina*, that the prologue comes from a revival, and other prologues may well have been altered for productions taking place after Plautus's death. It is, however, noteworthy that Plautus never indulges in polemics against other writers, or feels it necessary to justify his own professional technique. In this respect he is, of course, quite different from Terence, but it is not now possible to say whether this is because Plautus reacted less sensitively to criticism, or whether, in Plautus's time, the hey-day of the *fabula palliata*, there was less bitterness in professional rivalry than was to develop later in the time of Terence.

Since we do not possess any of the Greek originals, it is impossible to say with certainty what alterations Plautus felt it necessary to make in the plot and characterization to make them acceptable to a Roman audience. It has frequently been argued, on the basis of Terence's remarks in the *Andria* prologue (18-21), that Plautus indulged in the practice of combining more than one Greek original in order to make one Latin play. However, it is by no means certain that this is what Terence means. When he talks of imitating Plautus's *negligentia*, he may only mean that he wishes, like Plautus, to handle his material fairly freely. Moreover, although the hypothesis of combination might explain difficulties in some plays, e.g. the *Miles Gloriosus*, it is not the only possible solution.[47] One must remember that some inconsistencies in plot and treatment which seem obvious to the scholar, may not have been so obvious to the writer, possibly writing to a dead-line, or to the audience seeing the play performed.

We do not know how Plautus found his originals, but it seems reasonable to assume that he could choose from a large number of extant Greek plays. It is therefore probable that in making his selection he chose in particular plots which would be generally acceptable to his Roman audience. It has often been noted that, with the exception of the *Amphitruo*, and this is an exception which proves the rule, adulterous wives are never presented in his plays as a comic theme. However, as we have no evidence that they appeared frequently in Greek New Comedy, we can draw no conclusions about Roman taste from this fact. The taste of Plautus's audience was clearly not prudish, and the *Casina*, which is one of the least inhibited of his plays,[48] was apparently one of the most popular, to judge from the prologue (17)—*haec quom primum acta est, vicit omnis fabulas*. We may perhaps compare the popularity of Terence's *Eunuchus* which appears to have been his most successful play. On the other hand, there is nothing to indicate that the *Captivi* was not popular, although Plautus prides himself on the purity of its plot (*Capt.* 53-60 and 1029-36).

Plautus may well have avoided plays whose action turned on some fairly recondite point of Greek law or custom. An exception to this general rule is to be found in the allusion to slave-marriage in the *Casina* (68 ff). In this passage, by the jocular tone and the rather slighting reference to Apulia, he deftly avoids appearing didactic. It is possible that, on occasion, he may have altered the plot in order to omit material which would have been offensive or incomprehensible to his audience. It has been argued that in the *Epidicus* he altered the ending of the play in order to remove a marriage between half-brother and half-sister which would have been repugnant to the Romans.[49] But this is by no means certain and the suggestion has been strongly contested by several scholars.[50]

It is possible that Plautus might have been justified in making fairly radical changes in the plots. For instance, in view of the greater social freedom enjoyed by women in Rome than in Greece, he might conceivably have expanded the roles of the free-born women in his plays. Since he did not do so, we may assume that his audiences preferred to look on the *fabula palliata* as representative of Greek life, and to accept at least some of the limitations imposed by the foreign setting. Probably they did not expect their plays to be 'realistic', although, as Duckworth has pointed out,[51] the plots, however improbable, are usually possible. Kidnapping and child-exposure must have been known to happen, and so the basic situation of many of Plautus's plots must have been readily imaginable. The coincidences in the plots may often seem too good to be true, but Plautus is no more open to criticsm on this point than, say, Charles Dickens.

It would be very interesting to know whether Plautus's

depiction of his slave characters is to any great extent a reflection
of the social conditions of his time. We have already noted that
slaves were in all probability given a more prominent role in
Plautus's plays than they had had in the Greek originals. Plautus
might quite easily have given slaves more prominence purely
from considerations of comic effect, and in consequence it might
be the case that this feature supplies us with evidence about the
Roman sense of humour, but not about Roman social conditions.
Tenney Frank maintained[52] that in fact slaves were relatively
scarce in Rome in Plautus's lifetime, and, of course, no one would
suggest that the Romans of this period were nearly so dependent
on slave-labour as they were later to become after the great
periods of conquest. The process of acquiring slaves in large
numbers had already begun in Plautus's lifetime, and we may have
a reference to it in his allusion to the *patientia Surorum* in *Trin.*
542-6. But even before that happened it is quite possible that there
were considerable numbers of slaves in Rome. Mommsen held[53]
that in the frequent references to the punishment of slaves we have
a reflection of the policies advocated by the Elder Cato. This may
be an overstatement of the case, but the frequency of the references
to crucifixion and other servile punishments would seem to imply
that there must have been a sufficient number of slaves in Roman
territories to constitute a potential menace which had to be held
in check by the threat and infliction of brutal punishment. Plautus
in fact supplies us with some evidence which indicates that he
may have had Roman conditions in mind, at least to some extent,
in his depiction of slave characters. If we consider the words and
phrases which he puts in Greek, we find that the great majority
are spoken by slaves or other 'low-life' characters such as parasties
and procurers. Some are spoken by old men, but significantly,
usually by old men who are not behaving with appropriate
gravitas. It is clear, too, that some at least of these Greek words
and phrases cannot have come from the Greek originals; for
example, the punning allusions to Italian towns in *Capt.* 881-3.
The slaves and other low-life characters also use a higher
proportion of Latinized Greek words than do the more respectable
characters. It seems very likely that Plautus is reflecting the mode
of speech which was current among the slaves and freedmen of
his own time. Since some of the Latinized Greek words tend to
be used almost exclusively in one or two plays (e.g. *graphice* in

the *Persa* 306, 464, 843, and *Trin.* 767), it is possible that his language may be influenced by transitory fashions in 'slang '.[54]

The use of Greek words in a Latinized form is not confined to the 'low-life' characters. Such words are used fairly frequently, and, as Hough has pointed out,[55] Plautus appears to have employed them with an artistry which developed steadily throughout his professional career. Hough refers[56] to the work of Bostroem, who, in his analysis of Plautus's use of Greek words, concluded that such words are to be attributed to '*Graecam fabularum naturam*, *versum*, or *ioci causa*, but by far the greatest number to *linguae Latinae egestatem*'. Hough points out that the Greek character of the plays can only have affected 'particular episodes or topics of a Greek nature', and he rightly rejects the notion that metrical considerations may have induced Plautus to use a Greek word instead of a Latin one. Hough agrees that some words were taken over into Latin to make good deficiencies, but points out that many words such as *eleutheria* and *architecton*, which have been adduced as examples of this class, have sound Latin equivalents which are used by Plautus himself elsewhere. His own theory[57] is that Plautus 'used Greek primarily *ioci causa et elegantiae*'. Many Greek words at this time must have been quite comprehensible but still retained an aura of amusing elegance. It is quite possible, I believe, that some of the Greek words of this type may not have been widely understood by his audiences. This might more particularly be true of the occasional strings of Greek words such as occur in the list of articles of feminine luxury in the *Epidicus* (222-34), or in the long list of fish-names in the Fisherman's Chorus in the *Rudens* (290-305). Here Plautus probably hoped that they would seem funny just because they were only partially understood. This motive will possibly account also for the passages in alleged Punic in the *Poenulus*, as, even if Plautus did write correct Punic, it is very unlikely that even the veterans of the Punic War could have understood much of it. Shakespeare aims, I think, at the same kind of comic effect with his introduction of Katherine's French in *Henry V*, as does Dekker with the Dutch which he includes in *The Shoemaker's Holiday*.[58] But most frequently, the Greek words occur quite naturally in normal conversation, and were clearly meant to be comprehensible.

Many of the Greek words must, of course, have been introduced because they represented something for which Latin could not provide a suitable term. Some of these, such as *lanterna*, reveal by their altered appearance that they were popular and not literary borrowings.[59] The word *artopta* is particularly interesting. Pliny notes (N.H. xviii, 28) that, since the Romans did not have bakers until the time of the war against Perseus (which ended in 168 B.C.) some scholars of his time doubted the authenticity of the line in the *Aulularia* (400) in which it occurs. It seems most probable that Plautus used the word precisely because Latin had no equivalent, but nevertheless the word may have been familiar, particularly to the ex-servicemen in the audience. Plautus does not appear to have been a pedantic translator, and he is quite prepared to use a natural Latin word such as *lanius* when it suits the context even if it may not be a literal translation of the word used in the Greek original.[60]

Some of the Latinized Greek words may be mere transliterations of words in the original, but there is evidence that many were not. Fraenkel has pointed out[61] that some of the Greek words used, e.g. *thermopolium* and *anancaeum*, do not occur elsewhere in Greek literature, and so are unlikely to have come from the Attic original. He draws the inference that such words may have come from the Greek cities of Magna Graecia, and this seems reasonable. The adverb *basilice* would more probably have been in common use in monarchical Sicily than in Attica.[62] If this theory is right, it helps to reinforce the idea that perhaps the majority of the words of Greek derivation owe their presence in the plays to the fact that they had already been imported into Latin. Probably the most likely channels of importation were those we have already mentioned; the 'slang' of soldiers who had served in the South of Italy, the trade contacts of Rome with the cities in the Naples area, and the Greek slaves whose presence in significant numbers cannot be proved, but may reasonably be conjectured. It is, for instance, reasonable to infer from the frequency of Greek medical terms in the plays that Greek medicine had established itself in Rome. Pliny (N.H. xxix. 6) records that the first Greek doctor set up practice in Rome in 218 B.C. Cato (quoted by Pliny, xxix. 7) seems to speak in a letter to his son of the arrival of Greek doctors as a dire possibility in the future, but the fact that he himself uses such Greek terms as *dyspepsia* and *stranguria* in the *De agri cultura* (cxxvii.) suggests that Greek practitioners must already have been familiar in Rome, and thus confirms the Plautine evidence.

The assimilation of words by one nation from the language of another does not in itself establish that more important cultural borrowings have taken place. However, Plautus's plays provide a good deal of evidence that the Romans had indeed absorbed much more of the Greek cultural heritage. We have already noted the frequency of the mythological passages and the possibility that many of these may be the work of Plautus himself. The most frequent of these references are to the Trojan Cycle and to the Labours of Hercules. Tenney Frank has pointed out[63] that in the third century, the Romans were already becoming interested in the legend, first found in the work of Timaeus, that they were themselves descended from the Trojans, and this interest was of course fostered by the publication of the *Odisia* of Livius Andronicus. It is not at all probable that the circulation of this work can have been so widespread as to account for the familiarity with the Trojan legends which I am suggesting that Plautus could assume. Livius' poem, however, reveals that he was not introducing legends which were entirely novel to the Romans. Although his work is called the *Odisia*, his hero is referred to as *Ulixes*, which shows that that name was already well known in Rome. This form of the name cannot have come from Homer, but may have reached Rome, by way of the Etruscans, from the legends of West Greece and Illyria, as Phillips suggests.[64] In Plautus the *Ulixes* form is used, and similar transformations have also occured, e.g. with the name *Catamitus* for Ganymede (*Men.* 144). It is interesting to note too that Troilus is mentioned (*Bacch.* 954 and 960), a fact which suggests that the Romans were acquainted with versions other than the Homeric ones.[65] Roman interest in myths about Hercules is established by the frequency with which the exclamation *mehercle* is used and by the fact that payment of tithes to Hercules had been adopted as a custom.[66]

It seems fairly clear that the process of assimilating Greek mythology had already made considerable progress, and this is not surprising. The religious beliefs of the Romans were not too dissimilar from those of the Greeks, and so provided a common stem on to which more recondite detail could be grafted. They had very few myths of their own,[67] and at the same time they had not as yet adopted the gently cynical attitude towards mythology which was probably characteristic of the Greek New Comedy.[68] They probably acquired their knowledge of mythology in various ways. Their main sources may have been the normal channels of oral transmission. They may also have been familiar with works of art depicting mythological subjects either from Greece itself, or perhaps more probably of Etruscan workmanship. It would certainly seem reasonable to postulate an Etruscan provenance for the paintings referred to in *Capt.* 998 f (*Vidi ego multa saepe picta, quae Accherunti fierent cruciamenta*), as the horrors of the underworld appear to have been a popular subject for Etruscan art.[69] Moreover, the Romans' interest in, and knowledge of, Greek legend must have been greatly encouraged by the contemporary productions of translations from Greek tragedy. The *Amphitruo* prologue implies that the same audiences attended both comedies and tragedies, and it seems almost certain that Plautus frequently parodied the style of tragedy.[70] When, in *Rudens* 86, Plautus refers to the *Alcumena Euripidi*, he may, as Marx argues,[71] merely be repeating a reference originally made by Diphilus, but it is at least possible that a Latin version of this play was already familiar to the audience. The opening passage of the *Poenulus* prologue contains a reference to the *Achilles* of Aristarchus, and, as the passage as a whole bears all the marks of being from Plautus's own pen, one must conclude that this play had recently been performed at Rome. The evidence all suggests that Plautus's audiences had already by various means acquired a knowledge of Greek mythology, that Plautus was aware of their taste for it, and that he took steps to gratify that taste in his plays.

What is more surprising is that Plautus could apparently count on his audience being able to understand references to aspects of Greek culture which one would not have thought likely to make any great impact on them. There are, for instance, references to Greek historical events and personages, although they are not very numerous. In the *Menaechmi* (409 ff) the list of Sicilian kings is quite inaccurate and is presumably included merely to help to give local colour. In the *Mostellaria* (775-7), Alexander the Great and Agathocles appear, as it were, in double harness, and one wonders whether Plautus intended this incongruity as a joke, or whether he expected his audience to be aware of it. When no specific names are mentioned, it is often very difficult to decide whether references are to Greek or Roman history. For example, the diatribe against feminine extravagance in the *Aulularia* (498-535) might have come from the original Greek,[72] or it might have been inserted in order to refer to the repeal of the sumptuary *Lex Oppia* in 195 B.C., or again, conceivably both explanations might be true. Plautus might have retained a passage which had been topical in the Greek original, because it could be taken as a comment on the events of his own time. The fact that during the early years of the second century B.C. Rome became embroiled in wars in the territories which had been the scene of fighting among the successors of Alexander makes it peculiarly difficult to decide whether references, e.g. to Asia Minor, are Roman topicalities or survivals from the Greek original.[73] Most of the named historical Greek characters might perhaps have been heard of in Rome, but, as Fraenkel points out,[74] it is difficult to believe that the Romans were able to make much of the references to Clinias and Demetrius (*Bacch.* 912) or to Stratonicus (*Rud.* 932 ff). In this *Rudens* passage Gripus goes on to talk of having a city called after himself, and one wonders whether the retention of the reference may be explained on the hypothesis that the Romans had heard of the city of Stratonicea in Caria during their campaigns in 190 against Antiochus, and that this memory was fresh in their minds at the time of production of the *Rudens*.[75] This may be too subtle an explanation, and it would be impossible to prove. It is perhaps safer to admit the possibility that Plautus on occasion retained from the original references which were not fully comprehensible to his audience.

This may be true also of some of the references to Greek philosophers. Socrates, for example, is mentioned in the *Pseudolus* (465), but an allusion to clouds in line 463 suggests that the original had contained a joke about Aristophanes' *Clouds* which Plautus probably did not himself understand, but which he retained on the assumption that some of his audience had heard of Socrates. He certainly expected them to know about Thales, as, among other references, in *Capt.* 274 he has the line *Thalem talento non emam Milesium*, which, since it contains a Latin pun, must be his own work. Probably stories about the Seven Sages of Greece had become familiar in Rome. If so, this would account for the reference to Solon (*Asin.* 599).

Plautus also occasionally refers to Greek writers and artists. The names of Diphilus and Philemon (*Most.* 1149) would presumably be familiar to the audience because, as is apparent from the prologues both of Plautus and Terence, it was quite

44

usual for a Roman writer to tell the audience the name of the author of the Greek play on which his own Latin one was based. But what are we to make of the mention of the names of the artists Zeuxis and Apelles (*Epid.* 626 and *Poen.* 1271)? Fraenkel maintains[76] that these two would never have been mentioned in this way by any Greek author, and therefore that they must have been inserted by Plautus himself. Whether this is so or not, Plautus surely could only have mentioned them if he expected them to be recognized as leading exponents of the graphic arts, and this in turn indicates that his audience had begun to take an interest in Greek art.

There are, of course, in the plays numerous allusions to social and legal institutions which are undoubtedly Roman. These are primarily of value because they show clearly how successfully Plautus translated his originals, carefully avoiding a pedantic adherence to the letter of the Greek while at the same time retaining the general Greek atmosphere. There are also frequent 'Roman topicalities'. We have had occasion to mention some of these, and many more might have been included, e.g. the frequent references to victory in war in the prologues, and the allusion to the defeat of the Boii in *Capt.* 888. It is also probable that there are many topical references which nowadays must escape detection. There are indications that Plautus assumed that his audience took an interest in the general political situation. This may be inferred from the fairly frequent use of such words and phrases as *gloria*, *virtus*, and *mos maiorum*, which in his time had specific political connotations.[77] On the whole the Roman topicalities seem to presuppose an audience which was alert and quick-witted, but at the same time unsophisticated enough to take pleasure in manifest anachronisms and incongruities.

A great deal of the humorous element in the plays depends naturally on the plot and the characters, and so must have been taken over from the Greek. In the language of the plays, however, Plautus is able to make a special appeal to the Romans' sense of humour.[78] He is particularly fond of what one might term the '*para prosdokian*' joke, in which, for example, a question meets with a wholly unexpected reply. The frequent use made by Plautus of puns and similar plays on words, which must by their very nature be his own work, is a clear indication of the Roman taste in humour, a taste which appears in this respect to have been very similar to that of the Elizabethans. Puns do not appear to have been common in Greek New Comedy, and only one example is to be found in the *Dyskolos*,[79] an example so feeble that it would be more charitable to assume that it is accidental. Sometimes the puns of Plautus are very neat, when a word which is perfectly natural in the context of the dialogue reveals itself as having another, but still perfectly possible meaning. Sometimes the puns can only be described as bad, when the main statement seems to have been dragged in to provide a peg on which to hang an even more far-fetched secondary significance, and of course there are many intermediate stages. The pun as a form of humour never quite lost respectability at Rome, and Cicero, himself a frequent punster, virtually justifies the use of puns in the *De Oratore* (ii. 248 ff). Plautus exploits most of the obvious veins in the Latin language, and occasionally even includes plays on words in Greek (e.g. *Miles* 438 and *Stich.* 630 f). Sometimes the puns might more properly be termed *doubles entendres*, but this is not very frequent. In one such case, involving the two meanings of the verb *comprimere*, there is also a play on the words *eira* (an old form of *ira*) and *era* (*Truc.* 262-4). Here Astaphium points out that there is the difference of one letter between the two words. A similar remark is made about *medicus* and *mendicus* in *Rud.* 1305 f. This suggests that Plautus was able to assume at least a rudimentary degree of literacy on the part of his audience.

Some of the most interesting Roman jokes relate to other parts of Italy. We have already noted the allusion to the Hellenized customs of Apulia, and the probable reference to Etruscan immorality. Capuan extravagance is gently satirized in *Rud.* 631. The people of Praeneste seem to have been a special target for Plautus's humour. They are described as boastful (*Bacch.* 12), and on two occasions (*Trin.* 609 and *Truc.* 691) they are singled out for jokes at the expense of peculiarities of their dialect. This is particularly interesting as one of the surviving fragments of Naevius (*Ariolus* ii) alludes to their rustic manners. Praeneste was probably at this time one of the more important of Rome's neighbours,[80] and one might perhaps see in this little more than the kind of joke based on inter-city rivalry which recurs perennially in pantomime and music-hall humour. But there is also the implication that the Romans felt themselves to be more culturally advanced than their neighbours.[81]

This may well be an important clue towards the understanding of Plautus's audience. The Romans, particularly through their associations with the Etruscans and the Greeks of Italy, had probably for a long time been assimilating cultural elements from outside, but this process must have been considerably accelerated by the increased contacts produced by the First and Second Punic Wars. In many respects the Romans found that their own social life could be compared with that of the Greeks whom they then encountered, although at the same time they found features in the Greek way of life of which they disapproved. In the cultural and intellectual spheres, however, they perceived that they had much to learn from the Greeks. This feeling prompted them to embrace the *fabulae palliatae*, and in these, while they appreciated adaptations which had a specifically Roman flavour, they welcomed references to the culture which they were absorbing. At the same time they enriched their own language with neologisms which could convey *nuances* for the expression of which Latin was inadequate. This phase was probably most fully developed during the lifetime of Plautus, but there is evidence that it was not welcome in all quarters at Rome. The Elder Cato specifically objects to the Greeks referring to the Romans as *barbari*,[82] a practice which was a source of amusement to Plautus and his audience. The attitude of Hellenophobia which is typified by Cato probably spread more widely and became more influential when Rome was involved more and more in warfare with the Greeks. Later the process of the absorption of Greek culture continued in rather different ways and the comic theatre played scarcely any part in it.

If our initial assumptions, and our selection and interpretation of the evidence have been sound, it would appear that Plautus's audiences were intellectually awake and had a robust sense of humour and a keen zest for life. In these respects they remind us of the Elizabethans; and like the Elizabethans they were fortunate in having a writer of genius to cater for their tastes.

NOTES

For convenience, the following works will be referred to by the surnames of their authors: W. Beare, *The Roman Stage*² (1955); G. E. Duckworth, *The Nature of Roman Comedy* (Princeton, 1952); E. Fraenkel, *Elementi Plautini in Plauto* (Firenze, 1960)—a revised Italian translation of the same author's *Plautinisches in Plautus*; Tenney Frank, *Life and Literature in the Roman Republic* (Berkeley, 1930); F. Leo, *Plautinische Forschungen*² (Berlin, 1912); B. A.

Taladoire, *Essai sur le Comique de Plaute* (Monaco, 1956); K. M. Westaway, *The Original Element in Plautus* (Cambridge, 1917).

[1] Cf. V. Ehrenberg, *The People of Aristophanes* (Oxford, 1943), p. 29 f.

[2] Cf. H. B. Mattingly, 'The First Period of Plautine Revival', *Latomus* XIX (1960), p. 251. I am very grateful to Mr. Mattingly, my colleague, for his helpful discussion of a number of points.

[3] Cf. Leo, pp. 74 ff; and F. della Corte, *Da Sarsina a Roma* (Genova, 1952), pp. 15 ff.

[4] Cf. Beare, p. 13 f; Duckworth, pp. 8-10, and Taladoire, pp. 74-6.

[5] For a longer list, see Westaway, p. 31.

[6] Rome was, of course, also involved in wars in Greece from 212 to 205 and from 200 to 187, and in Asia Minor from 190 to 187 B.C.

[7] Cf. Duckworth, p. 42.

[8] Cf. H. B. Mattingly, 'Naevius and the Metelli', *Historia* IX (1960), pp. 414-39.

[9] Paulus, s.v. barbari.

[10] Cf. Mattingly (*art. cit.*, n. 8 above), p. 416.

[11] Ad *Eun.* 57. Cf. Duckworth, p. 69.

[12] Cf. Mattingly (*art. cit.*, n. 2 above), pp. 246 ff.

[13] Cf. R. W. Reynolds, 'Criticism of Individuals in Roman Popular Comedy', *CQ* XXXVII (1943), pp. 37-45.

[14] Beare, pp. 209 ff.

[15] W. B. Sedgwick, 'The *Cantica* of Plautus', *CR* XXXIX (1925), pp. 55-8.

[16] Cf. K. H. E. Schutter, *Quibus annis Comodeiae Plautinae primum actae sint quaeritur* (Groningen, 1952), p. 94 f, and G. Williams, 'Evidence for Plautus' Workmanship in the *Miles Gloriosus*', *Hermes* LXXXVI (1958), pp. 79 ff.

[17] Aulus Gellius, II, 23.

[18] Fraenkel, pp. 105 ff.

[19] pp. 7 ff.

[20] pp. 21 ff.

[21] pp. 55 ff.

[22] H. W. Prescott, 'Criteria of Originality in Plautus', *TAPhA* LXIII (1932), pp. 193-25. It is interesting to note that the mythological passage in *Duscolus*, 153 ff, is almost 'Plautine' by Fraenkel's criteria.

[23] pp. 223 ff.

[24] T. B. L. Webster, *Studies in Later Greek Comedy* (Manchester, 1953), p. 69.

[25] Westaway, pp. 49 ff.

[26] Cf. Beare, pp. 152 ff, and Duckworth, pp. 76-9.

[27] Cf. Beare, pp. 161 ff, and Duckworth, p. 79 f.

[28] Cf. Duckworth, pp. 132 fi.

[29] Cf. n. 12 above. Duckworth (p. 81) believes that both the *Amphitruo* and the *Poenulus* prologues are by Plautus.

[30] The changes which took place in the *fabula palliata* between the times of Plautus and Terence are ably discussed by H. Oppermann, 'Zur Entwicklung der Fabula Palliata', *Hermes* LXXIV (1939), pp. 113-29.

[31] Cf. Duckworth, p. 53.

[32] K. Schmidt, 'Griechische Personenname bei Plautus', *Hermes* XXXVII (1902), pp. 173-211 and 353-90.

[33] B. L. Ullman, 'Proper names in Plautus, Terence and Menander', *CPh* XI (1916), pp. 61-4.

[34] Leo, p. 110.

[35] Cf. W. M. Lindsay, *The Captivi of Plautus* (1900), p. 170.

[36] Frank, p. 71.

[37] Cf. G. Williams, 'Some Problems in the Construction of Plautus' *Pseudolus*', *Hermes* LXXXIV (1956), pp. 424-55, esp. p. 425.

[38] Plutarch, *Fabius*, 5.

[39] Leo, p. 140, n. 1. Cf. Frank, p. 81 f; but against this cf. K. Abel, *Die Plautusprologe* (Frankfurt, 1955), p. 116, n. 111.

[40] Fraenkel, pp. 139 ff. Cf. Williams (*art. cit.*, n. 37 above), p. 427.

[41] For a recent discussion of the probable sources of the *Amphitruo* see the edition by W. B. Sedgwick (Manchester, 1960), pp. 2-6.

[42] R. B. Lloyd, 'Two Prologues—Menander and Plautus', *AJPh* LXXXIV (1963), pp. 146-61.

[43] Cf. my note in *CPh* LVII (1962), p. 240.

[44] Leo, p. 197.

[45] Frank, pp. 106 ff.

[46] J. N. Hough, 'The understanding of Intrigue: A study in Plautine Chronology', *AJPh* LX (1929), pp. 422-35.

[47] For recent discussions of this problem in the *Miles* see Webster (*op. cit.*, n. 24 above), pp. 174-83, and Williams (*art. cit.*, n. 16 above). Cf. my 'Contaminatio', *CR* VII (1957), pp. 12-14.

[48] Cf. Beare, 'Plautus and his Public', *CR* XLII (1928), pp. 106-11, esp. pp. 109-110.

[49] The theory was put forward by K. Dziatzko in *RhM* LV (1905), pp. 104 ff.

[50] Cf. Fraenkel, pp. 300 ff and 434-5, and Duckworth, pp. 153-4.

[51] Duckworth, pp. 158-9.

[52] Frank, p. 80.

[53] T. Mommsen, *Römische Geschichte*[12] I (Berlin 1920), p. 900.

[54] The *Trinummus* has the adjective *graphicus* in lines 936 and 1024, and *pergraphicus* in 1139. *Graphicus* also occurs in *Epid.* 410, *Pseud.* 519 and 700, and *Stich.* 570. Cf. Fraenkel, p. 185, n. 1.

[55] J. N. Hough, 'The Use of Greek Words by Plautus', *AJPh* LV (1934), pp. 346-64.

[56] p. 347.

[57] p. 349.

[58] One might also instance the Latin of Sir Hugh Evans in *The Merry Wives of Windsor*, and the Spanish in Ben Jonson's *The Alchemist*.

[59] The Plautine form of the word may have been *laterna*. Cf. Sedgwick (*op. cit.*, n. 41 above), pp. 58-9 and 66.

[60] Cf. Fraenkel, pp. 124 f and 408 ff, and Prescott (*art. cit.*, n. 22 above), n. 21

[16] p. 149, n. 2.

[26] Asia Minor might be another possible source. On *basilice* see Franekel, pp. 183 ff.

[63] Frank, p. 15.

[64] E. D. Phillips, 'Odysseus in Italy', *JRS* LXXIII (1953), pp. 53-67, esp. p. 67, and L. R. Palmer, *The Latin Language*, (1961), pp. 40-1.

[65] Troilus is depicted on the Etruscan Tomb of the Bulls in Tarquinia. Cf. Pallottino and Hürlimann, *Art of the Etruscans* (1955), Pl. XII and pp. 133 ff.

[66] The form *mehercle* again suggests Etruscan influence. Cf. M. Pallottino, *The Etruscans* (1955), p. 160.

[67] Frank, p. 10.

[68] Cf. J. A. Hanson, 'Plautus as a Source Book for Roman Religion', *TAPhA* XC (1959), pp. 48-101, esp. p. 101.

[69] Cf. Fraenkel, pp. 170-1 and 424, and Pallottino (*op. cit.*, n. 66 above), p. 170 f.

[70] Cf. Leo, pp. 131 ff; Fraenkel, pp. 64 ff; W. B. Sedgwick, 'Parody in Plautus', *CQ* XXI (1927), pp. 88-9; T. Frank, 'Two Notes on Plautus', *AJPh* LIII (1932), pp. 243-51, and A. Thierfelder, 'Plautus and Römische Tragödie', *Hermes* LXXIV (1939), pp. 155-6.

[71] F. Marx, *Plautus Rudens* (Amsterdam, 1959), pp. 73-4.

[72] This would be especially likely if 503-4 contain a reference to the γυναικονόμος. Fraenkel thinks (pp. 131-2) that, even so, the passage is a Plautine insertion. At p. 413 he quotes Wilamowitz as supporting the theory that the passage dervies from Menander.

[73] Cf. della Corte (*op. cit.*, n. 3 above), pp. 181-2.

[74] p. 83, n. 3.

[75] This would be possible if the *Rudens* was produced in 189 B.C. as Sedgwick thinks. Cf. his 'Plautine Chronology', *AJPh* LXX (1949), pp. 376-83. On the other hand, F. Taeger in his *Charisma* I (Stuttgart, 1957), p. 407, thinks that this allusion to city-foundation would have been almost incomprehensible to Plautus's audiences.

[76] pp. 16 ff.

[77] Cf. D. C. Earl, 'Political Terminology in Plautus', *Historia* IX (1960), pp. 235-43.

[78] For discussions of Plautus's humour cf. Duckworth, pp. 331 ff, and Taladoire, 173 ff.

[79] Cf. L. A. Post's review of Martin's Dyscolus, *AJPh* LXXX (1959), p. 404.

[80] Cf. Fraenkel, p. 86 f.

[81] Cf. E. S. Ramage, 'Early Roman Urbanity', *AJPh* LXXXI (1960), pp. 65-72.

[82] Cf. Pliny, N. H. XXXIX, 7.

III

The Glorious Military

JOHN ARTHUR HANSON

A STOCK character is a scholar's delight. He may be traced backward and forward in time, across national boundaries from writer to writer, engendering Quellenforschungen and appreciations of our debt to classical culture. With a figure as frequent as the *miles gloriosus*, the mere tabulation of his occurrences in Western literature might exhaust a learned lifetime. Such a catalogue would have to follow the intrepid soldier through Greek Comedy, Old, Middle, and New, across the Adriatic to Republican Roman Comedy and around the Mediterranean through various forms of prose fiction, then up through Italy in the Commedia dell' Arte and across the spread of the Renaissance stage in Europe; thence multifariously through each nation's dramatic and fictional literature to the present moment.[1]

The present essay will not attempt to review this military parade in detail, from Lamachus to Sergeant Bilko, although the mere names on the roll call have their entertainment value: Therapontigonus Platagidorus, Horribilicribrifax, Ralph Roister Doister, Matamore, Chateaufort, Parolles, Bobadill, Bluffe, Bloody Five. . . .

The presence of a literary ancestor for a fictional character is of course in some measure critically significant: in so far as the author and audience can also be presumed to be aware of the ancestry, it is a contributing factor to the understanding of the character in his own environment. Thus Evelyn Waugh can make use of the classical education of his readers and add a Plautine reminiscence to the already anachronistic self-glory of Apthorpe in *Men at Arms* by entitling a chapter 'Apthorpe Gloriosus'. Thus Plautus himself can make use of his hearers' expectations embodied in the stock traits of the *miles gloriosus* by comically

disappointing these expectations: in the *Truculentus* he lets
Stratophanes, named and dressed for a conventional entrance of
boasting and threatening, tease the audience with his first line,
'Ne expectetis, spectatores, meas pugnas dum praedicem' (*Truc.* 482).

Yet in his quest for ancestral traits and family similarities,
the literary historian may unconsciously obscure other critical
questions which are raised by the iteration itself, by the very
repetitiveness of the stock character. One must try to answer, both
for the *miles gloriosus* as a type and for any specific embodiment of
that type, questions of both motive and means. What attracts a
playwright to the braggart warrior, and, once he has adopted him,
how does he fit him into the formal and thematic structure of his
play? What relation, if any, does he bear to the extra-literary world?
Specifically, given the fact that Pyrgopolinices in Plautus's *Miles
Gloriosus* is probably a copy in many essentials of a Menandrean
military braggart, what values does he have in Plautus's play in
Plautus's Rome? If the starting-point for this essay were
Shakespeare instead of Plautus, there would be little need to insist
on the primacy of these questions. Yet the sight of Latin sometimes
tends to obfuscate the critically obvious and the prejudices which
shape the directions of literary studies among classical scholars
have been especially strong in the case of Roman Comedy.
Critical opinion has in general valued Greek literature higher than
Latin and deprecated the latter as derivative. Since in addition
scholars manifest an unconquerable desire to reconstruct the
non-existent from the extant, the chief use to which Plautus and
Terence were put until 1958 was as a tool for the hypothetical
reconstruction of Greek New Comedy. In that year the publication
of Menander's *Dyskolos* ensured the world at least one genuine
example of a Greek New Comedy, and lifted from Plautus and
Terence the unreasonable burden of simultaneously permitting
their critics both to divine their sources and measure their departure
from those same sources.[2]

One may not of course ignore completely the problem raised
by the derivative nature of Roman Comedy, since both Plautus and
Terence freely admit, even proudly advertize the fact that they
have 'translated' Greek originals. Terence in the prologue to his
Eunuchus first cites his model as Menander's *Eunuchus*, then
counters the charge that he has stolen his soldier and parasite
from Plautus and Naevius.

si id est peccatum, peccatum imprudentiast
poetae, non quo furtum facere studuerit.
id ita esse vos iam iudicare poteritis.
Colax Menandrist: in east parasitus Colax
et miles gloriosus: eas se hic non negat
personas transtulisse in Eunuchum suam
ex Graeca. (27-33)

But that he 'transferred' the character of the soldier Thraso from
Menander does not prevent Terence from translating him into
Roman terms, at least in details of military terminology, as in the
following dialogue during the siege of Thais's house:

Thraso: ubi centuriost Sanga et manipulus furum? *Sanga:* eccum
adest.
Thraso: quid ignave? peniculon pugnare, qui istum huc portes,
cogitas?
Sanga: egon? imperatoris virtutem noveram et vim militum; sine
sanguine hoc non posse fieri: qui abstergerem volnera.
Thraso: ubi alii? *Sanga:* qui malum 'alii' solus Sannio servat domi.
Thraso: ti hosce instrue; ego ero hic post principia: inde omnibus
signum dabo.
Gnatho: illuc est sapere: ut hosce instruxit, ipse sibi cavit loco.
Thraso: idem hoc iam Pyrrhus factitavit. (776-783)

Thus even Terence, agreed by all to be more faithful to the tone of
his Greek originals than Plautus to his, has Romanized the scene
with technical words like *centurio, manipulus, imperator*, and *principia*,
and with the appropriate historical example of Pyrrhus. Such
relatively minor adaptation of detail, found even more abundantly
though less consistently is Plautus, along with the ebullient
linguistic expansion that is so characteristic of Plautus's style, is
usually what is meant by the 'originality' of Roman comedy, but
this is hardly sufficient to establish its own validity in its Roman
cultural milieu, and hardly consonant with what we know of other
Roman adaptations of Greek forms, where individualization
permeates far below surface translation.

There are numerous theories about the fundamental characteristics of good comedy and the causes of laughter. Central to many
of these theories, and axiomatic in the rest, is the notion of
familiarity. From the paradigmatic vaudeville joke—'Why does a
chicken cross the road? To get to the other side'—to the fantasy
of Aristophanes' *Birds*, the comic involves the rhetorical figure of

para prosdokian, the cheating of expectations. As in reading an old issue of *Punch* or the *New Yorker*, much of our difficulty in properly understanding Plautus results from our failure to 'get the point', that is, our failure to recognize the expected in such a way that we may appreciate the unexpected.

Comedy always alludes in some degree to its environment, but the allusiveness of Plautus, since it does not name names in Aristophanic style, is difficult to prove. We have little contemporary material for comparison: the *senatus consultum de Bacchanalibus* and a handful of other inscriptions of meagre content. Our view of the social and ideological history of the period is based almost entirely on two writers: Polybius, writing analytically a generation later of Rome's and the Scipios' rise to imperial glory, and Livy, who had Cato and Ennius, Augustus and Virgil between himself and the realities of the early second century B.C.

Although it is now generally conceded that in small things Plautus is Plautine and Terence even Terentian, the view is still often held that the larger world of Roman drama, including the moral, philosophical, and psychological framework within which the characters act and speak, is foreign. Yet when Plautus's characters issue pronouncements such as 'alii, Lyde, nunc sunt mores' (*Bacch.* 437) and 'haec huius saecli mores in se possidet' (*Truc.* 13), he cannot have expected his audience to hear the words *nunc* and *huius saecli* in terms of the Athens of a century before. If so, Plautus should have continued working as a stage hand. If so, then the Roman audience was indeed a collection of strange bumpkins who would keep coming back to laugh at what was incomprehensible and not pertinent to their own experiences. In this light the stock soldier, a borrowed character who intrinsically need have no allusive relation to the life around him, forms an interesting test case. The aspects of real life which he embodies, the military and the glorious, are an important phase of Roman ideology, treated with the utmost seriousness by Romans and Roman historians. It thus matters greatly in our evaluation of Plautus as a comic playwright whether the repeated portrayal of military glory in his plays is to be taken as an academic allusion to the mercenary armies of Alexander and the Diadochoi or as a commentary on the military ideals of his own time.

The *miles* appears in seven of the twenty preserved plays of Plautus, with his fullest development in the *Curculio, Truculentus*, and *Miles Gloriosus*.[3] His function is that of the young hero's rival for a girl, a role which could be filled as well by several other occupational types, as long as they were rich enough to contrast to the young hero's lack of ready cash. It is not the rivalry itself and the personal confrontation of the two suitors that makes up the stage intrigue. Most often it is the necessity for the young man to obtain money, usually from his father, with the help of a clever slave. Once he gets the money, the girl is effectively his, and the rival *miles* seldom need appear on stage. Far from being an unavoidable necessity of the plot, then, the role of the braggart soldier was a flexible element which could be expanded or contracted as Plautus chose; the very frequency of its appearance must itself be regarded as a deliberate preference of Plautus, not an accident of his sources.

Plautus's *miles gloriosus* had seen new and exotic-sounding lands in the Greek East, had conquered many of them with incredible rapidity, and had been courted by their kings. He had come back laden with riches and extravagant honors, nor was he reticent about his miraculous feats. On his return men might find him vain, hard to approach, ready to threaten instead of reason, yet they might also flatter him, even to the point of finding a reason for his success in some special relationship to the gods. All this can be said as well of Rome's historic heroes of Plautus's time, who had taken Rome up from the disastrous trough of Cannae through the battles of Zama and Cynoscephalae into the Seleucid Empire.[4] This fantastic series of successes brought with it an extravaganza of wealth and glory which the historian glimpses largely through the tradition of Cato's stern censorship. Both historian and literary critic should profit by a more detailed examination of the Plautine soldier to discover whether the parallelism between stage and contemporary reality that is clear in its broad outlines may be confirmed in particulars as well.

The soldiers' names, Greek or pseudo-Greek according to the conventions of the Roman stage, are Cleomachus, Stratophanes, Antamoenides, Pyrgopolinices, Polymachaeroplagides, and Therapontigonus Platagidorus. Pyrgopolinices also names an opponent, Bumbomachides Clutomestoridysarchides. In addition to a Rabelaisian relishing of the name itself, Plautus underscores the point of its length in the *Curculio* by having the banker Lyco say of Therapontigonus Platagidorus:

novi edepol nomen, nam mihi istoc nomine,
dum scribo, explevi totas ceras quattuor.

(*Curc.* 409-10)

One may well see an allusion here to the extra heroic military cognomina which accrued to Roman generals in Plautus's time, like Cunctator and Africanus; or perhaps even the specific occasion in 188 when the younger brother of Africanus, not to be left behind in a contest of name length, took the cognomen Asiagenus. That Plautus is not afraid of an even more pointed allusion to a name is clear from the joke in the *Miles Gloriosus* at the expense of the easily satirized cognomen of the Claudii. The maid greets Pyrgopolinices, 'Pulcher, salve', to which he confidently replies, 'meum cognomentum commemoravit' (1037-38).

The polysyllabic Therapontigonus Platagidorus is introduced to us largely through the imaginary description of the parasite Curculio, who has acquired the soldier's seal and must now draw a sufficiently boastful picture of the soldier to convince the banker that he is his *bona fide* representative. Asked why the *miles* was not there in person to retrieve his money, Curculio answers that he had just arrived in Caria from India, and there

nunc statuam volt dare auream
solidam faciundam ex auro Philippo, quae siet
septempedalis, factis monumentum suis.

(*Curc.* 439-41)

This passage gains point in the light of contemporary phenomena such as the honors paid Flamininus in Greece after the liberation proclamation, which, if they did not include seven-foot solid gold statues, did include his portrait on gold coinage. One of Cato's censorial speeches was entitled 'De signis et tabulis' and dealt with the violation of propriety in the proliferation of statuary in Rome, and Plautus gains a touch of the prophetic in view of the fact that the first gilded statue of a human was set up by Acilius Glabrio to himself in the temple of Pietas in 181. Plautus might well be less than prophetic, since this temple was dedicated by Acilius after the battle of Thermopylae and the routing of Antiochus in 191, and plans for the gilt statue 'made from Philip's money' might well have been known soon thereafter, before the traditional date of Plautus's death in 184.

Lyco the banker then asks Curculio why the general needs a commemorative statue. The answer:

> quia enim Persas, Paphlagonas,
> Sinopas, Arabes, Caras, Cretonas, Syros,
> Rhodiam atque Lyciam, Perediam et Perbibesiam,
> Centauromachiam et Classem Unomammiam,
> Libyamque oram omnem, omnem Conterobromniam,
> dimidiam partem nationum usque omnium
> subegit solus intra viginti dies.
>
> (Curc. 442-48)

Despite attempts to date the Greek original by explaining this geographical buffoonery in terms of Alexandrian conquests or the career of Demetrius Poliorcetes, the best formal parallels are Roman honorific inscriptions. Although the sepulchral *elogia* of the great Scipios of Plautus's time are not among the famous inscriptions found in the Tomb of the Scipios, the family style can be demonstrated even from the *factis monumentum suis* of the earlier Lucius Cornelius Scipio Barbatus, despite his limited geographical range:

> Taurasiam Cisauriam Samniom cepit,
> subegit omnem Loucanam opsidesque abdoucit.

Even the farcical counting scene at the beginning of the *Miles Gloriosus*, where the parasite Artotrogus stands with a tablet and stylus doing the sums of the enemy soldiers killed by Pyrgopolinices on various battlefields:

in Cilicia	150
in Scytholatronia	100
Sards	30
Macedonians	60
total	7000

has its somewhat embarrassing analogy in the marked desire for numerical precision of official Roman monuments of conquest, from the *Res Gestae Divi Augusti* to the *Columna Rostrata*, where Duilius about 260 B.C. described his feats in part as follows:

. . . and all the Carthaginian hosts and their most mighty chief after nine days fled in broad daylight from their camp; and he took their town Macela by storm. And in the same command he as consul performed an exploit in ships at sea, the first Roman to do so; . . . and by main force he captured ships with their crews, to wit: one septireme, 30 quinqueremes and triremes; 13 he sank. Gold taken: 3,600 pieces; silver: 100,000; total in sestertii: 2,100,000.

Such reckoning of the commander's victims continues both in official and popular tradition. In Vopiscus's life of Aurelian we find this account:

Aurelian alone with three hundred guardsmen smashed the Sarmatians as they were breaking out in Illyricum. Theoclius, a writer of imperial times, states that in the Sarmatian war Aurelian by his own hand on one day killed forty-eight, and more than nine hundred and fifty on various other days. The result was that boys made up verses and ditties for Aurelian which they used to dance to on holidays:

> mille mille mille decollavimus
> unus homo mille decollavimus
> mille bibat quisquis mille occidit
> tantum vini nemo habet quantum fudit sanguinis.

(S.H.A., *Vita Aureliani*, 6-7)

Another theme of the soldier's ditty, the so-called *versus Fescennini* which were a traditional part of triumphal processions of famous generals, was the sexual prowess of the commander. Julius Caesar's troops chanted

> urbani, servate uxores: moechum calvum adducimus;
> aurum in Gallia effutuisti, hic sumpsisti mutuum.

(Suet. *Iul.* 51)

Although Plautus's braggart soldiers are not usually taunted about their love-making, except in so far as they end up as the unsuccessful rival for the girl, Pyrgopolinices in the *Miles Gloriosus* is the butt of teasing about his amorousness: he is *inpudens, plenus adulterii* (90), *magnus moechus mulierum* (775), *moechus unguentatus* (924), has long curly locks (64, 923), thinks himself handsomer than Alexander (777), is a 'skilled stud horse for the mares, both male and female' (1112-3), and is tricked in the finale and threatened with the standard penalty for adultery because of his belief in his own irresistibility.

> ipsus illic sese iam impedivit in plagas;
> paratae insidiae sunt: in statu stat senes,
> ut adoriatur moechum, qui formast ferox,

> qui omnis se amare credit, quaeque aspexerit
> mulier: eum oderunt qua viri qua mulieres. (1388-92)

The hero believes himself both bold and handsome, and his double vanity, military and amatory, accounts for much of his comic appeal. The underscoring of Pyrgopolinices' double pride— in great deeds and good looks—seems almost formulaic:

> fortem atque fortunatum et forma regia. (10)
> virtute et forma et factis invictissumis. (57)
> cum hac forma et factis. (1021)
> formam et facies et virtutes. (1027)
> hominem tam pulchrum et praeclarum virtute et forma, factis.
> (1042)
> saltem id volup est quom ex virtute formai evenit tibi. (1211)
> forma huius, mores, virtus. (1327)

The pairing of *virtus* and *forma*, seemingly un-Roman, can best be paralleled in the epitaph of Scipio Barbatus, whose 'forma virtutei parisuma fuit'.

Beauty aside—since few military heroes might legitimately boast of such an endowment—Plautus's soldiers are normally labelled with epigrammatic tags of civic *virtus:*

> virtute belli armatus promerui ut mihi
> omnis mortalis agere deceat gratias.
>
> (*Epid.* 442-42)

Stratophanes in the *Truculentus*, refusing to tell tall stories, philosophizes instead about the sufficiency of *virtus:*

> facile sibi facunditatem virtus argutam invenit,
> sine virtuti argutum civem mini habeam pro praefica,
> quae alios conlaudat, eapse sese vero non potest. (494-96)

But his boasting comes a few lines later in his pride for the baby whom he thinks is his new-born son. He is told that immediately after birth the infant reached for sword and shield, and expresses wonder that the child is not now away in battle winning booty: He congratulates Phronesium for adding to the glory of his name.

> gratulor, quom mihi tibique magnum perperisti decus. (517)
> filium peperisti, qui aedis spoliis opplebit tuas. (522)

This parallels the projected progeny of Pyrgopolinices:

PALAESTRIO: meri bellatores gignuntur, quas hic praegnatis fecit, et pueri annos octingentos vivunt. MILPHIDIPPA: vae tibi, nugator!

PYRGOPOLINICES: quin mille annorum perpetuo vivunt ab saeclo ad saeclum.

(*Mil.* 1077-79)

One thinks too of Hercules, the other miraculous babe in Plautus, of whom Jupiter tells Amphitryon, 'suis factis te inmortali adficiet gloria' (*Am.* 1140), and again of the epitaphs of the Scipios:

> facile faceteis superases gloriam maiorum.
> virtutes generis mieis moribus accumulavi,
>   progeniem genui, facta patris petiei.
> maiorum optenui laudem, ut sibei me esse creatum
>   laetentur; stirpem nobilitavit honor.

The divine aura which formed around Scipio Africanus and which Polybius was at such pains to rationalize is also drawn around Stratophanes and Pyrgopolinices. The latter is a self-styled *nepos Veneris* (1265), comically turned into *Venerius nepotulus* (1413, 1421) after his ill-fated attempt to seduce the supposed wife of Pleusicles. The best statement of his divinity occurs in an earlier exchange between Milphidippa and Palaestrio:

> MILPHIDIPPA: ecastor hau mirum si te habes carum, hominem tam pulchrum et praeclarum virtute et forma, factis. deus dignior fuit quisquam homo qui esset? PALAESTRIO: non hercle humanust ergo—
> nam volturio plus humani credo est. (1041-4)

All the Scipionic parallels adduced up to this point are not meant to create a picture of Plautus as a political pamphleteer opposing the Scipionic faction in government. The modern critic is at the mercy of his sources, which are disproportionately concentrated on the Scipios—accidentally in the case of the inscriptional evidence and deliberately in the case of historians. Although to his contemporaries Africanus probably was a leading symbol of Rome's new heroism, the effects of the rapid military and diplomatic success of the period not only were visible in the other ruling families, but also permeated other social levels. The typical Roman soldier of the early second century was not the yeoman leaving his plough for an occasional short campaigning season, but a professionalized military man who saw nearly regular service in several theatres of war. One can see the pride of such a campaign veteran in Livy's version of a speech by Spurius Ligustinus, a centurion of Sabine origin, who in the period from 200 to 171 B.C. had served twenty-two years in the army, been *primus pilus* four times, had been rewarded thirty-four times by various generals *virtutis causa*, and had won six civic crowns (Livy, xlii. 34).

The impact of the returning hero, whether general, centurion, or common soldier, on Roman society is clearly revealed in Plautus. There is no reason to doubt the realism of his description in the *Epidicus* (208-15) of the streets full of soldiers carrying their weapons and leading their pack-animals, and being met by fathers looking for their own sons and by crowds of prostitutes, all dressed for the occasion. Nor is there any reason to doubt the justice of one of his few explicit criticisms of war greed at the beginning of the same play, where the slave Thesprio, returning well-fed from an overseas campaign, remarks that the wars have converted him from a sneak thief to an open robber (*Epid.* 10-12).

Plautus's *miles gloriosus*, then, is relevant to his own society. If originally he reflected the early Hellenistic mercenary captain, his traits as we meet him in Plautine comedy have become thoroughly congruent with the native Roman general turned world conqueror in Plautus's time.

Artistically, however, one must further question the relevance of the *miles* to the play or plays within which he occurs. Although satirizing society by stringing together a number of socially recognizable characters may be interesting in itself and provide good fun, great comic drama is more than this. The critic demands—and finds—unifying elements of structure, whether they be formal or thematic, imagistic or psychological. On the other hand, the usual critical *comparanda* of Plautus are vaudeville and Gilbert and Sullivan: his plots are thin, his construction loose, he will do anything for a laugh. Yet some understanding of the coherence of Plautine comedy may be gained by studying the role of the *miles gloriosus* in its dramatic context.

This coherence is not primarily a factor of the plot as such. The soldier is neither a prime mover of the action, nor is he, except in the case of Pyrgopolinices in the *Miles Gloriosus*, an important antagonist who must be met and overcome. In the

Curculio, Therapontigonus is deceived *in absentiâ* by the eponymous hero in order to deceive the banker to pay the *leno* to get the girl who turns out to be Therapontigonus's sister anyway. The soldier meanwhile returns and rages ineffectually at both banker and *leno*, but all ends happily when he is invited to dinner, getting neither girl nor retribution. In the *Epidicus*, the soldier enters only after the father has been deceived, is incidentally discomfited in a brief scene, and leaves the stage never to be mentioned again. In both *Poenulus* and *Bacchides*, the soldier, although an absent rival for the hand of the heroine, is not the effective enemy of the hero and arrives on stage only after the battle is essentially over. He struts and threatens for a time, and in the *Poenulus* returns at the happy ending to help gloat over the *leno*. In the *Pseudolus*, the Macedonian *miles* never appears in person, being replaced by his slave Harpax. Even in the *Truculentus*, a love-story without a hero in the usual sense, Stratophanes is merely one of Phronesium's three fools, whose deception by her leads to no *peripeteia*, but who is instead given a half share of the booty at the end.

Clearly, then, whatever organic quality the *miles* may have in Plautus does not depend on the dramatic exigencies of plot. It depends rather upon the parallelism of roles, the thematic repetition in other characters of the traits of the braggart warrior. In the *Bacchides*, for example, the role of Cleomachus seems perhaps more nearly fortuitous than that of any Plautine soldier. He appears in one short scene in which he is merely a tool used by the slave Chrysalus to defraud the old man Nicobulus, But the soldier's appearance is framed by the character of Chrysalus, who dominates the stage for a long period both before and after the brief apparition of the professional swaggerer with his identifying sword and shield. Chrysalus's entrance in this portion of the play is highly revealing. The young man Mnesilochus has just sung a monologue of utter despair. Although his friend Pistoclerus tries to console him, he only makes matters worse by mentioning the recent arrival of a parasite from Cleomachus to demand either the soldier's money or his girl.

PISTOCLERUS: tace modo: deus respiciet nos aliquis. MNESILOCHUS: nugae!
PISTOCLERUS: mane. MNESILOCHUS: quid est? PISTOCLERUS: tuam copiam eccam Chrysalum video.

CHRYSALUS: hunc hominem decet auro expendi, huic decet statuam
statui ex auro;
nam duplex facinus feci hodie, duplicibus spoliis sum adfectus.
(638-41)

Pistoclerus's assurance that some god will help them is answered
immediately by the appearance of Chrysalus, who begins with a
claim that his glory warrants him a golden statue, like
Therapontigonus in the *Curculio*, and clearly identifies himself with
the military profession in the next line by a reference to his
'double-dealing spoils'. In heroic style he tells of the splendid
wealth—'regias copias aureasque optuli' (647)—gained through
his bravery—'mea virtute parta' (647). When he discovers that
Mnesilochus has given the money back to his father in a
sentimental rage because of a foolish misunderstanding, the slave
becomes the commander in earnest to devise a new strategy,
scheming in military metaphor:

de ducentis nummis primum intendam ballistam in senem;
ea ballista si pervortam turrim et propugnacula,
recta porta invadam extemplo in oppidum antiquom et vetus:
si id capso, geritote amicis vostris aurum corbibus,
sicut animus sperat.   (709-13)

He tells the young men not to rise from their banquet until he
gives the battle cry, to which Pistoclerus replies, 'o imperatorem
probum' (758-9). After his preliminary skirmish with the
conventional soldier Cleomachus, Chrysalus produces a truly
epic piece of self-glorification, comparing his past and future
exploits to those of the Greek heroes at Troy.

Atridae duo fratres cluent fecisse facinus maxumum,
quom Priami patriam Pergamum divina moenitum manu
armis, equis, exercitu atque eximiis bellatoribus
milli cum numero navium decumo anno post subegerunt.
non pedibus termento fuit praeut ego erum expugnabo meum
sine classe sineque exercitu et tanto numero militum.
cepi, expugnavi amanti erili filio aurum ab suo patre . . .
ego sum Ulixes, quoiius consilio haec gerunt . . .
poste cum magnifico milite, urbis verbis qui inermus capit,
conflixi atque hominem reppuli; dein pugnam conserui seni:
eum ego adeo uno mendacio devici, uno ictu extempulo cepi
spolia . . .
sed Priamus hic multo illi praestat: non quinquaginta modo,

quadringentos filios habet atque equidem omnis lectos sine
  probro:
eos ego hodie omnis contruncabo duobus solis ictibus.   (925-75)

After the besieged old man gives the slave money for the second
time, Chrysalus-Ulysses comments:

> hoc est incepta efficere pulchre: veluti mi
> evenit ut ovans praeda onustus cederem;
> salute nostra atque urbe capta per dolum
> domum redduco iam integrum omnem exercitum.
> sed, spectatores, vos nunc ne miremini
> quod non triumpho: pervolgatum est, nil moror;
> verum tamen accipientur mulso milites.   (1068-744)

Thus exists the slave, at once more boastful and more military
than the *miles gloriosus* whom he has overcome. The physical
caricature of resplendent militarism momentarily introduced on to
the stage in Cleomachus is only one statement of a theme which
is repeated more fully in the extravagant language of the slave-hero.
Artistically Cleomachus and Chrysalus reinforce one another, the
soldier being a literal embodiment of the figurative language and
behaviour of the slave, and the slave generalizing the specific
humorous traits of the soldier.

In the *Miles Gloriosus*, where Pyrgopolinices' role is the most
extensive of all Plautus's soldiers and would not seem to need
reinforcement from outside, the slave Palaestrio again acts as
his counterpart in mock heroism. When he learns that his fellow-
servant Sceledrus has seen Philocomasium kissing Pleusicles, he
first calls a council with himself to plot his strategy:

> paullisper tace,
> dum ego mihi consilia in animum convoco et dum consulo
> quid agam, quem dolum doloso contra conservo parem.
>   (196-98)

After much painful thought accompanied by tragic gesture, he
devises a plan and is warned by his young master of the dangers
in the enemy forces:

> viden hostis tibi adesse tuoque tergo opsidium? consule,
> arripe opem auxiliumque ad hanc rem: propere hoc, non
>   placide decet.
> anteveni aliqua, aliquo saltu circumduce exercitum,
> coge in opsidium perduellis, nostris praesidium para;

interclude inimicis commeatum, tibi muni viam
qua cibatus commeatusque ad te et legiones tuas
tuto possit pervenire. (219-25)

Palaestrio accepts his *imperium* and storms Sceledrus with siege
machines:

si invenio qui vidit, ad eum vineam pluteosque agam:
res paratast, vi pugnandoque hominem caperest certa res.
(266-67)

Next he throws him from the bastions:

meus illic homo est. deturbabo iam ego illum de pugnaculis.
(334)

Then after a new council of war (597 ff) Palaestrio leads his
maniples against Pyrgopolinices:

quantas res turbo, quantas moveo machinas!
eripiam ego hodie concubinam militi,
si centuriati bene sunt manuplares mei. (813-5)

Although he is viewed momentarily as a shipbuilder laying the
hull of a fine trick (915 ff), when the time for launching comes he
returns to his proper métier of imperator:

PLEUSICLES: oppidum quodvis videtur posse expugnari dolis.
date modo operam. ACROTELEUTIUM: id nos ad te, si quid velles,
venimus.
PALAESTRIO: lepide facitis. nucn hanc tibi ego impero provinciam.
ACROTELEUTIUM: impetrabis, imperator, quod ego potero, quod
voles.   (1157-60)

Of all the speeches of these slave generalissimos, perhaps the
most effective is that of Pseudolus just before he meets Harpax,
the slave of Polymachaeroplagides.

nam ego in meo pectore prius ita paravi copias,
duplicis, triplicis dolos, perfidias, ut, ubiquomque hostibus
congrediar
(maiorum meum fretus virtute dicam, mea industria etmalitia
fraudulenta),
facile ut vincam, facile ut spoliem meos perduellis meis
perfidiis.
nunc inimicum ego hunc communem meum atque vostrorum
omnium

Ballionem exballistabo lepide: date operam modo;
hoc ego oppidum admoenire ut hodie capiatur volo.
atque hoc meas legiones adducam; si hoc expugno facilem hanc
    rem meis civibus faciam,
post ad oppidum hoc vetus continuo meum exercitum protinus
    obducam:
ind' me et simul participes omnis meos praeda onerabo atque
    opplebo,
metum et fugam perduellibus meis me ut sciant natum.
eo sum genere gnatus: magna me facinora decet ecficere
quae post mihi clara et diu clueant.
sed hunc quem video quis hic est qui oculis meis obviam
    ignobilis obicitur?
lubet scire quid hic venit cum macchaera et huic quam rem
    agat hinc dabo insidias. (579-92)

Military activities are here combined with more serious attributes of the Roman nobility: dependence upon the *virtus* of one's ancestors and confidence in one's future fame, as well as high-minded concern for the citizenry (although 'vostrorum omnium' and 'meis civibus' become merely 'participes meos' when it comes to sharing the boodle). The *para prosdokian* in the first lines is biting, with the long heroic phrases culminating in *dolos, malitia, perfidiis,* and *Ballionem.* Such in general is this Plautine heroic type, who with legions of perfidious machinations besieges the stronghold of an old man or pimp for the booty of a prostitute which he brings home in triumph to a dissolute and spendthrift young man. Boaster of his talents, he is clearly one of Plautus's most popular creations, on whom the playwright lavished his verbal imagination to a high degree. If one includes his parasite counterpart Curculio, he appears in nine plays, and it is significant that all but one of the plays in which a *miles gloriosus* appears also boasts a *servus gloriosus.* The exception is the *Truculentus,* and in this play the meretricious Phronesium and her maid Astaphium play the role usually afforded a Pseudolus or Palaestrio, devising the tricks and managing the action. They are in fact called *gloriosae* (157). The *militia* which forms a pendant to the stage soldiery of Stratophanes is here the *militia amoris.*

ASTAPHIUM: amator similest oppidi hostilis. DINIARCHUS: quo
    argumento?

ASTAPHIUM: quam primum expugnari potis, tam id optumum est
amicae. (170-71)

ASTAPHIUM: numquam amatoris meretricem oportet caussam
noscere, quin, ubi det, pro infrequente eum mittat militia domum.
(229-30)

As in the elegiac poets of Augustan times, where love is the
preferred soldiery and foreign service is deprecated because it
detracts from the service of one's mistress, so Plautus' young men
may occasionally express their passion in military metaphor.
The *Curculio* opens with the following dialogue between the young
Phaedromus and his slave Palinurus:

PALINURUS: quo ted hoc noctu dicam proficisci foras cum istoc
ornatu cumque hac pompa, Phaedrome?

PHAEDROMUS: quo Venus Cupidoque imperat, suadetque Amor:
si media nox est sive est prima vespera, si status, condictus cum
hoste intercedit dies, tamen est eundum quo imperant ingratiis.
(1-6)

If it is not quite true in Plautus that 'militat omnis amans', it is
still the conquest of hearts or of money that motivates most of the
heroism. *Virtus* is presented full-blown upon the stage. Whether
it wins or loses is irrelevant: it usually does both. Palaestrio
conquers, Pyrgopolinices falls; Chrysalus defeats Cleomachus;
Phronesium cheats Stratophanes of his money but Stratophanes
still gets his spoils of the girl. Both hero and dupe are *gloriosus*,
and on both sides the *gloria* is perverted. (Falstaff and Hotspur
lie side by side on the battlefield.) In Plautine comedy—and
probably in all comedy—glory can only appear as vainglory. The
tall tales of the hyperbolic stage soldier, as well as the pronouncements of slaves and mooning lovers, are equally incongruous
settings for the language of official military dispatches. Critics have
varied in interpreting Sosia's long announcement of victory in
the *Amphitruo*. It has been considered both a serious ode of
victory addressed by Plautus to his fellow-Romans and a comic
parody of Ennius. It is both: a lavish pronouncement of official
res gestae delivered in epic style through the mask of a cowardly
slave who was drunk in his master's tent during the entire battle.
Such is the mask of military glory in Plautine comedy, a mask
assumed by other characters as well as the *miles gloriosus* himself.
The comic playwright deals as extensively with *hybris* as the

writer of tragedy. Man boasts, and the hollowness of the boast brings terror or laughter, but is never allowed to stand unanswered. The mighty shall fall, whether they be mighty in wealth, manners, learning, or war. The sentimental shell is cracked, and what is left is that 'A man's a man'. In warfare the gap between the sentimental slogan and the reality behind it is enormous. The Roman legionnaire as well as the modern infantryman exists for the messy business of shedding blood and letting blood. Although there have been revolutions in the technique and even the sociology of warfare, this fundamental gap has never narrowed. War may still give rise to heroic sentiment and men may glory in a machine gun as much as in a *machaera*, may count the victims of an automatic rifle as proudly as those of a sword.

> When lunchtime arrived on the front lines on Guam, a Marine automatic rifleman, picking off Japs caught in a pocket, mixed business with pleasure.
> With precise rhythm, he fired, rolled over, took a mouthful of rations, rolled back, fired, rolled to the food, ate, and so on, until simultaneously both rations and Japs gave out.

> Before we started it was great fun. We grinned and chortled. . . . I recalled Major Mill's instructions: 'We don't intend to neutralize the island. We don't intend to destroy it. We will annihilate it'. . . . At dawn our planes came in. We could see them disappear into the smoke and flame. We could hear the sputter of their machine guns. We could see the debris raised by their bombs. It was wonderful.[5]

One might have supposed that the trench warfare of World War I killed the romanticism of combat, but a new generation became aces with new weapons, and unfortunately there is no intrinsic reason to suppose that a button pusher might not boast of his expertize in some future atomic conflagration. If war appears on the comic stage, it appears perforce as *alazonia*, and the great soldier cannot be drawn otherwise than as the great boaster, the *miles gloriosus*. There may indeed be times in which war is not a subject for comedy. A defeated nation may be too depressed and a militant government too jealous.[6] But there have been surprisingly few periods in the national literatures of Europe when the *miles* has been long absent from the stage, although, for example, Abraham Cowley felt it necessary in 1658 to append the following defence to the preface to *Cutter of Coleman Street*.

This play was a revised version of *The Guardian* which he had produced in 1641; the years between had clearly been difficult ones for the spirit of comedy.

> And it has been the perpetual privilege of Satyre and Comedy to pluck their vices and follies though not their persons out of the Sanctuary of any Title. A Cowardly ranting Souldier, an Ignorant Charlatanical Doctor, a foolish Cheating Lawyer, a silly Pedantical Scholar, have alwayes been, and still are the Principal Subjects of all Comedy, without any scandal given to those Honourable Professions, or ever taken by their severest Professors; And, if any good Physician or Divine should be offended with me here for inveighing against a Quack, or for finding Deacon *Soaker* too often in the Butteryes, my respect and reverence to their callings would make me troubled at their displeasure, but I could not abstain from taking them for very Cholerique and Quarrelsome persons. What does this therefore amount to, if it were true which is objected? But it is far from being so; for the representation of two Sharks about the Town (fellows merry and Ingenious enough, and therefore admitted into better companyes than they deserve, yet withall too very scoundrels, which is no unfrequent character at *London*) the representation I say of these as Pretended Officers of the Royal Army, was made for no other purpose but to show the World, that the vices and extravagancies imputed vulgarly to the Cavaliers, were really committed by Aliens who only usurped that name, and endeavoured to cover the reproach of their Indigency or Infamy of their Actions with so honourable a Title. So that the business here was not to correct or cut off any natural branches, though never so corrupted or Luxuriant, but to separate and cast away that vermine which by sticking so close to them had done great and considerable prejudice both to the Beauty and Fertility of the Tree.

Cowley further fitted action to his words by changing the description of Cutter in the *personae* from 'a sharking souldier' in *The Guardian* to a 'merry, sharking fellow about the town, pretending to have been a Colonel in the King's Army'. Such an elaborate protestation of innocence does far more than any citation of parallels to prove the relevance of stage soldier to his contemporary counterparts in real life. Although the best comic playwright does not explictly moralize, the comic vision is *per se* pacifistic. Shaw the essayist, however, annotates Shaw the dramatist. In the preface to the four 'pleasant plays' of *Plays:*

Pleasant and Unpleasant, he writes thus of *Arms and the Man*, with its ironic Vergilian title:

> In spite of a Liberal Revolution or two, I can no longer be satisfied with fictitious morals and fictitious good conduct, shedding fictitious glory on over-crowding, disease, crime, drink, war, cruelty, infant mortality, and all the other commonplaces of civilization which drive men to the theatre to make foolish pretences that these things are progress, science, morals, religion, patriotism, imperial supremacy, national greatness and all the other names the newspapers call them.

Neither Plautus nor Shakespeare wrote explanatory prefaces, and of all the alleged literary descendants of Pyrgopolinices none has perhaps raised more critical problems than Falstaff. To begin with, there is little agreement as to whether he is properly to be called a *miles gloriosus*. While the majority of literary historians would view him as a version, albeit a distinctive one, of the conventional *miles*, most critics feel that the appellation limits and lightens the more complex character of Sir John. They follow in part the lead of Maurice Morgann's *Essay on the Dramatic Character of Sir John Falstaff*, written in 1777 to vindicate his courage and deny the propriety of calling him a *miles gloriosus*. The particular arguments, however, which Morgann adduces indicate a misunderstanding, not of Falstaff, but of the Plautine *miles*. 'If Falstaff had been intended for the character of a *Miles gloriosus*, his behaviour ought and therefore would have been commented upon by others.' But except for the asides of the parasite Artotrogus which characterize Pyrgopolinices as a liar— a fact which the audience does not need to be told and which serves to characterize the parasite more than the *miles*—Plautus does not make use of other characters to point up the falsity of his soldier's boasted *virtus*. Further, Morgann feels that Falstaff's character is not that of a real braggart, because his lies are 'too extravagant for practised imposition', a description certainly equally apt for the Plautine feats of scattering legions with a breath (*Mil.* 16-18), breaking elephants arms with a fist (*Mil.* 25-30), bringing down 60,000 flying troops by shooting bird-lime at them with slingshots (*Poen.* 470-87). Finally, the critic examines Falstaff's battle experience to show that it does not prove his cowardice. Yet none of Plautus's *milites gloriosi* are convicted of cowardice on the stage.

The worst one can say is that they show Falstaffian 'discretion',
like Terence's Thraso in his siege of Thais' house:

> omnia prius experiri quam armis sapientem decet.
> qui scis an quae iubeam sine vi faciat?
>
> *(Eun.* 789-90)

In a scene which would have given a natural opportunity for a
portrayal of real cowardice, the confrontation between the cook
Cyamus and the soldier Stratophanes in the *Truculentus*, the soldier
ought to have run off in fright at the sight of the cook's butcher
knife, but he actually drives off the cook with his longer sword.
Although Pyrgopolinices gets a beating at the end of the *Miles
Gloriosus*, it is not a coward's but a lecher's punishment, and he
is held by a group of slaves while he takes his blows. Despite the
fact that the sensitivity of Roman audiences was not shocked by
watching a good stage beating, there is nothing in Roman comedy
to correspond to the cringing cudgelling in English Comedy of
Bessus or Bluffe or Bobadill.

Although in his polemic Morgann takes too narrow a view of
the dramatic values of the *miles gloriosus* before Shakespeare's
time, he understands that Falstaff must be understood, if at all,
in terms of the incongruities of his character and his relations with
other roles in the play.

> To this end, Falstaff must no longer be considered as a single
> independent character, but grouped, as we find him shewn to us in
> the play;—his ability must be disgraced by buffoonery, and his
> courage by circumstances of imputation; and those qualities be
> thereupon reduced into subjects of mirth and laughter:—his vices
> must be concealed at each end from vicious design and evil effect,
> and must thereupon be turned into incongruities, and assume the
> name of humour only;—his insolence must be repressed by the
> superior tone of Hal and Poins, and take the softer name of
> spirit only, or alacrity of mind; . . . he must thrive best, and
> flatter most, by being extravagantly incongruous; and his own
> tendency, impelled by so much activity, will carry him with
> perfect ease and freedom to all the necessary excesses.

What else is this but a definition of the comic *alazon* at his best,
a definition which would fit Plautus's Pyrgopolinices or Shaw's
Sergius equally well? Coward and no-coward, Falstaff is an
embodiment of military glory who raises the question of

cowardice. On his lips, 'the better part of valour is discretion; in the which latter part I have saved my life', may be a comic proposition, but it has a serious relevance to the corpse beside him. 'Zounds, I am afraid of this gunpowder Percy, though he be dead; how if he should counterfeit too, and rise? I am afraid he would prove the better counterfeit.' In a play which begins and ends with plans for war, Hotspur is the example which King Henry wished Prince Hal to follow:

> He doth fill fields with harness in the realm;
> Turns head against the lion's armed jaws;
> And, being no more in debt to years than thou,
> Leads ancient lords and reverend bishops on
> To bloody battles and to burning arms. . . .
> Thrice hath this Hotspur Mars in swathing-clothes,
> This infant warrior in his enterprise
> Discomfited great Douglas.

Hotspur's first appearance in the play is in a short scene framed between the two parts of Falstaff's inglorious robbery, between the deed at Gadshill and the boast at Eastcheap. He enters reading a letter and reviling the cowardice of his correspondent: 'You are a shallow, cowardly hind, and you lie. . . What a frosty-spirited rogue is this. . . . O, I could divide myself, and go to buffets, for moving such a dish of skimmed milk with so honourable an iron.' Lady Percy reveals that even in his sleep he thinks of the heroics of war:

> In thy faint slumbers I by thee have watched,
> And heard thee murmur tales of iron wars;
> Speak terms of manage to thy bounding steed;
> Cry, Courage!—to the field!—And thou hast talked
> Of sallies and retires, of trenches, tents,
> Of palisadoes, frontiers, parapets,
> Of basilisks, of cannon, culverin,
> Of prisoners' ransom, and of soldiers slain,
> And all the currents of a heady fight.

At the tavern, while they await Falstaff's return, Prince Henry thus characterizes Hotspur:

> I am not yet of Percy's mind, the Hotspur of the North; he that kills me some six or seven dozen Scots at a breakfast, washes his hands, and says to his wife, 'Fie upon this quiet life! I want

work'. 'O my sweet Harry', says she, 'how many hast thou killed today?' 'Give my roan horse a drench', says he; and answers, 'Some fourteen', an hour after, '—a trifle, a trifle', I pr'ythee, call in Falstaff: I'll play Percy, and that damned brawn shall play Dame Mortimer his wife.

Enter Falstaff with 'A plague of all cowards'. The valorous boast of the comic *miles*—'Why, thou knowest I am as valiant as Hercules: but beware instinct; the lion will not touch the true prince'—illumines the valorous boast of the historic *miles*. Which of the two glories is the vainer is decided on the battlefield: '. . . for worms, brave Percy'.

> who lined himself with hope,
> Eating the air on promise of supply,
> Flattering himself with project of a power
> Much smaller than the smallest of his thoughts:
> And so, with great imagination,
> Proper to madmen, led his powers to death,
> And, winking, leaped into destruction.

As Falstaff illumines Percy in Part I, so Pistol illumines Falstaff in Part II. Pistol, with his name, his military title—'Captain! thou abominable damned cheater, art thou not ashamed to be called captain?'—his learnedly heroic language—'shall packhorses, and hollowed pampered jades of Asia, which cannot go but thirty miles a day, compare with Caesars, and with Cannibals, and Trojan Greeks? nay, rather damn them with King Cerberus'—is the more obvious swaggerer, whose swaggering is both called and proved hollow by Sir John:

> He's no swaggerer, hostess; a tame cheater, i' faith; you may stroke him as gently as a puppy greyhound: he will not swagger with a barbary hen, if her feathers turn back in any show of resistance.

Falstaff rises above his own vanity, as it were, to become the touchstone of the vanity of others. Yet the same extravagant mythology that was a part of Pistol's boast is turned immediately upon Falstaff in Doll's congratulations on his bravery in driving off Pistol:

> ah, rogue! i' faith, I love thee. Thou art as valorous as Hector of Troy, worth five of Agamemnon, and ten times better than the nine worthies: ah villain!

Caveat lector. Again it is Falstaff who 'see's the bottom of Justice Shallow'. He is *alazonia* looking at itself. Like the *milites gloriosi* of Plautus, he remains detached from the central action of the play, yet concentrates in his own character the theme of the vanity of honour and military glory which is crucially relevant to the central action and reiterated in other characters. His range is wider than that of any Plautine *miles*, and in this he is rather more like the Plautine slave. That he is a greater figure than either is in part simply due to the fact that his creator is Shakespeare, but in part because his context is not comedy. The heroes with whom he shares the stage are Hotspur and Prince Henry, not the *adulescentuli* of the Roman stage.

Much of the same dramatic use, if less subtle, is made of the *miles gloriosus* in Beaumont and Fletcher's melodramatic treatment of incest between brother and sister, *A King and No King*. Bessus, 'valiant enough upon a retreat', opens the play by boasting of his accomplishments at a place now called 'Bessus' Desperate Redemption'. Mardonius, King Arbaces' friend and counsellor, informs the audience of Bessus' cowardice:

> Thou knowest, and so do I, thou meanedst to flie, and thy fear making thee mistake, thou ranst upon the enemy, and a hot charge thou gavst, as I'll do thee right, thou art furious in running away, and I think, we owe thy fear for our victory; if I were the King, and were sure thou wouldst mistake always and run away upon the enemy, thou shouldst be general by this light.

His comic boasting continues to be displayed and convicted throughout the play. When the king twits him on his cowardice, he shows his sword and maintains: 'If I do not make my back-biters eat it to a knife within this week, say I am not valiant.' When he is later disgracefully beaten by Bacurius and has his sword taken from him, he begs at least for his knife back, so that he can show it to the king and assert that this was all that was left uneaten of his sword. When the king's sister asks for news of the king, he talks only of himself:

Panthea: And is he well again?
Bessus: Well again, an't please your grace: why I was run twice through the body, and shot i'th'head with a cross-arrow, and yet am well again.
Panthea: I do not care how thou do'st, is he well?

Bessus: Not care how I do? Let a man out of the mightiness of his
   spirit, fructifie Foreign Countries with his blood for the good
   of his own, and thus shall he be answered; why I may live to
   relieve with spear and shield, such a lady as you distressed.

Now styled a hero, he must defend his honour in duels, and all
those whom he has boorishly insulted before the war come to
challenge him. He joyfully proclaims in a monologue that he is
really a coward and then escapes another duel by telling the
challenger's second that he is already engaged

   . . . 'upon my faith Sir, to two hundred and twelve, and I have a
   spent body, too much bruised in Battail, so that I cannot fight, I
   must be plain, above three combats a day: All the kindness I can
   shew him, is to set him resolvedly in my rowle, the two hundred
   and thirteenth man, which is something, for I tell you, I think
   there will be more after him, than before him, I think so; pray
   you commend me to him, and tell him this'.

After he has been kicked and cudgelled by Bacurius, two sophistical
teachers of swordmanship attempt to prove by argument that he
was really brave in being beaten, as long as he laughed enough to
show that he contemned the beating:

>   If he be sure he has been kicked enough.
>   For that brave sufference you speak of brother,
>   Consists not in a beating and away,
>   But in a cudgelled body, from eighteen
>   To eight and thirty; in a head rebuked
>   With pots of all size, degrees, stools, and bed-staves,
>   This shows a valiant man.
>   *Bessus:* Then I am valiant, as valiant as the proudest,
>   For these are all familiar things to me;
>   Familiar as my sleep, or want of money,
>   All my whole body's but one bruise with beating,
>   I think I have been cudgelled with all nations,
>   And almost all Religions.

Through all this beating, the braggart buffoon learns no lesson,
remains undaunted, since, as he himself remarks, 'A base spirit has
this vantage of a brave one, it keeps always at a stay, nothing brings
it down, not beating'. But King Arbaces, Bessus' heroic counterpart, does not 'have this vantage'. In him, because he *is* a brave
man, the exaggeration of military boastfulness is no comic folly,
but a tragic distortion.

Bessus: Come, our King's a brave fellow.

Mardonius: He is so, Bessus, I wonder how thou camst to know it.
But if thou wert a man of understanding I would tell thee, he
is vain-glorious, and humble, and angry, and patient, and merry,
and dull, and joyful and sorrowful in extremity in an hour. . . .
Here he is with his prey in his foot.

Arbaces enters, glorying over the fallen Tigranes:

> Be you my witness earth, need I to brag,
> Doth not this captive prince speak
> Me sufficiently, and all the acts
> That I have wrought upon his suffering land;
> Should I then boast! where lies that foot of ground
> Within his whole realm, that I have not past,
> Fighting and conquering; far then from me
> Be ostentation. I could tell the world
> How I have laid his kingdom desolate
> By this sole arm propt by divinity,
> Stript him out of his glories, and have sent
> The pride of all his youth to people graves,
> And made his virgins languish for their loves,
> If I would brag, should I that have the power
> To teach the neighbour world humility,
> Mix with vain-glory? . . .

Mardonius: 'Tis pity that valour should be thus drunk.

Then Beaumont and Fletcher repeatedly display the braggart
coward and braggart king together, with the effect of making
the one more ludicrous, the other more pitiable. At first, the
experience of seeing himself caricatured does not abate Arbaces'
boastfulness. To Mardonius in defence of his earlier speech:

> There I would make you know 'twas this sole arm.
> I grant you were my instruments, and did
> As I commanded you, but 'twas this arm
> Moved you like wheels, it mov'd you as it pleased.

After promising not to insult the captive king Tigranes any
further, he delivers another self-laudatory speech at his own
triumphal procession. Yet as the drama is about to become tragic,
as his vanity is about to ruin him irrevocably by making him
flaunt moral law and make love to his sister, he once more
confronts Bessus, whom he has asked to play the pander for him.

Bessus' eagerness to be of service is expressed in what is perhaps the most shocking sentence in English drama: '. . . and when this is dispatched, if you have a mind to your mother, tell me, and you shall see I'le set it hard'. The king recoils at this incredibly vulgar image of himself, and the play begins to move toward the comic conclusion implicit in its title.

Falstaff and Bessus are unusual *milites gloriosi* in that the effect of their comic military boasting is enhanced by being set in the dramatic context of serious military heroism. Their *alazonia* finds both contrast and tragic counterpart within the play itself. More frequently the *miles gloriosus* in Western literature is less ambiguously comic in his setting. His military analogies lie in real life and epic literature, but his stage world is a world of pure comic bluster. His heroism need never be matched against heroism of another level of value, but only against other follies as comic as itself: flattery, pedantry, social pretentiousness, romantic sentimentality. Thus, for example, appear Bobadill in Jonson's *Every Man in his Humor*, Don Armado in Shakespeare's *Love's Labour's Lost*, Cutter in Cowley's *The Guardian*, Bluffe in Congreve's *The Old Bachelor*, Matamore in Corneille's *L'Illusion Comique*. They keep pace with the times in their weapons, their fashions in dueling, their historical allusions. Like the Plautine soldiers, they raise laughter with their incredible feats, their inaccurate arithmetic, their unfulfilled threats, their epic comparisons. Like Pyrgopolinices, they are perhaps most amusing when they combine military vanity with vanity in the amorous sphere.

Every reader will have his favourite exponent of such 'un-in-one-breath-utter-able skill'. Jacob von Tyboe, a creation of the eighteenth-century Danish playwright and scholar Ludvig Holberg, may serve as an example. In an explanatory prologue, Jesper Oldfux, a combination of counsellor, confidant, and spy, reveals that his young friend Leonard, currently penniless and in love with Lucilia, has two rivals for her hand.

> The first one's name is Jacob von Tyboe, a man with a screw loose in his head, as far as I can tell. He says he's done service overseas, but can't show service papers or an honourable discharge. The other officers here in town put on a good face with him, and call him Captain, or Major, or even General, depending on his pretensions. When he talks about his campaigns, they pretend to listen with astonishment; when he gets in trouble with the law,

they go to court for him; and when he needs some soldiers, they lend him some of their own and order them to treat him with respect and reverence. *En somme*, he is a *divertissement* for the whole garrison.

In encouraging Leonard not to lose hope, Jesper assures him that von Tyboe

is so stark raving mad that I can easily convince him that he has fought far greater campaigns than Alexander the Great, that Prince Absalom was no comparison for him in beauty, and that every time he hears the church bells ringing it's to bury some woman who has died of unrequited love of him.

The other rival is the Magister Tychonius, and the stage is superbly set for the confrontation of the braggart pedant and the braggart warrior by a debate between their respective servants, Jens and Peer, on the relative merits of the suffix '-us' and the prefix 'von' in ennobling Tycho and Tyboe. The real obstacle in the way of Lucilia, explains Tychonius, is her chambermaid Pernille, who is 'the outwork that must be stormed before one can reach the fortress, and this can only be accomplished *aureis et argentis armis, id est* with gold and coin'. Jesper, much as a Plautine slave might do, devises a trick to get each of the *gloriosi* in trouble with Lucilia. Since von Tyboe cannot read or write, but wishes to send his love a name-day verse in Latin, Jesper arranges to have an obscenely insulting verse written for him by a certain Petronius posing as a poet; Tychonius is cleverly disposed of by turning the *aurea et argenta arma* with which his servant is trying to bribe Pernille into copper pennies, the distinction of the deceit lying in the fact that Tychonius' servant himself is made to trade the sack of silver which he is carrying with the larger sack of worthless coins carried by von Tyboe's man Christoff, who pretends to be in a drunken stupor. Meanwhile the *miles* boasts in accordance with our expectations and assisted by Jesper:

Tyboe: Yes I guess they do know me all over Holland, what with the siege and the great engagement near Amsterdam, where I singlehandedly slew over six hundred.
Jesper: Oh, you must add another zero.
Tyboe: Let someone else do it. I've never been concerned about the count. In those days another hundred more or less didn't matter to Jacob von Tyboe. What I can't understand is how my broadsword held out so long.

Jesper: Oh, you could cut people in half with a penpoint. It isn't the sword that matters, but the hand of the man who wields it. I was reading in an old history book about Alexander the Great who could cut the head off the biggest English bull with one stroke. Alexander was Nebuchadnezzar's field-marshal at the time, and when he heard about this he wanted Alexander to lend him his sabre so that he could try it too. But Nebuchadnezzar missed and got mad and said, 'Das ist nicht die rechtet Sabel, Herr General', to which Alexander replied: 'I lent your Imperial Majesty my sabre, not my arm'.

Of the two braggarts, the maid Pernille prefers the military one, because she likes red clothes and the plumes in his hat send chills up and down her spine. His language of courtship follows the best heroic traditions:

I am no longer the invincible hero and lion-hearted von Tyboe of a moment ago. The cannons of your eyes have shot such a breach into the fortress of my heart that I am forced to surrender at discretion. I lay at you feet that sword with which I have brought a million men to their grave. If the King of Holland should see me in this posture, he would say, 'Where is your former courage, your Herculean bravery, Wohlgebohrener Herr von Tyboe'? And I would answer him that even Hercules, who had subjected the five zones of the world, had to have his Delilah to trick him.

The climax is reached in a stichomythy in which Tycho follows Tyboe boast for boast:

Tyboe: Perhaps you have not met Herr von Tyboe?
Tycho: Perhaps you have not met Herr Magister Tychonius?
Tyboe: I have won more than twenty battles.
Tycho: I have disputed *absque praesidio* more than twenty times.
Tyboe: Everyone knows me in Holland and Brabant.
Tycho: All *literati* know me in Rostock, Helmstad and Wittenberg.
Tyboe: I have laid the strongest heroes low with my bare hand.
Tycho: I have laid the strongest *opponentes* low with my bare mouth.
Tyboe: In half a second I can set a man like you on your rump.
Tycho: With half a syllogism I can reduce a whole army *ad absurdum.*

At the end, *miles* and *magister* line up on opposite sides of the stage with four soldiers each. Since neither wants to fight, Jesper easily arranges a truce, while preserving the pride of each. They decide to unite forces and storm Lucilia's house, but both armies are driven off by one pistol shot in the air from Leonard, who himself collects the booty.

Holberg's comedy was written in a period when Denmark was trying to disentangle herself from military alliances and simultaneously assert her cultural independence. He alone contributed much to both these goals through his *History of Denmark* and numerous other works, both serious and satirical. His comedies, although derivative in the same sense that Plautus's were, are not without relevance to these same goals. Holberg especially liked to ridicule the German orientated culture of the bourgeois, as is apparent in von Tyboe. The satire of soldiery will have had a specific timeliness for his audience since Jacob von Tyboe was produced in 1723, only three years after the Treaty of Copenhagen had ended, ingloriously for Denmark, a series of political involvements with the Netherlands that had sent Danish troops into battle throughout northern Europe.

It is only natural that Shaw, who wrote, 'Idealism, which is only a flattering name for romance in politics and morals, is as obnoxious to me as romance in ethics or religion', should make use of the *miles gloriosus* in his 'general onslaught on idealism'.[7] Sergius, in *Arms and the Man*, led a magnificent cavalry charge, which, like Bessus', succeeded by a lucky accident. As his fiancée's mother tells it:

> You can't guess how splendid it is. A cavalry charge—think of that! He defied our Russian commanders—acted without orders— led a charge on his own responsibility—headed it himself—was the first man to sweep through their guns. Can't you see it, Raina; our gallant splendid Bulgarians with their swords and eyes flashing, thundering down like an avalanche and scattering the wretched Servian dandies like chaff.

As his less romantic opponents see it:

> He did it like an operatic tenor—a regular handsome fellow, with flashing eyes and lovely moustache, shouting a war-cry and charging like Don Quixote at the windmills. We nearly burst with laughter at him; but when the sergeant ran up as white as a sheet, and told us they'd sent us the wrong cartridges, and that we couldn't fire a shot for the next ten minutes, we laughed at the other side of our mouths.

Shaw then confronts Sergius with his 'realistic' counterpart, and the stage directions define the contrast: The chest of drawers in Raina's bedroom 'is covered by a variegated native cloth, and on it there is a pile of paper backed novels, a box of chocolate creams, and a miniature easel, on which is a large photograph of an extremely handsome officer, whose lofty bearing and magnetic glance can be felt even from the portrait'. Into this room walks a man whose unromantic name, Shaw later informs us, is Bluntschli:

> A man of about 35, in a deplorable plight, bespattered with mud and blood and snow, his belt and the strap of his revolver case keeping together the torn ruins of the blue coat of a Servian artillery officer. As far as the candlelight and his unwashed, unkempt condition make it possible to judge, he is a man of middling stature and undistinguished appearance, with strong neck and shoulders, a roundish, obstinate looking head covered with short crisp bronze curls, clear quick blue eyes and good brows and mouth, a hopelessly prosaic nose like that of a strong-minded baby. . . .

With this, the 'chocolate cream soldier', the son of a Swiss hotel owner, begins to win the novel-reading Raina, while Sergius, true to his stage character and therefore convinced of his own intense attractiveness to women, wins the vulgarly practical maid Louka for his wife. Each deserves his match, and, with typical Shavian irony, the play ends as romantically as it had begun.

Shaw permits Bluntschli speeches of realistic bitterness relatively untempered by comic distance.

Bluntschli: You never saw a cavalry charge, did you?
Raina: How could I?
Bluntschli: Ah, perhaps not—of course. Well, it's a funny sight. It's like slinging a handful of peas against a window pane: first one comes; then two or three close behind him; and then all the rest in a lump.
Raina (her eyes dilating as she raises her clasped hands ecstatically): Yes, first One!—the bravest of the brave!
Bluntschli (prosaically): Hm! you should see the poor devil pulling at his horse.
Raina: Why should he pull at his horse?
Bluntschli (impatient of so stupid a question): It's running away with him, of course: do you suppose the fellow wants to get there before the others and be killed? Then they all come. You can tell the young ones by their wildness and their slashing. The old

ones come bunched up under the number one guard: they know that they are mere projectiles, and that it's no use trying to fight. The wounds are mostly broken knees, from the horses cannoning together.

The fact that soldiers are 'mere projectiles' and *a fortiori* incapable of individual heroism, although it probably underlies any great comic vision of war since Aristophanes, has been more often implicit than explicit until modern times. An exception is Goldoni, whose *La Guerra* is perhaps the bitterest indictment of military glory possible within the framework of comedy. Here, a disillusioned courtesan and ruthless profiteer form the background against which romantic young braggart warriors fight duels and speak of the honour of war. The comedy was not successful, audiences having preferred the more gallant and less shocking *L'Amante Militare*. Yet the realistic tone of parts of *La Guerra* accurately predicts the way in which war has most often appeared in the twentieth century.

Bertolt Brecht's *Mother Courage* has this same collocation of the boast of glory and the sordidness of reality. Eilif, the 'brave son' of the titular heroine, is as truly a *miles gloriosus* in his swagger as any Plautine soldier. Yet his *alazonia* is immediately negated on the stage, not by the impossibility of the boast, but by its frightful truthfulness. His great feat was the theft of cattle from peasants.

> *Eilif:* The rest was a snap. Only the peasants had clubs—and outnumbered us three to one. They made a murderous attack on us. Four of them drove me into a clump of trees, knocked my sword from my hand, and screamed: Surrender! What now? I said to myself, they'll make mincemeat of me.
> *Commander:* So what did you do?
> *Eilif:* I laughed.
> *Commander:* You what?
> *Eilif:* I laughed. And so we got to talking. I came right down to business and said: 'Twenty guilders an ox is too much, I bid fifteen'. Like I wanted to buy. That foxed 'em. So while they were scratching their heads, I reached for my good sword and cut 'em to ribbons. Necessity knows no law, huh?

Mother Courage, while taking inventory of her provision wagon, disposes of the *alazonia* of another of the play's representatives of military glory.

Pity about the Chief—twenty-two pairs, socks—getting killed that way. They say it was an accident. There was a fog over the fields that morning, and the fog was to blame. He'd been telling his men to fight to the death, and was just riding back to safety when he lost his way in the fog, went forward instead of back, found himself in the thick of the battle, and ran right smack into a bullet. . . . I feel sorry for a commander like that—when maybe he had something big in mind, something they'd talk about in times to come, something they'd raise a statue to him for, the conquest of the whole world for example—Lord, the worms have got into these biscuits. . . .

In Brecht's *A Man's a Man*, 'Nothing is sacred any more unless it's identity cards.' The porter Galy Gay has the makings of a *miles gloriosus* with his 'famous self-conceit'. 'So big and fat on the outside, you'd never guess he had an inside like a raw egg,' says Mrs. Gay. The transformation is easy, requiring only a uniform and a new identity card: 'A man like that does the turning all on his own. Throw him into a puddle and he'll grow webs between his fingers in two days.' And the transformation is complete: he accepts the identity of Jeraiah Jip, the attentions of the widow Begbick, his comrades' rations, and the crushing of the Sir el Dchowr fortress as his due. 'Then you're the greatest man the army has, Jeraiah Jip! The human fighting machine'.

In a close structural relationship, reminiscent of the relation between slave and soldier in Plautus, Galy Gay's counterpart, Bloody Five, goes through precisely the opposite process, losing his identity, and then his literal manhood, because he loses his uniform. Early in the play, after he recounts the story of his heroics against the Sikhs, his men chorus, 'What a great soldier you are, Bloody! You give off sparks! Thrilling! The strength of those loins must be terrific too'! But after he is tied up and thrown on the transport train in civilian clothes, his powers are transferred to Galy Gay, and Bloody Five can only threaten and boast and worry about his name:

The eyes of the whole country are upon me. I was a big wheel. A cannon wheel. My name is Bloody Five. A name that is to be found three times over all through the pages of history! . . .
Galy Gay: On account of his name, this gentleman did something very bloody to himself. He shot his sex away. I was very fortunate to see it, for now I see where pigheadedness leads, and what a

bloody thing it is for a man to be dissatisfied with himself and make such a fuss about his name!

The self-inflicted castration of Bloody Five, which might strike the reader as shockingly modern, is a literary reiteration of the threatened punishment of Pyrgopolinices, in the last scene of the *Miles Gloriosus*.

Brecht is enjoying enormous posthumous success in our generation, although we might seem to be living in a period when it is difficult to obtain a comic perspective on war. It is interesting to observe that in *A Man's a Man*, which has been produced several times in recent years, the figure of the *miles gloriosus* is still remarkably close to his Plautine ancestors. Eric Bentley has remarked that 'Brecht's final attitude would be vehemently anti-tragic. The newfangled notion of Epic Theatre can be construed as a synonym for traditional comedy'.[8] Bloody Five and Galy Gay are not only 'synonyms' of the stock braggart warrior, but they are simultaneously a commentary on the possibility of this stock figure maintaining itself in the twentieth century, concerned as it is with the problem of preserving individual identity in the face of mass numbers and mechanization.

NOTES

[1] One may refer, with gratitude, to several excellent studies which have laid the historical groundwork for this and any treatment of the *miles gloriosus*. Otto Ribbeck, *Alazon—Ein Beitrag zur antiken Ethologie* (Leipzig, 1882), collects the Greek material illustrating the various forms of *alazonia*, enabling one to see the predominance of the braggart warrior over other braggarts: doctor, cook, soothsayer, etc. Karl von Reinhardstoettner, Plautus, *Spätere Bearbeitungen plautinischer Lustspiele* (Leipzig, 1886), collects and liberally quotes from later adaptations of the *Miles gloriosus*, as of all the Plautine plays, showing incidentally the relative popularity of this particular comedy, second only to the *Amphitruo* and perhaps the *Menaechmi*. Daniel C. Boughner, *The Braggart in Renaissance Comedy*, *A study in Comparative Drama from Aristophanes to Shakespeare* (Minneapolis, 1954), although perhaps over-ambitious in its sub-title, discusses with critical insight the vast number of *milites gloriosi* who appear in Renaissance comedy in Italy, Spain, France, and England; the reader who is troubled by the jump in this present essay from Plautus to Jonson and Shakespeare will read Boughner with pleasure and illumination. The best guide through the morass of scholarly literature on Plautus is George E. Duckworth, *The Nature of Roman Comedy* (Princeton, 1952), with its extensive bibliography. Of critical works published subsequently Raffaele Perna, *L'originalita di Plauto* (Bari, 1955), is excellent.

My own views on the subject of Plautine originality are discussed in detail in 'Plautus as a Source-Book for Roman Religion', *TAPA*, XC (1959), pp. 48-60. D. C. Earl, in two recent articles, 'Political Terminology in Plautus', *Historia* ,IX (1960), pp. 234-43, and 'Terence and Roman Politics', *Historia*, XI (1962), pp. 469-85, has had the courage to use Roman comedy to illustrate Roman political concepts, and I owe much to his example.

² The state of Plautine criticism previous to 1958 may perhaps best be described by imagining what Virgilian criticism would be if only a few scattered fragments of Homer and Apollonius of Rhodes were extant. It is still too soon (in 1963) to measure fully the impact of the *Dyskolos*, and in the light of announcements that more Menander is forthcoming it would show *alazonia* indeed to attempt in this essay a re-evaluation of the role of the braggart in Menander. Although there are a half-dozen passages in our fragments referring to a *miles*, this is scarcely enough on which to base any valid critical judgment.

³ The other four are *Bacchides, Epidicus, Poenulus,* and *Pseudolus.*

⁴ Twenty-three triumphs and ovations are known from the period 200-184 B.C.

⁵ Taken from *Semper Fidelis: The U.S. Marines in the Pacific*—1942-1945, edit. by Patrick O'sheel, USMCR, and Staff Sgt. Gene Cook, USMCR (New York, 1947), pp. 62 and 30.

⁶ The following sample may give one pause. In 1878 the German scholar J. Thummel wrote in an essay on the *miles gloriosus*: 'After the recent wars, which have clearly revealed to the people the seriousness of the situation and the significance of the army, we no longer have any taste for this sort of witless absurdity.'

⁷ In the preface to Volume II of *Plays, Pleasant and Unpleasant.*

⁸ *Seven Plays by Bertolt Brecht*, edit. by Eric Bentley (New York, 1961), p. xvii.

IV

The Amphitryo Theme

C. D. N. COSTA

THE *Amphitruo* of Plautus, itself a most interesting and important play, is particularly remarkable for the extent and variety of its literary progeny. From at least the time of Vitalis of Blois in the twelfth century, who wrote a narrative version of the story in Latin elegiacs, until the present day there has been a succession of poems, plays, operas and, latterly, films, to illustrate the tremendous hold which the theme has had on the imaginations of writers as great as Molière and Dryden. Of these categories of imitation and adaptation of the Plautine material the plays are by far the most numerous and important, and this essay will attempt to consider, as well as the great original, four of its most successful followers: the versions of Molière, Dryden, Kleist, and Giraudoux.

There were clearly rich comic possibilities in the old story which told of Jupiter's infatuation with Alcmena, and his assuming the form of her absent husband in order to visit her and gratify his passion. Clearly too a skilful and discerning dramatist could make much more of the situation than simply underline its humour: he could analyse the effect of Jupiter's adventure upon a hitherto happy marriage, and, in particular, probe the psychological state of perplexity and suffering which the situation produces in Alcmena. One of the most interesting and instructive points of contrast to be seen in the many versions of the story is the different treatment of Alcmena's personal feelings, and the various degrees of subtlety with which her character is drawn by different dramatists. Often in this one point lies their most significant resemblance to, or departure from, the Plautine version. The wronged wife has always been a favourite subject of tragedy and comedy; but when the culprit is not the husband, nor indeed any other mortal, all sorts of moral complications arise in addition to the farcical circumstances of the plot, and offer a wide scope for treatment with levity tempered with seriousness in proportions dictated by the writer's outlook. That is why, centuries after anyone even pretended to believe in the myths of Greece or the existence of Jupiter, the old story has continued to offer not only good (if not always clean) fun on the stage, but some often profound observations on the psychology of women.

Of course, Plautus and many of his successors have made the most of the obviously comic elements of the situation. His audience, like Shakespeare's and, to a lesser extent, those of our own day, relished the ludicrous scenes of farce and perplexity which abounded in the 'comedy of errors', and the particular theme of the Amphitryo story added to knockabout possibilities an almost endless scope for bawdy innuendo. There is no doubt that obvious potentialities for humour and a very real moral dilemma were an inspired formula for great comedy, and both features combined in one work always command a wider reception than either in isolation.

Who first discovered the formula? We do not know, and for our present purposes it does not matter. It was certainly not Plautus, whose work, however adapted and improved, is always derivative. This is not the place to go into the very vexed question of the sources of his *Amphitruo*, but it is worth pointing out that, as this play of all his *oeuvre* has fathered the most numerous imitations, so it presents the most interesting problems of origin. It is the only extant example of a mythological parody, and the consensus of modern scholarship on the whole suggests that it derives from Plato Comicus' νὺξ μακρά ('Long Night') *via* some New Comedy adaptation, and that it perhaps borrowed elements from the popular South Italian *phlyakes*, or tragic burlesques. (There is good evidence that the story of Amphitryo was a popular theme in these farces.)

The uncertainty of its origin and the impressiveness of its progeny must not side-track us from observing that Plautus' play is in its own right a highly skilful and successful production. Probably a work of his later years (we can, with some hesitation, date it 191-189 B.C.), it contains some of his finest versification, especially in the narrative style, and, compared with many of his other works, it is less strewn with those gratuitous verbal quibble. and banalities which try our patience and frustrate the translators

There is, unfortunately, a long lacuna in the text of the order of 250-300 lines, though the existing fragments allow us to reconstruct the action. This is a notable loss, as the missing lines continued the very promising scene in which Mercury on the roof taunts and flouts Amphitryo, and we are deprived, also, of the scene in which Amphitryo and Jupiter first confront each other, and Blepharo is given the impossible task of distinguishing them. (This lacuna, needless to say, has presented a challenge to all would-be imitators of Plautus, but, interesting as the attempts to fill it have been, we meet few surprises of incident or characterization in subsequent versions.)

To deal first with the play's weakness, the main criticism of the poet's treatment of his plot has always been that he has got into a hopeless confusion over the number and occasion of Jupiter's visits to Alcmena. We find Jupiter coming to her the very night before the birth of their son Hercules, which necessitates at least one previous visit, as is implied anyway in lines 107 ff, 479 ff, and 1122. Apart from a certain lack of consideration on Jupiter's part in so timing this visit, it is fairly clear that the divinely prolonged night of the legend was originally the night of Hercules' conception,[1] whereas here the purpose is to give Jupiter more time to enjoy Alcmena. Moreover, the important rôle as a proof of identity played by the goblet, a prize of war which Amphitryo intends to, and Jupiter actually does, give to Alcmena, more naturally suggests Jupiter's first visit to her.

This difficulty is part of the larger problem of Plautus' use of his sources, and we cannot now discuss it in detail; but two essential points can be made. First, it may not have been Plautus, but one of his sources, who conflated incongruous details of Jupiter's visits. Secondly, if it was Plautus who did so, we have good evidence that he never bothered his head about sticking rigidly to his models. Terence, for example, tells us that Plautus left a whole scene out of one of his received plots,[2] and it is clear that where the pace, humour, and convenience of his own versions demanded changes he made them without hesitation. In his *Amphitruo* he wanted to end with the very fine climax of the reported birth of Hercules and the attendant miracles, and this seems cheaply bought at the cost of a few earlier inconsistencies.

One of the play's great merits (and this is characteristic of Plautus' best work) is the pace and vigour with which the plot advances. Although, for example, the prologue (Plautus' longest) and first scene between Mercury and Sosia take up two-fifths of the whole play, there is no tedium, provided that we can read the language fairly rapidly: we need not pause to worry about the occasional repetition of a scene-setting detail (which some scholars have found obnoxious), and we take in our stride Sosia's sometimes pathetic quibbles with Mercury. Apart from interest in the plot, Plautus' technical virtuosity in the use and variation of his metres keeps the reader always on the move. When sense and emotion require it he passes skilfully and naturally from the usual iambics and trochaics into more excited lyric metres. Thus, Sosia appears on the stage for the first time grumbling about the dangers of having to walk alone late at night, and suddenly irritation at his master as the cause of this makes him burst forth into ionics:

> ita peregre adueniens
> hospitio puplicitus accipiar.
> haec eri inmodestia
> coegit me . . . (161 ff)

Again, in his very fine description of the fight against the Teleboae, an impressive and oratorical passage in iambics telling of the preliminaries gives way to more excited cretics when he comes to the battle itself:

> postquam utrimque exitum est maxuma copia,
> dispertiti uiri, dispertiti ordines . . . (219-20)
>
> consonat terra, clamorem utrimque ecferunt.
> imperator utrimque, hinc et illinc, Ioui
> uota suscipere, < utrimque > hortari exercitum.
> < tum > pro se quisque id quod quisque potest et valet
> edit, ferro ferit, tela frangunt, boat
> caelum fremitu uirum . . . (228-33)

This is good narrative verse by any standards, and in showing us his metrical paces Plautus shows also his sheer enjoyment in letting himself go. Nor must we forget the overall irony of the fact that this tremendous account of the battle is delivered by a slave who was not even present at the time—'nam quom pugnabant maxume, ego tum fugiebam maxume' (199).

Another fine narrative passage occurs at the climax of the play, when the maid Bromia enters, dazed in mind (but not in speech) by the thunder and supernatural marvels which have attended Alcmena's *accouchement*. She gives an account of her mistress' divinely assisted delivery, while Amphitryo interjects appropriate astonished comments and queries. Her description is vividly pictorial, and, considering the circumstances, economically worded; and the pace is modified by the use of anapaestic, trochaic, and iambic metre:

> ita erae meae hodie contigit. nam ubi parturit, deos inuocat,
> strepitus, crepitus, sonitus, tonitrus: ut subito, ut prope, ut
>   ualide tonuit!
> ubi quisque institerat, concidit crepitu. ibi nescioquis maxuma
> uoce exclamat . . . (1061-4)

The character of Alcmena is central in the play: the whole action is set in train by her beauty and attraction for the god, and any dramatist who deals with this theme must succeed or fail according to his treatment of her psychology and her reactions to her dilemma. The point is that, grotesque as is the situation portrayed in the legend, there is enough probability in it, enough likelihood of the events occurring in an all-human milieu, for the effect upon Alcmena to be of real interest to us. This is partly responsible for the play's constant re-birth in so many different ages and languages. Though the incidental details of the story have usually suggested a comic treatment, yet Alcmena's dilemma has a basic seriousness and universality which would qualify it for a place in Greek tragedy. Plautus showed his awareness of the two levels of feeling in his own play by calling it, for ostensibly flippant reasons, a tragi-comedy (Prologue, 59 ff).

It is impossible to dissent from the unanimous verdict of generations of commentators on the characterization of Plautus' Alcmena. She is indeed a noble, dignified and very sympathetic woman, and the jester in Plautus gives way to the discerning observer of human character when he portrays this ideal of the young *matrona*. In the catalogue of Plautine women, who consist very largely of older *matronae*, slave girls, and ladies of the town, there is a small group of young wives to which Alcmena belongs, and of which she is perhaps the most notable creation.[3] To point the contrast between Alcmena's simple dignity and the prevailing frivolity of the play, one need only quote the much admired speech of rebuke to her husband, who has just questioned the reality of her *pudicitia*:

non ego illam mi dotem duco esse quae dos dicitur
sed pudicitiam et pudorem et sedatum cupidinem,
deum metum, parentum amorem et cognatum concordiam,
tibi morigera atque ut munifica sim bonis, prosim probis.   (839-42)

Again, her straightforward denial of infidelity is expressed in
simple and moving words:

per supremi regis regnum iuro et matrem familias
Iunonem, quam me uereri et metuere est par maxume,
ut mi extra unum te mortalis nemo corpus corpore
contigit, quo me inpudicam faceret.   (831-4)

Yet she is never sanctimonious, and does not dissolve into a flood
of self-centred wailing. We have the firm impression here of a
strong character deeply hurt, who in the midst of her misery
can yet round curtly upon the impertinent Sosia, and send him
packing with the words 'abin hinc a me, dignus domino seruos?'
(857). Similarly, when she next appears she has resolved to take
matters into her own hands, to leave Amphitryo's house and to
divorce him. This scene (882 ff), in which she is in fact confronting
the disguised Jupiter, is one of fine psychological insight, when
Jupiter skilfully mollifies her by humbling himself and asking
pardon for the harsh words Amphitryo had recently used against
her. He plays upon her piety and wifely affection, which become
obvious when (with typical Plautine irony) he appeals to himself
against himself:

id ego si fallo, tum te, summe Iuppiter,
quaeso Amphitruoni ut semper iratus sies.   (933-4)

Quickly she tries to avert the omen ('a, propitius sit potius'), and
as her unchanged love for her husband thus gives itself away, he
presses the advantage: 'iam nunc irata non es?', and she can only
reply 'non sum'. A woman's tenderness and quick change of mood
are here drawn with a sure hand.

It is worth pointing out that Alcmena also manages to utter
truisms which do not seem, coming from her, to be sententious.
After parting from her supposed husband she reappears on the
stage, sadly reflecting on the disproportion of blessings and
troubles in human life:

satin parua res est uoluptatum in uita atque in aetate agunda
praequam quod molestum est? ita quoiq' comparatum est in
    aetate hominum;

> ita dis est placitum, uoluptatem ut maeror comes consequatur:
> quin incommodi plus malique ilico adsit, boni si optigit
> quid. (633-6)

Innumerable characters in tragedy have spoken these not very
original thoughts, but somehow, knowing Alcmena's position
and the trick that is being played on her, we feel that they have a
particularly genuine and ironic relevance to her. Even the later
lines of this speech, with their very Roman praise of *uirtus*, are
softened and made more personal by being linked in thought with
the husband she loves:

> feram et perferam usque
> abitum eiius animo forti atque offirmato, id modo si mercedis
> datur mi, ut meus uictor uir belli clueat.
> satis mi esse ducam.
> uirtus praemium est optumum;
> uirtus omnibus rebus anteit profecto:
> libertas, salus, uita, res et parentes, patria et prognati
> tutantur, seruantur:
> uirtus omnia in sese habet, omnia adsunt
> bona quem penest uirtus. (645-53)

The last *quem* is, of course, general, but the thought harks back to
meus uir of 647.

Having seen in some detail that Alcmena is one of Plautus'
greatest, if least characteristic, creations, we need not linger over
the other main characters in the play. Mercury and Jupiter are
irreverent and moderately amusing caricatures of these gods, and
Plautus has little trouble in presenting Mercury as a domineering
bully assailing the wretched Sosia (the stage convention demanded
at least some slapstick buffoonery), and Jupiter as the wily and
unscrupulous pseudo-husband. Amphitryo is a strong and
forthright character, very much on his dignity, who is caught
up in a baffling situation that eventually throws him off balance,
so that, at the climax of the play, just before the *coup de théâtre* of
the thunderclap, he rushes towards his own house raving:

> certumst, intro rumpam in aedis: ubi quemque hominem
> aspexero,
> si ancillam seu seruom siue uxorem siue adulterum
> seu patrem siue auom uidebo, optruncabo in aedibus.
> (1048-50)

In the end his natural feelings as husband and father get the better
of him after Bromia's account of Alcmena's delivery, and we know
she is already forgiven:

> iam istuc gaudeo,
> utut me erga merita est.   (1100-01)

Sosia has an unusually subdued rôle for a Plautine slave. His
big moment comes in the first scene, when he delivers the great
account of the battle he never witnessed; thereafter he is completely
quelled by Mercury as his double, though he holds his own for a
time with some essential Plautine quibbles. He is neither *callidus*
nor a rogue, and his chief function in the plot is as an instrument of
mystification.

Is Plautus's play funny? The answer for most readers and by any
standards should be Yes, though this play more than any other in
the Plautine corpus depends for its success on a 'suspension of
disbelief', on account of the mythological element. As with most
of Plautus' plays, we must accept that from a distance of two
millennia and a widely different society we have sometimes to
meet him halfway. We must try to understand the language in
order to appreciate (even if we do not always enjoy) the quibbles;
and as the humour often arises from parody, we must know what is
being parodied. For example, when Mercury dashes on to the
stage at line 984, calling out 'concedite atque apscedite omnes,
de via decedite', the point eludes us unless we realize that this
speech is a parody of innumerable *servi currentes* of Roman
comedy—the slaves who appear running helter-skelter on an
errand of their master, or announcing some juicy piece of news.
More obviously funny is the scene between Mercury and Sosia
at the beginning of the play; and we should not forget that we
have lost a promising scene in which Mercury taunts the hapless
Amphitryo from the roof of his own house, and no doubt
drenches him with water. On the whole the play does not very
often descend to feeble vulgarity (as at 348-9, 665-7), and it is
reasonable to suppose that Plautus was able to hold the interest
of even the crudest of his audience by the character of Alcmena,
and by showing them the king of the gods at play. If we read him
sympathetically the formula still works.

Molière's *Amphitryon* (1668) was not the first French version, though most would agree that it is still the most important. In 1636 Rotrou had produced his *Les Sosies* (he also adapted Plautus' *Captivi* and *Menaechmi*), and Molière, though of course his main debt is to Plautus, owed a good deal to him.[4]

While following the main outlines of the deception in the Plautine story, Molière introduced some significant features suited to his own inclination and the taste and convention of the French theatre of his day. We see this in the prologue, for example, which by nature lent itself particularly well to adaptation for the purpose of setting the scene and mood of a play. Rotrou had introduced Juno to speak his prologue in place of Plautus' Mercury, and Molière's prologue is an amusing dialogue between, Mercure, sitting on a cloud, and Night in her chariot. Mercure is giving her Jupiter's instructions to prolong the dark hours of his visit to Alcmène, and the dialogue incidentally acquaints the audience (if need be) with the background details of the story. There is also some amusing by-play between the two speakers. Mercure complains of feeling tired, and upbraids the poets for giving all the other gods some means of transport, while he has to go about on foot. To Night's reminder that he has been endowed poetically with wings on his feet, he gives the unanswerable reply:

> Oui; mais pour aller plus vite,
> Est-ce qu'on s'en lasse moins?

This introductory scene sets the tone of a play which is always lively and often brilliant.

The most important single innovation is the introduction of a wife for Sosie, Cléanthis, the maid of Alcmène.[5] She is a nagging scold who, after her amorous advances have been repulsed by Mercure (disguised as her husband), upbraids and rants against the real Sosie when next she meets him. The humour here is very much of its period, and very like that of English Restoration Comedy. Mercure had said that as far as he was concerned she could take a lover, if only this stopped her nagging—'Oui, si je n'étais plus de tes cris rebattu', (I. 4)—and the burden of Cléanthis' complaint thereafter becomes 'Oh, that I weren't an honest woman':

> Ah! que dans cette occasion
> J'enrage d'être honnête femme!

and again, later on (II. 7):

Va, va, traître, laisse-moi faire:
On se lasse parfois d'être femme de bien.

On the whole Molière brings off this further comic entanglement,
and the 'below stairs' scenes between Mercure (Sosie) and
Cléanthis reflect and contrast with those between Jupiter
(Amphitryon) and Alcmène.

Two other related changes are important, as they shift the
emphasis and interest of Molière's treatment slightly off the
course pursued by Plautus' plot. These are placing Jupiter's visit
very early in the marriage of Amphitryon and Alcmène, and the
greatly decreased importance of the birth of Hercules as a
consequence of his adventure. Mercure in the prologue tells
Night:

> L'état des mariés à ses feux est propice:
> L'hymen ne les a joints que depuis quelques jours;
> Et la jeune chaleur de leurs tendres amours
> A fait que Jupiter à ce bel artifice
>   S'est avisé d'avoir recours.

Again, whereas in Plautus the climax of the play is the birth of the
great hero Hercules and its attendant wonders, this birth merely
occurs in the prophecy of Jupiter at the very end of Molière's
play, when he says that Amphitryon will one day enjoy the
reflected glory of the great deeds of his 'son' Hercules:

> Chez toi doit naître un fils qui, sous le nom d'Hercule,
> Remplira de ses faits tout le vaste univers.   (III.10)

This change of emphasis is highlighted by the fact that at the end
of Plautus' play we find Amphitryo acquiescing in Jupiter's will,
and preparing a sacrifice; while Molière ends with Sosie cynically
cutting short Naucratès' congratulations, and saying that though
Jupiter has certainly done them honour, silence about these
matters is best.

It is not difficult to see the point of these changes. Originally,
if any justification for Jupiter's underhand *amour* were needed, it
was provided by the birth of the hero who should deliver mankind
of many evils: this side of the legend was perhaps as important
even to a comic writer like Plautus as the grotesque story of the
impersonation. But by the seventeenth century interest in the play
would centre on its possibilities as a simple comedy of intrigue,

and Molière adapts it accordingly. Indeed, it has always been clear to readers of the play that Jupiter talks the sophisticated language of Louis Quatorze gallantry. This is nowhere more obvious than in the emphatic and repeated passages in which he tries to induce Alcmène to accept him emotionally as a lover and not as a husband. With sophistical ingenuity he argues that to a lover is shown ardour 'de pure source', while a husband is gratified only through a wife's duty arising from the 'noeuds de l'hyménée'. (There is very involved irony here, for of course he is a lover pretending to be a husband asking to be received as a lover. We shall see that Molière's introduction of this husband-lover antithesis proved popular with later adaptors of the story.) All this mystifies the simple and affectionate Alcmène, who can but answer:

> Je ne sépare point ce qu'unissent les Dieux
> Et l'époux et l'amant me sont fort précieux.   (I.3)

In a later scene, after the quarrel between Alcmène and the real Amphitryon, Jupiter tries to ingratiate himself again with the excuse that it is the husband in him who has done her wrong, not the lover:

> Haïssez, détestez l'époux,
> J'y consens, et vous l'abandonne.
> Mais Alcmène, sauvez l'amant de ce courroux. . . .   (II.6)

We can but agree with her rejoinder:

> Ah! toutes ces subtilités
> N'ont que des excuses frivoles.

This is a fine, blistering speech of Alcmène. Again she refuses to distinguish husband and lover, and she ends:

> Tous deux de même sorte occupent ma pensée,
> Et des mêmes couleurs, par mon âme blessée,
>   Tous deux ils sont peints à mes yeux:
> Tous deux sont criminels, tous deux m'ont offensée,
>   Et tous deux me sont odieux.

However, her fundamental tenderness (as in Plautus) does not allow her anger to last, and the wily Jupiter wins her over in the end, when she says resignedly:

Pour vouloir soutenir le courroux qu'on me donne,
Mon coeur a trop su me trahir:
Dire qu'on ne saurait haïr,
N'est-ce pas dire qu'on pardonne?

The early scene between Mercure and Sosie follows Plautus fairly closely, and can well stand comparison with its Plautine counterpart for the skill and wit with which Sosie is persuaded that he is not himself. Proof after crushing proof gradually convinces him that the man he is talking to must be himself, until, bereft of identity, he at last bursts out desperately: 'But if I'm not Sosie, who am I? I must be somebody':

Je ne saurais nier, aux preuves qu'on m'expose,
Que tu ne sois Sosie, et j'y donne ma voix.
Mais, si tu l'es, dis moi qui tu veux que je sois?
Car encor faut-il bien que je sois quelque chose. (I.2)

This is an example of Molière's making a good, long scene out of a long one in Plautus, because the humour of it is timeless and could appeal to a seventeenth-century French audience as much as to the Roman audience of Plautus. By contrast, although Sosie's first speech follows Plautus fairly closely, Molière adjusts it to contemporary taste by shortening his account of the battle, and by enlivening the whole speech by having Sosie use his lantern to represent Alcmène in his imaginary conversation with her. This device successfully avoids what might be on the stage a tediously long monologue, and in the hands of a good comic, alternately telling his impressive story to the lantern, and interjecting falsetto comments on its behalf, the scene should be really successful.

Molière added little to the dimensions of the characters which he took over from Plautus. In fact, as we saw earlier, by minimizing the Hercules element in the story he took away something of the dignity of Jupiter, and virtually reduced him to an adventurer pure and simple. He becomes an experienced gallant, who has little difficulty in winning Alcmène from her anger by contrition and threatened suicide—though he would have been hard put to it had she called his bluff. To this extent he is a more colourless character than Jupiter in Plautus.

Again, Molière was not much interested (as later writers were) in the psychology of Alcmène. Although his play is a great deal longer than that of Plautus, Alcmène has a proportionately smaller rôle, and she does not appear at all in the third act. (To judge from the extant fragments she appeared in the missing section of Plautus.) We cannot say more than that she is a normally affectionate and tender wife, who when roused can defend herself, as we have seen, with great spirit (II. 6).

Mercure, Amphitryon and Sosie follow their Plautine models fairly closely. Cléanthis, the chief addition to Plautus' *personae*, is deftly drawn and adds much humour to the play. In a smaller compass, the same can be said of one of Amphitryon's henchmen, the Theban captain Argatiphontidas, who is very much the blustering, hit-first-ask-questions-afterwards type, and may owe something to the *miles gloriosus* of Latin comedy.

By and large, the obvious humour of the piece lies in the subsidiary characters, like Mercure, Sosie, and Cléanthis. This is natural, but it is noteworthy, considering the nature of the subject, that Molière has managed to keep the humour remarkably clean. Whether this was by natural inclination or by design, he is in strong contrast here with Dryden, and even with Plautus, who is not notably salacious. In reading the play one has to remind oneself, in the midst of its elegance and sophistication, that it is about adultery and a cruel trick played by an Olympian god: a good example of the treatment of a work of art transcending its subject-matter.

We have already looked briefly at the end of the play, and marked the contrast between Plautus' and Molière's finales. There is an interesting problem of staging in Molière's play, caused by Amphitryon's curious silence at the end, when Jupiter appears and reveals everything, prophesying the birth of Hercules and future glory to his house. Amphitryon's last words (though he does not subsequently leave the stage) are in Act III, Sc. 8, when he asks the astonished Cléanthis:

> Qui t'épouvante ainsi?
> Quelle est la peur que je t'inspire?

There is no reaction, whether of acquiescence or rebellion, to Jupiter's revelation, and it is left to Sosie to acknowledge guardedly that honour has indeed been done them by 'le grand Dieu Jupiter'. Apart from the difficulty of acting a leading rôle in silence at a climax when all the preceding action demands some verbal reaction, we are left with a puzzle, an unresolved chord in the play: why did the poet not commit Amphitryon to some attitude about his wife's adventure with the god? It may be that a good actor could mutely indicate some such emotion as sullen acceptance of the situation, but Amphitryon's silence together with Sosie's concluding speech (his last words are 'Sur telles affaires, toujours/ Le meilleur est de ne rien dire'), and some of his remarks to Night in the prologue, have been used to suggest that the play has a contemporary reference. It has been interpreted as a satire on the behaviour and attitudes of the aristocracy in general, and as referring in particular to the recently formed liaison between Louis XIV and Madame de Montespan, portrayed by Jupiter and Alcmène.[6] Mercure's last words recall Night in the prologue:

> N'apprêtons point à rire aux hommes
> En nous disant nos vérités;

and Mercure's previous lines to her have a gratuitously pointed ring:

> Lorsque dans un haut rang on a l'heur de paraître,
> Tout ce qu'on fait est toujours bel et bon.

If this interpretation is correct, it might be supposed that the significant silence of Amphitryon, the aggrieved husband, is a comment by the poet on what may be called the general theme of the play, expressed here (we note) by Jupiter himself ('Un partage avec Jupiter / N'a rien du tout qui déshonore' (III. 10)), while in Plautus the thought comes from the mollified Amphitryo ('pol me hau paenitet, / si licet boni dimidium mihi diuidere cum Ioue' (1124-5)). However, this is not the place to discuss in detail this theory, which is certainly not established: it is sufficient to note the possibility that Molière added a satiric dimension to the received story.

Two last points may be mentioned: the skill and beauty of Molière's lyrical verses, which have been universally admired; and the scenic effects, which no doubt were spectacular. The stage directions of the prologue tell us that Mercure appears on a cloud, meeting Night, who is in a chariot drawn by two horses; and that at the end of their colloquy Mercure descends from the cloud to earth, while Night departs, still in her chariot. Again, in the penultimate scene Mercure is finally wafted off to the sky; and

Jupiter at the end speaks from a cloud, into which he eventually disappears. We are a long way from the comparative simplicity of the Roman stage, though few would suggest that in other respects Molière has been able greatly to improve on his model.

In 1690 appeared Dryden's *Amphitryon: or, The Two Sosias,* based largely on Molière, but with Plautus still looming recognizably in the background. Dryden's own view of his play is given modestly in his Dedication to Sir William Gower:

> It is true, were this comedy wholly mine, I should call it a trifle, and perhaps not think it worth your patronage; but when the names of Plautus and Molière are joined in it, that is, the two greatest names of ancient and modern comedy, I must not presume so far on their reputation, to think their best and most unquestioned productions can be termed little. I will not give you the trouble of acquainting you what I have added, or altered, in either of them, so much, it may be, for the worse; but only that the difference of our stage from the Roman and the French did so require it. But I am afraid, for my own interest, the world will too easily discover that more than half of it is mine; and that the rest is rather a lame imitation of their excellences than a just translation. . . . As for Plautus and Molière, they are dangerous people; and I am too weak a gamester to put myself into their form of play.[7]

He goes on to give high praise to Purcell for his musical settings of the three songs which the poet added to the old story.

Dryden's version is much longer than Molière's, and is written in both verse and prose—the prose predominating, and verse appearing in passages of emotional elevation or excitement. His most important innovations are in the addition of characters and sub-plots, the key to which can be seen in his alternative title *The Two Sosias* (cf. Rotrou's title *Les Sosies*). For here the by-play involving Mercury / Sosia is much increased in complexity by the introduction of a second maid of Alcmena's, Phaedra, a type of the venal and unscrupulous lady-in-waiting, with whom Mercury falls in love while trying to avoid Sosia's wife Bromia. The latter is an Anglicized Cléanthis, domineering and insistent on her wifely dues, who plays exactly the rôle Cléanthis had in Molière's play. Further complications arise from another new character, Judge Gripus, uncle of Alcmena, who is an old admirer of Phaedra, and hence a rival to Mercury much to his own discomfiture. There is a strong satiric element here, for Gripus is portrayed as completely corrupt and self-seeking, and a contemporary reference must be more than probable. One more new character is Phoebus, who in the opening scene and by way of prologue discusses with Mercury the reason for their summons by Jupiter: they surmise correctly that "tis some petticoat affair', and soon the great god himself descends to give them the details of his new passion. Dryden's Phoebus and Night (who presently appears) thus between them play the part of Night in Molière.

The play has justly been accused of coarseness and ribaldry, and Sir Walter Scott's verdict has often been quoted with approval:

> The modern poets have treated the subject, which they had from Plautus, each according to the fashion of his country; and so far did the correctness of the French stage exceed ours at that period, that the palm of the comic writing must be, at once, awarded to Molière. For, though Dryden had the advantage of the French author's labours, from which, and from Plautus, he has translated liberally, the wretched taste of the age has induced him to lard the piece with gratuitous indelicacy. He is, in general, coarse and vulgar, where Molière is witty; and where the Frenchman ventures upon a double meaning, the Englishman always contrives to make it a single one.[8]

Yet Scott went on to speak well of the work, and there is certainly no lack of vigour, good cut-and-thrust dialogue, some really poetic lines, and some very funny ones. One does not expect or find any real subtlety or depth of characterization: the piece, in spite of the antiquity of its theme, must be judged by the standards of Restoration Comedy, of which a reasonable verdict would pronounce it a fair, if not brilliant, specimen. Certainly it proved popular, and up to the nineteenth century was thought worthy of no fewer than three bowdlerizations—an operation which, to be worth while, presupposes considerable qualities in the subject.

As far as the coarseness goes, which we find chiefly in the 'lower' characters, in particular Mercury and Phaedra, standards of taste of course vary enormously, and what a sophisticated Restoration or mid-twentieth century audience would accept, a Victorian audience would find (or claim to find) revolting. Therefore, judgment on such a point can hardly avoid being relative. However, it is worth pointing out that Dryden's vulgarity is not much worse than Shakespeare's in places, and that no doubt he included this feature among the changes which he said he introduced into his play because 'the difference of our stage from the Roman and the French did so require it'. This topic belongs more to sociology than to literature, and his society must share with Dryden any censure we give to his bawdy humour. It is more interesting and worth while to examine the play's good qualities.

Apart from some changes like those mentioned above, Dryden in general follows Molière, and in fact imitates closely some details in the latter's treatment of the story. For example, his Jupiter too tries to get Alcmena to distinguish husband and lover in their relationship; and his Alcmena is equally baffled by the subtlety of the distinction:

> I comprehend not what you mean, my lord;
> But only love me still, and love me thus,
> And think me such as best may please your thought. (II.2)

Later on, angrily,

> How vainly would the sophister divide,
> And make the husband and the lover two! (IV.1)

Again, as in Molière, in their scene of mutual recrimination Amphitryon and Alcmena accuse each other of suffering respectively from a 'dream' and a 'vapour'.

Molière:	*Amph.*:	Cette vapeur, dont vous me régalez
		Est un peu, ce me semble, étrange.
	Alc.:	C'est ce qu'on peut donner pour change
		Au songe dont vous me parlez. (II.2)
Dryden:	*Amph.*:	I thank you for my melancholy vapour.
	Alc.:	'Tis but a just requital for my dream. (III.1)

There are other verbal echoes, but this will serve as an example of Dryden's indebtedness in points of detail to Molière's play of twenty-two years earlier.

In one respect Dryden harked back rather to Plautus than to Molière. He lays more stress than did Molière on the birth of Hercules as a result of Jupiter's escapade with Alcmena. In the first scene, when Mercury and Phoebus are twitting Jupiter with this misuse of his omnipotence to satisfy his own desires, he angrily justifies his behaviour on this occasion by prophesying the birth of Hercules, champion of mankind.

Merc.: Here's omnipotence with a vengeance! to make a man
       a cuckold, and yet not to do him wrong! . . .
Phoe.: If there be no such thing as right and wrong
       Of an eternal being, I have done;
       But if there be—
Jup.: Peace, thou disputing fool!
       Learn this: If thou couldst comprehend my ways,
       Then thou wert Jove, not I; yet thus far know,
       That, for the good of humankind, this night
       I shall beget a future Hercules,
       Who shall redress the wrongs of injured mortals,
       Shall conquer monsters, and reform the world. (I.1)

Again, at the end, when Jupiter reveals himself he repeats the
prophecy :

> From this auspicious night shall rise an heir,
> Great like his sire, and like his mother fair:
> Wrongs to redress, and tyrants to disseize;
> Born for a world that wants a Hercules.
> Monsters, and monster-men he shall engage,
> And toil, and struggle, through an impious age.
> Peace to his labours shall at length succeed;
> And murmuring men, unwilling to be freed,
> Shall be compelled to happiness, by need. (V.1)

Molière, as we saw, may have had his own reasons for replacing
certain traditional elements of the myth by contemporary ones;
at all events, Dryden allows Jupiter more of the old high purpose,
however cynically Mercury and Phoebus receive the news of it,
though he does not repeat Plautus' chronological confusion by
bringing the birth of Hercules into the action.

Despite the slightly greater prominence of the Hercules theme,
Dryden's play is still essentially, like Molière's, a comedy of
intrigue. Amphitryon is the duped cuckold (as he thinks) of
innumerable Restoration farces, Phaedra the saucy, scheming,
below-stairs flirt, Gripus the pompous 'Justice', ripe for deflation,
and so on; while Dryden has written a Prologue and Epilogue
(again typical of productions of this period), spoken outside of the
action and linking it, more or less loosely, with contemporary
life and events. To this fusion of old story and contemporary
treatment Dryden added, with Purcell's aid, the very attractive
songs and the 'fantastic Dance', which must have contributed

notably to the popularity of his play. Mercury's song to Phaedra is worth quoting for its charm and witty parody of a swain's song to his mistress:

> Fair Iris, I love, and hourly I die,
> But not for a lip, nor a languishing eye:
> She's fickle and false, and there we agree;
> For I am as false and as fickle as she.
>
> We neither believe what either can say;
> And, neither believing, we neither betray;
> 'Tis civil to swear, and say things of course;
> We mean not the taking for better for worse.
>
> When present, we love; when absent, agree:
> I think not of Iris, nor Iris of me:
> The legend of love no couple can find,
> So easy to part, or so equally joined.   (IV.1)

There is good comic pace and vigour in the piece, and that Dryden aimed at this can be deduced from his invention of Phaedra and Gripus, who are responsible for much of the humour, clean and otherwise. The scenes between Mercury and Phaedra have a continual liveliness worthy of Beatrice and Benedick, as illustrated by the following passage, in which Mercury is trying against odds to induce Phaedra to accept his love:

Merc.: All this notwithstanding, I must tell you, pretty Phaedra, I am desperately in love with you.

Phaed.: And I must tell thee, ugly Sosia, thou hast not wherewithal to be in love.

Merc.: Yes, a poor man may be in love, I hope.

Phaed.: I grant a poor rogue may be in love, but he can never make love. Alas, Sosia, thou hast neither face to invite me, nor youth to please me, nor gold to bribe me; and, besides all this, thou hast a wife, poor miserable Sosia!—What, ho, Bromia!

Merc.: O thou merciless creature, why dost thou conjure up that sprite of a wife?

Phaed.: To rid myself of that devil of a poor lover. . . .   (II.2)

Even Mercury has met his match, and her technique does not alter when she later learns his real identity, and insists on her own conditions in the articles of marriage that Gripus draws up for them.

Again, to increase the farcical, knock-about humour of the play Dryden, as well as making use of the inherited scene between Mercury and Sosia, added one between Mercury and Gripus, when the former induces the Judge by physical violence to renounce his present of a goblet to Phaedra, and his pretensions to her person. Scenes such as these, like the bawdy humour, are a matter of taste, but they no doubt contributed to the play's success on the stage.

At the other pole from slapstick and coarseness, we find some lines of fine, if not great, poetry, in particular in the earlier scenes between Jupiter (Amphitryon) and Alcmena, when they express their love for each other. Alcmena sets the tone of their dialogue in Act II, Sc. 2, with her words:

> So long an absence, and so short a stay!
> What, but one night! one night of joy and love
> Could only pay one night of cares and fears,
> And all the rest are an uncancelled sum!—
> Curse on this honour, and this public fame;
> Would you had less of both, and more of love!

The thought of this and other speeches is not at all original, but the lines do not limp, and occasionally they take wing:

> Ye niggard gods! you make our lives too long;
> You fill them with diseases, wants, and woes,
> And only dash them with a little love,
> Sprinkled by fits, and with a sparing hand:
> Count all our joys, from childhood even to age,
> They would but make a day of every year.
> Take back your seventy years, the stint of life,
> Or else be kind, and cram the quintessence
> Of seventy years into sweet seventy days;
> For all the rest is flat, insipid being.[9] (II. 2)

Piece-meal quotation is unsatisfactory, and extensive quotation impossible; but perhaps some indication has been given that the reader can sometimes forget the ridiculous plot in his enjoyment of the poetry.

Dryden has added little depth or subtlety to the characters he inherited from Plautus and Molière. His Alcmena, like theirs, is a tender, virtuous wife, who yet defends herself with spirit when her honour is called in question. But to the received pattern of

Alcmena scenes he adds an ironic one, in which Amphitryon and Jupiter are both on the stage, and Alcmena, apparently seeing only Amphitryon, goes to him as to her 'proper choice'. Repulsed by him, she is welcomed by Jupiter, and this makes her decide that he is really her husband:

> The face might have deceived me in my choice,
> Thy kindness is a guide that cannot err. (V. 1)

The scene is effective, and an interesting comparison can be made with a variation on it which we shall find in Kleist.

Alcmena can probably claim any sympathies the author may be thought to have had with his characters, though we should not read too much into the Virgilian quotation under the title of the play ('egregiam vero laudem, et spolia ampla refertis, / una dolo divum si femina victa duorum est'), or into the very feminist sentiment of the Prologue. At any rate, the Epilogue suggests that Alcmena had a fair deal—and that Jove the lover has set an example of tact to his mortal imitators.

One last point about Amphitryon's behaviour at the end of the play. As in Molière he has nothing to say after Jupiter's appearance and revelation, but he does not have to stand silently on the stage until the curtain for as long as in Molière, and there is at least a comment on his behaviour from Mercury:

> Amphitryon and Alcmena both stand mute, and know not
> how to take it. (V. 1)

(Alcmène is not on stage at this point in Molière.) Therefore, mingled astonishment and acquiescence seem a reasonable deduction about his (and her) reaction, and Mercury's remark may be an attempt by Dryden to tie up a loose end in Molière's finale. In Dryden, Mercury delivers Sosie's advice (rather more shortly) to be silent and not offer congratulations on the event, but it is Sosia who has the last word with the audience: he moralizes knowingly on wives, husbands, and lovers, and firmly resolves to beget a squire to attend on the unborn Hercules.

Heinrich von Kleist's *Amphitryon: ein Lustspiel nach Molière* appeared in 1807 and introduced into the old legend a depth and subtlety not found in previous versions. It is a very complex play, and more difficult to discuss in a short compass than its predecessors, so that we shall confine ourselves to examining only its more interesting and important variations on the theme.[10] Some idea of the difficulty of assessing its merits may be given by the totally opposite reactions it provoked from critics as notable as Goethe and Thomas Mann. Goethe disliked the play and criticized it sharply, while Mann in a long essay[11] gave it fulsome and almost worshipful praise. Judgment of the play's merits depends largely on one's views of Kleist's much fuller treatment of the characters of Alkmene and Jupiter in the traditional context, and on whether one feels that this produces too great an incongruity of mood and style in the work. It can be argued, for example, that Kleist has been caught between his own preoccupations in psychological character-study and the rigid framework of a traditional and famous plot, and in consequence has produced a work of conflicting comic and tragic elements.

The sub-title suggests, correctly, that the play for the most part follows Molière in structure and many details. The main characters are the same, except that there is no equivalent to Night (there being no prologue), and Cléanthis has been ironically re-named Charis. The Merkur-Sosias-Charis situation, as in Molière, is a humorous foil to that of Jupiter, Amphitryon, and Alkmene. Jupiter reveals himself at the end amidst thunder and lightning, but the prophecy of Hercules' birth here comes as a result of a request from Amphitryon:

> Was du dem Tyndarus getan, tust du
> Auch dem Amphitryon: Schenk einen Sohn
> Gross wie die Tyndariden ihm.   (III. 11)

('What you have done for Tyndarus do also for Amphitryon: grant him a son as great as those of Tyndarus.')

We need not linger on those parts of the play which Kleist adopted without significant alteration. The main interest and importance of the piece lie in the character and greatly increased rôle of Alkmene, who in Molière does not appear at all in the third act. A central figure here, unlike her forerunners she is shown tortured by doubts about her faithfulness to her husband; and Jupiter is filled with an obsession to prove to her and to himself that her love for him surpasses that for her husband. Thus the lover-husband distinction in Molière is taken over and strongly emphasized. The scenes between these two, especially

Act II, Scenes 4 and 5, which are almost entirely Kleist's invention, form the core of the play and Kleist's really significant variation on the old theme. It is worth looking in some detail at these scenes.

The fourth scene of Act II occurs soon after the scene of violent recrimination between Alkmene and Amphitryon, when it becomes clear to him that someone else has visited his wife. In a state of extreme mental turmoil Alkmene had gone back to her room and looked again at the diadem which the pretended Amphitryon had given her as a memento of his victory. The initial *A* had been engraved upon it, and this to her horror she finds has inexplicably changed now to a *J*. She now appears in her misery to show the diadem to Charis, and pitiably tries to get the latter to persuade her that the initial is still an *A*. Charis, believing the evidence of her senses, insists that it is a *J*, and this miraculous event is the third blow to Alkmene's mental stability, coming on top of Jupiter's emphatic insistence on the distinction between lover and husband, and Amphitryon's accusation of infidelity. Jupiter had been quite fierce in his denunciation of the husband *vis-à-vis* the lover, and in his rôle of Amphitryon had referred ambiguously to the real Amphitryon as a 'popinjay' (Laffe), 'vain Theban general', and 'that obvious fop' (I. 4). These words, which she had dismissed at the time as frivolous, now come back to haunt Alkmene, and she tells Charis of the terror and despair with which she recalls the ambiguous jest (doppelsinn'ge Scherz) by which Amphitryon her lover showed his scorn for Amphitryon her husband. Now her own mind seems to separate these rôles, though she still insists she could not mistake her own husband—her husband who appeared to her, she admits, a transcendental and exalted version of himself:

> Ich hätte für sein Bild ihn halten können,
> Für sein Gemälde, sieh, von Künstlershand,
> Dem Leben treu, ins Göttliche verzeichnet.   (II. 4)

('I could have taken him for a portrait of himself, a painting, mark you, from an artist's hand, true to life but sealed to divine proportions'.) She goes on to say with innocent irony:

> ich hätt' ihn fragen mögen,
> Ob er mir aus den Sternen niederstiege.

('I might have asked him whether he had descended from the stars to me'.) (It is just this sublimer-than-life appearance of Jupiter-Amphitryon which induces Alkmene, with sad irony, to select him as her real husband at the climax of the play.) Charis tries to comfort her, but without success, as Alkmene now feels that the diadem which was formerly a proof of her honour now testifies against her:

> Bin ich wohl sicher, sprich, dass ich auch gestern
> Das *Zeichen*, das hier steht, von ihm empfing?

('Can I be certain, tell me, that yesterday I also received from him the *sign* (i.e. the *J*) now before me?') On this despairing question Jupiter enters for the fifth scene of Act II, in which his sophistry and ambiguities continue to confuse Alkmene, but do not shake her love for Amphitryon the husband.

In this long and crucial scene Jupiter-Amphitryon intensifies and completes what Goethe called the 'Verwirrung des Gefühls' (confusion of feeling)[12] of the wretched Alkmene. To her agonized question whether it was really he (whom of course she takes to be her husband) who came to her the previous night, he answers ambiguously 'Ich war's. Sei's, wer es wolle' ('It was I, no matter who it was'): whoever came, she only received himself. Somewhat naturally this evasion only increases her distraction (though Jupiter need only have answered truthfully and without qualification in the affirmative); and when she says that they must now part forever he says, with irony familiar to us from other treatments of the story, that he would not have foregone the previous day for Zeus' immortal life, and that if he were Zeus he would bring her in triumph among all the gods.

Alkmene's devotion to her husband makes her reject Jupiter, whom she takes to be the husband she has unwittingly betrayed. She feels she cannot stay with him after what has happened, so Jupiter tries another tack and tells her that her visitor was none other than Jupiter himself. At first aghast at the very suggestion, she is gradually won over to the possibility by his argument that only Jupiter could have deceived her so completely and appeared to her so boldly. He points also to the evidence of the changed initial on the diadem, and when she objects that she is quite unworthy of such grace he answers:

Ob du der Gnade wert, ob nicht, kömmt nicht
Zu prüfen *dir* zu. Du wirst über dich,
Wie er dich würdiget, ergehen lassen.

('Whether you deserve the grace or not is not for *you* to examine:
you have only to accept patiently the honour he confers on you'—
lines that Thomas Mann thought almost the finest in the play.)
At length Alkmene accepts the possibility with relief and happiness
in such a solution, but her sufferings are by no means over.
Jupiter now suggests that the reason for Jupiter's visit is that
whenever Alkmene prays to him she has the image of Amphitryon
in her mind, and it is her husband whom she is really adoring.
Consequently Jupiter has played this trick in order to make her
think of him, and to punish her for her forgetfulness. The
wretched woman, thus made responsible for her unfaithfulness,
has to admit the charge, and her *cri du coeur* at this point epitomizes
her predicament:

Ach, ich Unsel'ge, wie verwirrst du mich.
Kann man auch Unwillkürliches verschulden?

('Ah, unhappy that I am, how you confuse me. Can one be guilty
of an involuntary feeling?') She then promises that hereafter she
will think of Jupiter in her prayers, but she refuses to admit that
she could give up Amphitryon in his favour. Thus Jupiter has
failed in his ultimate aim, and it is his turn to exclaim in despair,
'Verflucht der Wahn, der mich hieher gelockt!' ('Accursed be the
delusion that lured me hither!'). He then paints a pathetic picture of
the great father of the gods yearning for love, and not just the
worship of mortals ('Auch der Olymp ist öde ohne Liebe'—'Even
Olympus is desolate without love'); yet the utmost admission he
can extract from her is that, if he were the god now holding her in
his embrace and if Amphitryon the husband were to appear, she
would wish that Amphitryon were the god, and that he (Jupiter)
would remain Amphitryon for her. This satisfies Jupiter, though
the admission stems only from the intense feeling she experiences
for this divine pseudo-husband: the lover is better than the husband,
but Alkmene would have the rôles reversed.

This intense feeling for the false Amphitryon, arising from his
supernaturally exalted appearance, betrays Alkmene when she is
faced with the necessity of choosing her real husband in the
confrontation of the two Amphitryons at the climax. She chooses

Jupiter (as she did in J. D. Falk's German version of 1804), rejecting her real husband with tragic irony because by comparison with the other he cannot be Amphitryon. She now sees herself as grossly betrayed and deceived, and with her mind now nearly unhinged she rails at him with terrible words, curses herself for succumbing, and resolves to flee away to mountain peaks and desert. Thus she addresses her real husband, and her 'Verwirrung des Gefühls' is complete.

In this way Alkmene is present at the dénouement and Jupiter's revelation, and her reactions when the truth is finally known form one of the play's puzzling complexities. Jupiter stands revealed, and with him her last and greatest error, the spurning of her real husband. At the theophany she sinks into Amphitryon's arms, calling on the gods' protection; Jupiter prophesies the birth and fame of Hercules, restores her to her husband and vanishes; the Theban generals cluster round offering congratulations, Amphitryon calls his wife by name, and the curtain falls on her only reply, a single 'Ach!' This confused and poignant exclamation is not easy to interpret. Does it express relief that all errors are resolved, and joy that husband and wife are together again, or rather resignation in her lot, tinged with sadness that things will never be the same again between them? After the maelstrom of emotional turmoil that Alkmene has experienced, culminating in her terrible denunciation of her husband, perhaps her 'Ach!' is simply the reaction of a woman emptied of feeling, who does not yet really grasp the meaning of what has happened to her, and who, like Dido, needs a *tempus inane* in which to learn to live after a shattering emotional experience. Molière did not introduce Alcmène at the dénouement of his play, so we cannot compare her and Alkmene's reactions, though we can assume that she would have been fully reconciled. However, we must remember that Kleist called his play a 'Lustspiel', so we must beware of reading too much into the closing scene.

Even if Alkmene is not fully reconciled, Amphitryon certainly is, but the manner of his reconciliation is one of the least satisfactory features of the play. There is in Kleist a seriousness and tragic element in Amphitryon's ordeal that we have not found in the previous versions under review. This is largely because much more is made of the eradication of his identity at the climax, when Alkmene chooses wrongly and denounces him with unwitting cruelty. Amphitryon is really more of a tragic than a comic figure, and, throughout, his conduct on the whole is dignified and wins our sympathy. He uses bitter words to his wife in their first scene together, but he never seriously doubts her integrity and her honour. In his soliloquy at the beginning of the third act he remarks:

> Zu argem Trug ist sie so fähig just
> Wie ihre Turteltaub'; eh' will ich an
> Die Redlichkeit dem Strick entlaufner Schelme
> Als an die Tücke dieses Weibes glauben.

('She is no more capable of wicked deception than her turtledove; I will sooner believe in the honesty of rogues who have escaped the gallows than in this woman's treachery'.) She must be crazed, and he must send for the doctor tomorrow. At the end, such is his faith in her that he says that if she acknowledges Jupiter as her husband Amphitryon, he will agree with this; and, true to his word, after her verdict he makes the ultimate sacrifice of his own identity:

> O ihrer Worte jedes ist wahrhaftig,
> Zehnfach geläutert Gold ist nicht so wahr. . . .
> Jetzt einen Eid selbst auf den Altar schwör ich
> Und sterbe siebenfachen Todes gleich,
> Des unerschütterlich erfassten Glaubens,
> Dass er Amphitryon ihr ist.   (III. 11)

('O each of her words is true; gold ten times refined is not so true. . . . Now I swear an oath on the altar and die seven times over in the unflinching belief that, for her, he is Amphitryon'.) (But a last spark of resistance surely prompts the reservation in 'ihr'.)

It is at this point that Jupiter reveals himself, and Kleist's original treatment of Amphitryon's character gives way to the demands of the received plot. Jupiter offers Amphitryon personal fame as a token of his gratitude, and, if this does not satisfy him, fulfilment of his dearest wish. Amphitryon replies that he is not satisfied, and asks for a son as great as those of Tyndarus. Whereupon Jupiter promises him the future birth of Hercules. It is this development which critics, with some justice, have seen as an uncharacteristic distortion of Amphitryon's behaviour in order to follow the tradition: a character of tragic stature descends almost to the rank of complaisant cuckold. Goethe[13] thought the ending slovenly, though he pointed out that Amphitryon had to accept Jupiter's adventure and its outcome as an honour, in order to make his own and Alkmene's situation bearable.

Thus the ending shows the enforced mingling of original tragic with traditional comic elements, and Kleist's play truly fits Plautus' description of his own as a 'tragi-comedy'. There is humour in the Merkur-Sosias-Charis scenes, but the enduring impression of the play is of the ordeals of Alkmene and Amphitryon which shatter their faith in their own deepest feelings.

The *Amphitryon* 38 of Jean Giraudoux appeared in 1929, and is the most important recent version of the theme. The title indicates that Giraudoux knew he was heir to a long tradition, but in fact his work is in many ways the most original treatment so far.

The play is in prose, with several major innovations and omissions, both of incident and of characterization. Giraudoux shows no very strong links with earlier versions, though, as in Kleist, his Alcmène is the central character. She does not, however, suffer the agonized internal conflict of Kleist's heroine, and is much more mistress of the situation, in so far as she understands it. Giraudoux dispenses with the slapstick scenes between Sosie and Mercure, and the latter's function, when disguised as Sosie, is simply to announce to Alcmène her so-called husband's return to her. In fact Sosie and pseudo-Sosie do not confront each other, and instead of these scenes, which figure largely in the previous treatments we have examined, there are scenes of much quieter humour between Sosie and a Trumpeter. The latter is a droll character who prides himself on his craftsmanship, though this consists of blowing just one note on his trumpet. Again, Sosie and Alcmène's maid Ecclissé are not connected, and there is no reflection at this level of the Jupiter-Amphitryon-Alcmène situation. It is clear that Giraudoux's talents and interest lay in the witty, sophisticated, and often ironic humour of the conversations between Alcmène and Jupiter.

One of Giraudoux's important innovations is that Alcmène, while unaware that Jupiter has already visited her as Amphitryon, knows that he is planning to visit her the following night. Much to Jupiter's dismay, Mercure has announced this fact to Thebes and the world in general, as he tells his father, 'Comme votre

désir de passer une seconde nuit dans les bras d'Alcmène éclatait
à travers toutes les murailles' (II. 3). In the event Alcmène
persuades Jupiter on his second arrival to forgo spending the
night with her, and at this point the Hercules theme necessarily
receives a new twist. He had, of course, been conceived on the
night of Jupiter's first (and unknown) visit; subsequently Mercure
(as himself) announces to Alcmène, and a Celestial Voice announces
to a crowd outside the palace, that a child, Hercule, will be born
as a result of Jupiter's proposed (second) visit. Finally, when
Jupiter is prevailed upon to restore Alcmène untouched to her
husband, the arrangement is that she and Amphitryon are to have
a son whom they will call Hercule, 'puisque vous (Jupiter) aimez
ce nom' (III. 6). Alcmène is rather suspicious of Jupiter's eventual
agreement to give her up, and asks him whether he has ever
visited her before disguised as her husband: this the god brazenly
denies, and, at her request, he grants her troubled feelings the
relief of forgetfulness.

With some idea now of the scale of Giraudoux's originality,
we can look at his treatment of his two major characters, Alcmène
and Jupiter. Alcmène is the most human and feminine heroine we
have yet had: utterly devoted to her husband (like the others), she
also wins us over by her quick-witted and artful turn of mind,
and is fully a mental match for Jupiter, though she declines to be a
physical one. For example, in the scene already mentioned (III. 5),
in which she tries to persuade Jupiter to give her up, she suggests
that she can offer him something better than love—friendship!
Jupiter has not even heard the word:

Alc.: Oh! Jupiter, laissez-moi vous proposer mieux que l'amour.
Vous pouvez goûter l'amour avec l'autres. Mais j'aimerais
entre nous un lien plus doux encore et plus fort: seule de
toutes les femmes je puis vous l'offrir. Je vous l'offre.
Jup.: Et c'est?
Alc.: L'amitié.
Jup.: Amitié? Quel est ce mot? Explique-toi. Pour la prémière
fois, je l'entends.
Alc.: Vraiment? Oh! alors je suis ravie! Je n'hésite plus! Je vous
offre mon amitié. Vous l'aurez vierge. . . .
Jup.: Qu-entends-tu par là? C'est un mot courant sur la terre?
Alc.: Le mot est courant.
Jup.: Amitié. . . . Il est vrai que de si haut, certaines pratiques
des hommes nous échappent encore. . . .

So she explains to him as best she can, tells him how and when she would enjoy his friendship, and eventually with amused resignation he gives way to her courage and stubbornness, and accepts her friendship 'sans réserves'. In any case he has had his night of bliss. This is an amusing invention of Giraudoux, perhaps suggested by the husband-lover distinction of earlier versions, a distinction he also retains in Act I, Sc. 6, as we shall see.

More generally, Alcmène is seen typifying not only the contentment of a wife in her very happy bourgeois marriage, but the contentment of a human being in her mortal lot. Not for her the attractions of divinity or immortality repeatedly offered to her by Jupiter—they are not in fact attractions in her eyes. Her life and her love for her husband, set within the limits of mortality laid down for all animals and plants, suffice for her complete happiness. After their night together the disguised Jupiter asks her:

> Tu n'as jamais désiré être déesse, ou presque déesse?
>
> *Alc.:* Certes non. Pourquoi faire?
> *Jup.:* Pour être honorée et révérée de tous.
> *Alc.:* Je le suis comme simple femme, c'est plus méritoire.
> *Jup.:* Pour être d'une chair plus légère, pour marcher sur les airs, sur les eaux.
> *Alc.:* C'est ce que fait toute épouse, alourdie d'un bon mari.
> *Jup.:* Pour comprendre les raisons des choses, des autres mondes.
> *Alc.:* Les voisins ne m'ont jamais intéressée.
> *Jup.:* Alors, pour être immortelle!
> *Alc.:* Immortelle? A quoi bon? A quoi cela sert-il?
> *Jup.:* Comment, à quoi! Mais à ne pas mourir!
> *Alc.:* Et que ferai-je, si je ne meurs pas?
> *Jup.:* Tu vivras éternellement, chère Alcmène, changée en astre; tu scintilleras dans la nuit jusqu'à la fin du monde.
> *Alc.:* Qui aura lieu?
> *Jup.:* Jamais.
> *Alc.:* Charmante soirée! . . . (II. 2)

Again she says:

> Je ne crains pas la mort. C'est l'enjeu de la vie. . . . Je sens trop mes fibres continuer celles des autres hommes, des animaux, même des plantes, pour ne pas suivre leur sort. Ne me parle pas de ne pas mourir tant qu'il n'y aura pas un légume immortel. Devenir immortel, c'est trahir, pour un humain. (II. 2)

In her later scene with Jupiter (III. 5) when she persuades him to give her up, he offers her even a quick glimpse of eternity and the world, freed of all illusion, and a glimpse of her own future.

> *Alc.:* Je sais ce qu'est un avenir heureux. Mon mari aimé vivra et mourra. Mon fils chéri naîtra, vivra et mourra. Je vivrai et mourrai.
> *Jup.:* Pourquoi ne veux-tu pas être immortelle?
> *Alc.:* Je déteste les aventures; c'est une aventure, l'immortalité! . . . Non, Jupiter, je ne suis pas curieuse.

In the earlier scene Jupiter obliquely sounds out her reaction to the arrival of the infant prodigy and god-elect, Hercule: would she like an immortal son who from earliest infancy would grapple with lions, monsters, and serpents? Alcmène acknowledges the human desire for an immortal son, but at the mention of serpents in his cradle, this practical mother-to-be remarks:

> Il ne serait jamais seul. Ces aventures n'arrivent qu'aux fils des femmes de ménage. . . . Non, je le veux faible, gémissant doucement, et qui ait peur des mouches. . . . (II. 2)

This effectively kills the topic.

It must be obvious by now that the king of the gods undergoes some discomfiture in his verbal exchanges with Alcmène. Generally speaking, as Alcmène is a less intense creation in Giraudoux than her counterpart in Kleist, so Giraudoux's Jupiter is a more 'comic' figure than Kleist's. There is, to be sure, an echo of Kleist's love-starved god in Jupiter's remark to Mercure, 'Un dieu aussi peut se plaire à être aimé pour lui-même' (I. 5), but we do not take him very seriously. We enjoy seeing the almighty deceiver two or three times put in his place and thwarted, though his obvious dejection in the scene with Mercure (II. 3) invites our amused sympathy; for example, when he says:

> Alcmène, la tendre Alcmène, possède une nature plus irréductible à nos lois que le roc. C'est elle le vrai Prométhée;

and again,

> Pour la première fois, Mercure, j'ai l'impression qu'un honnête dieu peut être un malhonnête homme. . . .

He receives a temporary set-back in Act I, Sc. 6, when he approaches the palace disguised as Amphitryon. This is a variation on the familiar husband-lover theme, for when he announces himself to Alcmène first as 'un général', and then as her lover, he is refused admission with the curt words

C'est à Alcmène que vous parlez, non à sa chambrière. Je n'ai pas d'amant. . . .

(Alcmène has, of course, been warned of the arrival of her 'husband' by Mercure disguised as Sosie.) Jupiter has to call himself her husband before she eventually admits him— and then she tells him that the door was open all the time.

A similar rebuff is delivered to Jupiter in Act II, Sc. 2, when, after the night of his visit, he tries to persuade Alcmène that it has been the most 'agréable' or the most 'étonnante' that 'they' have had together. She refuses to admit this, and mentions instead a succession of other nights, which of course she had spent with the real Amphitryon, and which she thinks more deserve these adjectives. Finally, she twists the knife in Jupiter's wounded pride by saying that the adjective she would apply to the past night would be 'conjugale'. Jupiter's next conversational opening can rise no higher than 'Quelle belle chambre!'

One other important innovation by Giraudoux is the visit of Léda to Alcmène (II. 6), and their connivance to deceive Jupiter. Léda, who had once received the attentions of Jupiter in the form of a swan, has heard the rumour of his intended visit to Alcmène, and curiosity impels her to pay a visit. Alcmène persuades her to take her place when Jupiter arrives, and there is a good touch here with Alcmène's query, 'Ne se rend-on pas de ces services entre amies?', and Léda's answer, 'Sans se le dire, oui, souvent'. Léda decides that he will appear in 'la forme qui hante vos désirs et vos rêves', that is, in the shape of Amphitryon; but with unfortunate irony it is the real Amphitryon who next appears, only to be trapped into going to bed with Léda by his own wife, who thinks he is Jupiter. The scene between these two ladies is witty and entertaining, and they are well contrasted types, Alcmène eagerly questioning the sophisticated Léda about her affair with Jupiter, and unaware that she herself is equally experienced in this direction. Léda's attitude, in contrast with Alcmène's, is well brought out when she describes her husband's reaction to her own adventure:

Mon mari ne croit pas aux dieux. Il ne peut donc voir, dans cette aventure, qu'une imagination ou le sujet de jeux de mots. C'est un avantage.

This incident, and its ironic outcome, are a happy addition to the old legend.

There are some other, less important, novelties. For example, it is Mercure who, in the first scene, in which he and Jupiter are watching Alcmene and Amphitryon through a window, suggests that Jupiter take Amphitryon's form and decoy him away from home by stirring up a war. The epiphany of Jupiter at the end is not very dramatic, compared with earlier versions, as both Amphitryon and Alcmène have been expecting him, and debating what to do in the situation facing them. Again, it is Jupiter who has the final word, addressing the spectators and invoking a blessing upon the re-united couple.

Without more extensive quotation than is here possible, it is more difficult to give an idea of *Amphitryon* 38 than of any of the other plays we have considered. This is owing as much to the uniformly lively, often brilliant, quality of its dialogue, as to Giraudoux's structural alterations in the old plot. He is the most modern of the really significant adaptors of the legend: this fact as well as the reflections which he invites on marriage, contentment, and immortality, ensure for his play perhaps a wider audience than the others enjoy.

These five plays of Plautus, Molière, Dryden, Kleist, and Giraudoux are the great milestones in the astonishing history of the legend of Alcmèna and Amphitryo. Accordingly we have looked at them in some detail, but this is not to suggest that there are not other important and interesting versions.[14] Of the numerous imitations and adaptations of the story the following are well worth mentioning.

In the late twelfth century Vitalis of Blois wrote his *Geta*, a narrative version in Latin elegiacs, in which Amphitryon is a student of Philosophy returning from Athens. The whole piece is a satire on the scholasticism of the time,[15] and became extremely popular, inspiring French and Italian paraphrases.

In the sixteenth century Dolce wrote an Italian imitation, *Il Marito* (1545), in which Amphitryo and Alcmena become Mutio and Virginia; and Camões himself wrote a Portuguese version (*c.* 1550). In England Plautus' *Amphitruo* was one of the first two of his plays (the other being the *Menaechmi*) to be translated in the late sixteenth century; the story also provided material for the interlude *Jacke Jugeler* (*c.* 1550), and was utilized by Thomas Heywood in *The Silver Age* (*c.* 1600).

The seventeenth century saw the fine French version of Rotrou (1636, already mentioned), which influenced Molière; and also one of the most remarkable variants of the legend, Burmeister's Christianized paraphrase, published at Lüneburg in 1621.[16] In this work the setting is Nazareth, and Alcmena is transformed into the Virgin Mary, with corresponding alterations in the other *dramatis personae*.

The eighteenth century produced, among others, the Portuguese imitation of José da Silva (1736); and in the early nineteenth century appeared the German *Amphitryon* of J. D. Falk (1804), which may have influenced Kleist. Finally, in our own day, Georg Kaiser wrote a very original version, *Zweimal Amphitryon*, which was first performed in 1944.

And so the legend goes on, surely one of the most versatile in the whole range of Greek myths. We have seen how many writers, of both great and little stature, felt the appeal of the old story after Plautus had shown its possibilities, and found in it material for sensitive character study as well as comedy. The genius and bent of each writer has dictated the proportions of these elements in the various versions, and we have seen the trend towards ignoring or adapting the Hercules theme, and focusing the interest upon Alcmena's emotions and her relations with her real and spurious husbands.

NOTES

[1] Diodorus Siculus iv, 9, 2; Seneca, *Agamemnon* 825-6, *Hercules Oetaeus* 1864-6; Ovid, *Heroides* ix, 9-10; Lucian, *Dialogues of the Gods* x (cf. Apollodorus, ii. 4, 8). See also H. W. Prescott, 'The *Amphitruo* of Plautus', *CPh* VIII (1913), pp. 14-22.

[2] Terence, *Adelphi*, 6-10.

[3] Cf. Penegyris and Pamphila in the *Stichus*.

[4] Ironically, two of Molière's most famous lines derive from Rotrou. Sosie's criterion to distinguish the real and the false Amphitryon,

Le véritable Amphitryon
Est l'Amphitryon où l'on dîne,

recalls Rotrou's Second Capitaine:

Point, point d'Amphitryon où l'on ne dîne point;

and Molière's Sosie's cynical comment on Jupiter's revelation,

Le Seigneur Jupiter sait dorer la pilule,
adapts the words of Rotrou's Sosie:
On appelle cela lui sucrer le breuvage.

⁵ Sosie's wife may derive from Sosia's oblique reference to his *amica* in Plautus' play (659), and her name was possibly suggested by Alcmena's maid Galanthis in Ovid, *Met.* ix. 306 ff. See A. Ernout, 'Amphitryon dans Plaute et dans Molière', *Neophilologus* 33(1949), p. 115.

⁶ Cf. J. Michelet, *Histoire de France*, Vol. XV, Chap. 7 (Paris, 1899).

⁷ *The Works of John Dryden*, edited by Sir Walter Scott, Vol. VIII, pp. 8-9 (Edinburgh, 1884).

⁸ *Op. cit.*, p. 2.

⁹ An interesting contemporary criticism of this passage can be found in Laurence Echard's preface to his translation of Plautus (London, 1694). He singles out Alcmena's complaint in Act II of Dryden's version as 'one instance of what improvements our modern poets have made on the ancients, when they built upon their foundations'. (Quoted by Charles E. Ward, *The Life of John Dryden*, pp. 362-3 (Chapel Hill, University of North Carolina Press, 1961).)

¹⁰ Further and fuller discussion of the play can be found in E. L. Stahl, *Heinrich von Kleist's Dramas*, pp. 59 ff (Oxford, 1948); John C. Blankenagel, *The Dramas of Heinrich von Kleist*, pp. 81 ff (Chapel Hill, University of North Carolina Press, 1931); and W. Silz, *Heinrich von Kleist*, pp. 45 ff (Philadelphia, University of Pennsylvania Press, 1961). Classical scholars may note with interest Wilamowitz's derogatory judgment of Kleist's version in comparison with Molière's: see his edition of Euripides' *Herakles*, Vol. I, p. 53 (Berlin, 1895).

¹¹ 'Kleists Amphitryon: eine Wiedereroberung', written in 1926 and to be found in Mann's *Adel des Geistes*, pp. 56-103 (Stockholm, 1945).

¹² Diary for July 13th, 1807: *Goethes Werke*, hrsg. Grossherzogin Sophie, III Abt., Bd. 3, p. 239 (Weimar, 1887-1914).

¹³ In conversation with Riemer: *Gedenkausgabe der Werke, Briefe und Gespräche*, hrsg. Beutler, 22, p. 466 (Zürich, 1948-54).

¹⁴ Extensive lists and discussions of adaptations of the Amphitryo theme may be found in K. von Reinhardstoettner, *Plautus. Späterer Bearbeitungen plautinischer Lustspiele*, pp. 115-229 (Leipzig, 1886); and L. R. Shero, 'Alcmena and Amphitryon in Ancient and Modern Drama', *TAPha* LXXXVII (1956), pp. 192-238.

¹⁵ Cf. lines 451-8.

Birria subridens: 'accepit Graecia sanos
Hos', ait, 'insanos illa remisit eos.
Insanire facit stultum dialectica quemvis,
Ars ea sit nunquam, Birria, nota tibi.
Arte carere bonum est, quae per fantasmata quaedam
Aut homines asinos aut nichil esse facit.
Sit logicus quivis, tu, Birria, sis homo semper:
His studium placeat, uncta popina tibi.'

The text of the poem may be found in Thomas Wright's *Early Mysteries, and other Latin Poems of the Twelfth and Thirteenth Centuries*, pp. 79-90 (London 1838).

[16] *Plauti Renati sive Sacri Mater-Virgo Comoedia prima ex Amphitruone Ad Admirandum Conceptionis et Incarnationis Filii Dei Misterium inversa*. The *dramatis personae* are: Gabriel, Prologus; Sosia, Servos; Joseph; Maria, Virgo; Asmodes; Flamen Judaicus; Obstetrix; Pastores, tres. This work recalls Hrosvitha's imitations of Terence in the tenth century.

V

Shakespeare, Seneca, and the Kingdom of Violence

GARETH LLOYD EVANS

THE shadow of Seneca falls heavily across the arass of Elizabethan drama. In a thematic sense, and technically, it was his example which shaped the nature and traced the design of Elizabethan tragedy. Pre-Shakespearean plays, like Kyd's *The Spanish Tragedy*, are direct heirs of Senecan modes, deviating only slightly from the patterns of thought, feeling, and action which are present in his plays. Post-Shakespearean dramas, such as Ford's *The Broken Heart*, while they do not have the almost complete consanguinity with Seneca of the earlier dramatists, are not immune from the influence. Penthea, in Ford's play, is one of the most notable examples of Senecan stoicism in the whole corpus of Elizabethan / Jacobean drama.

It has become a truism of criticism of Shakespeare's tragedies to begin with the assumption that he, no less than many of his contemporaries, knew his Seneca well. Whether, with his presumed little Latin, he knew him in the original, or whether he relied upon the popular translations of the ten plays which appeared in 1581,[1] will remain a perpetual speculation. There are very few references to Senecan characters in Shakespeare's plays, and the immense number of verbal parallels suggested by Cunliffe[2] in one of the earliest studies of the influence, have been drastically reduced by later commentators. They have realized that the existence of a pervasive convention and tradition of mode in character, atmosphere, theme, and style can lead to typed verbal expressions which may appear unconsciously. Indeed, any speculation must include the possibility that Shakespeare's own Senecanism may, to a large extent, have been derived not from the source, but from early Elizabethan usages of the source—like *The Spanish Tragedy*. This is not to deny that Shakespeare had a direct contact with the source, but that the contact was mutated by his knowledge of what his predecessors had achieved in their use of the source. With caution it might also be suggested that, given a mind so varied and adhesive as Shakespeare's, other influences were constantly at their work of mutation and that if, by whatever process, Seneca was the dominant shaping figure on his tragedies, this was under pressure from a simpler and more rugged mediaeval legacy. *Richard III*, for example, so frequently attested as the most obvious issue of Senecan fertilization, throws out roots deep into the soil of the mediaeval vice-figure.

The exhaustive work of Cunliffe, Lucas, Eliot, Thorndike, Ribner, Fredson Bowers,[3] and others has definitively established the nature and the details of Seneca's influence. It has, with authority, speculated upon the way in which the influence was disseminated in Shakespeare and his contemporaries, and the mutations to which it was subjected. It has shown the extent to which the Elizabethans grafted upon a Roman ethos and Roman modes the living tissue of their own time.

There is no reason for further enquiry into these matters. There now exists a clear picture of those elements in Seneca which are characteristic of him, and which are to be found in a greater or lesser degree in the work of Kyd, Marlowe, Shakespeare, Tourneur, Webster, and Ford. The stoical behaviour and posturing of the tragic hero-villain, the rhetorical communication, the sensationalism of plot and incident, the implacable skeins of revenge, the demonstrations of cruelty, the descriptions of bloody acts, the reflectiveness of theme and tone in many speeches, the supernatural usages, the chorus, verbal devices, the five-act structure—all these lie clearly before us now, both as they appear in Seneca, and as they appear in the Elizabethans.

But it might be suggested that there remains one corner of study upon which some light may play. The most surprising feature of the Senecan influence on the drama is, despite the Elizabethan preoccupation in general with classical literature, that it exists at all. There is obviously much in Seneca which would appeal to a sophisticated intelligentsia, not least his often ponderous didacticism which seems designed to excuse his parade of sensationalism. There is much, too, in the melodramatic posturings of his characters to appeal to the histrionic imagination of an Elizabethan intelligentsia. Yet there would seem to be little in

Seneca to hold the patience of the hustling, commercially-minded theatre-world of the 1590's and 1600's. It remains a matter for investigation that Shakespeare, writing for the extrovert, critically horny-handed and demanding audience of the public theatre, should presumably have found his blood tingling to the stimuli of this ancient dramatist who wrote for no such audience. Seneca's plays lack much of what we find in Shakespeare's plays to stir us—dramatic interest, character development, subtlety, and variety of theme, plot, incident, and mood. They lack, in short, except intermittently, nearly all the qualities which we characterize by the name Drama.

One answer as to why Shakespeare looked to Seneca, especially in his formative years, brings us face to face with the oft-stated fact that he was possessed of the most predatory imagination of all the Elizabethan dramatists. He was a picker-up, not only of unconsidered trifles, the droppings from other men's tables, but reconnoitred for larger booty with a beguiling insouciance. Yet almost everything he touched he changed. It is at this point that his genius lies and it is at this point that further study of the Senecan elements in his plays might be profitable. The direction of Shakespeare's shaping imagination is always towards the animation of its material by the breath of dramatic logic and theatrical feasibility. His imagination transmutes the static into the mobile, the abstract into the concrete, the theoretical into the actual, the non-human into the human. How he achieves this with certain Senecan elements, making tractable much that is dramatically and theatrically intractable is the subject of this study.

Seneca's most compelling appeal for the Elizabethan playwrights lay in his exploitation of the themes and usages of blood, revenge, and cruelty. It was this 'kingdom of violence' which captured a good deal of Shakespeare's imagination in the early plays *Titus Andronicus*, *Henry VI*, and *Richard III*. The excitation of fear is a cliché of dramatic history, and Shakespeare's audience no less than modern audiences, were easy victims of an imagination which, nurturing itself upon Seneca, manipulated certain unchanging human responses to the spectacle of fearsome deeds and events. The attractiveness of being 'afraid' in the theatre is based perhaps on two conditions. Firstly, the desire to be as near as possible to the actual, or apparently actual, experience of what is unusual, without actively being involved in it; secondly the possible existence in humanity of a primordial streak of cruelty.

The response by audiences over the centuries to enactments of horror and cruelty has never abated. The Senecanism of the late sixteenth and early seventeenth centuries, the Gothic murk of the late eighteenth century, the melodramatic murder plays of the latter part of the nineteenth century, and the nameless horrors of modern quasi-scientific films, are a firmly-drawn line through the theatrical history of this country. The taste for horror has changed only in the sense-data provided for the feeding of audience's emotions. It might be suspected too that the Elizabethan audience was more vociferous in its response to depictions of horrific and cruel events than the modern audience, but this must be subjected to qualification. Evidence of the behaviour of audiences in the Elizabethan theatre strongly suggests that they reacted far less inhibitedly than the modern theatre audience, but it may be remembered that the twentieth century is not immune from extraordinary and violent response to the stimulus of fictional happenings. There is the infamous example of Orson Welles's radio-fantasy in 1938 which purported to depict the end of the world. The reactions in the United States are now a matter of bizarre history. Telephone lines were jammed by anxious citizenry ringing up priests, doctors, and relatives; many suicides were reported and, in many places, terrified men and women dug graves and kept a vigil by them, ready to fling themselves into their last rest at the first sign of calamity. Such events as this are rare in the modern English Theatre, though there is one notable recent example in Peter Brook's production of *Titus Andronicus* at the then Memorial Theatre at Stratford-upon-Avon in 1955. The usual small corps of St. John's ambulance personnel had to be reinforced to deal with cases of fainting and hysteria. Hardly a performance passed without the special ante-room set aside for this purpose being the scene of medication and comfort for those whose 'willing suspension of disbelief' had carried them too far into the realms of utter acceptance. But, in the theatre nowadays such reactions are rare. That Orson Welles on radio, and that, more recently television, in the B.B.C.'s quasi-scientific horror serial *Dr. Quatermass*, should occasion the reactions which they did—hysteria in the one, an unprecedented viewing-figure and countless letters to the press in the other—suggests that inhibitions are still easily removed. It may be that a medium having the quality of novelty, like the public theatre in the 1590's, the radio in the 1930's, and television in the mid 1950's, has the power to excite the most uninhibited reactions. When the medium becomes old and established that sophistication by and in which audiences and observers tend to hide emotion, lest it offend tradition and establishment, is in evidence. It is more easy to justify extrovert emotion in the presence of what is novel than in what is established.

With depictions arousing horror and fear it is the emotions rather than the intelligence which are aroused. Violent, bloody, and therefore horrific matters on the stage can embrace all kinds of illogicality because the intelligence of the audience is pushed into abeyance by the pervasive operation of certain emotions. Thus, the 'plots' of *Dr Jekyll and Mr Hyde*, of *Dracula*, of *Frankenstein*, and *The Spanish Tragedy* cannot stand up to the cool reflections of the rational mind. Their success depends on how far they are able to contain the reader or the watcher in an emotional cage. In horror plays, films, and novels we sometimes find ourselves laughing, and this is often said to be due to the release of nervous tension— nervous laughter purging horror of its rooted fever. But it may equally be true that often we laugh because, if only for a moment, the writer has relaxed his hold over our emotions, and has left a loophole for the intelligence to realize the ludicrousness of situation, plot, or character.

In the experience of horror fictionally, a complex of emotions is involved. Fear is the dominant—we are afraid of what we see in case it should harm us. Curiosity, the most adhesive of all the emotions, is the second. However frightened we may be, we have to 'know'. But interweaving these two dominants are others whose intensity varies from person to person, and which are of a contradictory nature. The experience of horror while it incites curiosity may also, paradoxically, create a withdrawal symptom. The results of this paradox may be observed in an audience in that equivocal reaction when a hand is placed over the eyes but a slight gap is left between two fingers for observation. Disgust is yet another of these errant emotions, sometimes accompanied by physical nausea, called up by the contemplation of cruelty or violently bloody spectacle. Yet again, a feeling of superiority may be involved. From time to time a part of us angrily stands back and declares that what is being seen is untrue, unreal, and unworthy of attention.

But mixed with themes which induce horror, the spilling of blood, and violence, there is very often, and certainly in Elizabethan times, the ingredient of revenge. Indeed it is revenge which is nearly always in drama the motivation for horror and violence. If justification they must be seen to have, then the so-called 'spirit' of revenge provides that justification—this is certainly true of all Senecan-inspired Elizabethan tragedy.

In the context of revenge we are face to face with one of the most popular devices in drama, indeed in the whole of verbal art. Greek, Roman, French, and English classical drama sustains a good deal of its dramatic impact by its inclusion. It would be easy to account for its popularity merely on the grounds that it appeals to a basic human impulse towards 'tit-for-tat'. This is certainly one of the most powerful impulses, baring its teeth with sharp simplicity in the world of children, and sinking them in even more tenaciously in the adult world. The impulse exactly opposite to 'tit-for-tat' is 'turning the other cheek', but this has always been, in drama at least, unpopular. The appearance of 'tit-for-tat' so frequently in drama can be, however, partly accounted for by the sheer dramatic and theatrical simplicity which it implies. A revenge play or scene needs only two characters—one who has done something and one who is going to get him because he has done it. There is no need even to see the initial deed performed—it can be reported and very often is in classical drama. But the spectacle of one character stalking another for purposes of revenge—the hunter and the hunted—is one of the most exciting and popular of dramatic situations.

This simplicity is not often found in modern drama though the American 'gangster' movie of the thirties exploited it with sensational effect. The reasons for its absence on the modern stage (except in the 'thriller' play) may lie in our obsessive preoccupation with the psychology of the single character. If there is a revenge motive in the anger of Jimmy Porter in *Look Back in Anger*, then it is very much an inward thing. In a sense Porter is taking revenge only upon himself in his emotional violence—so too, perhaps, is Stanley Kowalski in *A Streetcar Named Desire*. They themselves are their own worst enemies, and are expressly shown to be so by the playwrights. While they hurt what and who lies in their vicinity, their real revenge is upon themselves—the impulse is introverted. This is not to deny that there is, in Elizabethan drama, no concern for the revelation of personal psychology. Hamlet would be quite at home in the tortured world of Porter or Kowalski (mentally speaking). It may be suggested, however, that Richard III or any other of the monstrous avengers of the time would not be. Where Hamlet is more concerned with the motivations of a projected deed, and less with the deed itself, Richard III is more concerned with the deed. Hamlet is obsessed by the morality of revenge,[4] but most of his Elizabethan colleagues in the comprehensively inspired Senecan revenge plays are more concerned with the simple, mechanistic, and expedient justification for a decision already taken. Often, too, they will elaborate their plans for carrying it out with a species of ritual which involves a good deal of melodramatic posturing.

In Elizabethan tragedy, horror and revenge are glued together by a ritualistic exploitation of cruelty. If blood is not always spilled, its presence lurks behind every victim's shriek, every twist of a rope, every thrust of a dagger. Mankind has, however, a tendency to cover up its doubts and its conscience by acts of formalization in which they are encased in a flourish of theatrical ritual. There is a ritualistic quality about many of the scenes of cruel revenge-taking in Elizabethan and Jacobean drama in which the actual or metaphorical spilling of blood has the status of an elaborately stage-managed sacrificial act. In *Titus Andronicus* cruelty is encased in the ritual of a banquet; even in *Othello* the avenger surrounds his killing of Desdemona with a formalized lyricism of speech which gives the deed a 'nobility' of presentation. Iago, on the contrary, seems petty in his villainy not only because he does not have sufficient justification for his revenge, but because the mechanics and the surrounds of it are mean—a handkerchief, lies, a whore. Iago lacks the persona and the ability to give his revenge even a spurious ennoblement through ritual. Even the often clobbering deaths on battlefields in Shakespeare's plays are frequently accompanied by a set-piece speech over the dead antagonist—as if a ritual Q.E.D. were being written in letters of gold upon the tombstone of a man's stilled heart.

But this drive by the avenging figure to ritualise, even to stage-manage his deed, suggests other aspects of the matter—the reasons for the ritual and its nature.

If one examines in Shakespeare's plays certain aspects of revenge or apparent revenge—the blinding of Gloucester, the murder of Desdemona—it is noticeable that the amount of cruelty depicted is in proportion to the sense of ritual created. The bloodier the deed, the greater perhaps the need to make a set-piece out of it. So ritual insulates the consciences of the involved, if only temporarily, shrouding the vicious and the mean in a painted arass of spectacle.

To allay the pangs of conscience with a painted spectacle is an act of decadence—civilization's act of cowardice in the face of a moral sensitivity which it cannot expunge, but feels therefore that it must hide or disguise. Only so-called civilized man is capable of that 'refinement' by which acts of cruelty are prolonged by formalization and given a spurious dignity. Seneca is the main source of the assembly of blood, revenge, and cruelty in drama, and of this ritualization which so often accompanies it. From his plays the Elizabethans took actual incidents, and from them they learned the art of ritual. The decadent itch in the nervous system of a society which could encompass as much culture as that of the Elizabethans, found its natural counterpart in the Roman dramatist writing for an age whose upper class, like that of the Elizabethan period, was as prone to moral theorizing as it was to the gratification of the senses. The Elizabethans had just enough of the decadence which this complex creates to support a tragic drama intensified by a vital counterpoint between moral equivocation and sensuous indulgence.

There is no denying that one explicitly stated attraction of Seneca for the Elizabethans was in the realm of moral exemplar.[5] With that self-conscious high-mindedness which the Elizabethans no less than the Victorians were so fond of displaying, Alexander Nevile, in the preface to his translation of Seneca's *Oedipus*, wrote words which may stand for all the other translators of the Roman of this period. It is meant

> only to satisfy the constant demands and requests of a very few familiar friends, who thought to have put it to the same use that Seneca himself in his Invention pretended; Which was by the tragical and pompous show upon Stage to admonish all men. . . .

The admonishment of men is implicit in Seneca's high-sounding didacticism, but its currency was very limited in his own time, being confined to a kind of recitative before a small invited audience. His plays have the odour of a close privacy and, except intermittently, lack the dramatic and theatrical logic which would commend them to public performance. But the Elizabethans accepted them into the bloodstream of their culture with an astonishing comprehensiveness. Their didacticism was one reason for their popularity.

The characteristic stoicism, however, of the protagonists was yet another. This found a ready lodgement in the Elizabethan mind. When personal life is so much at the mercy and whim of a violently unpredictable political world, stoicism is perhaps a most comforting philosophy. In both Seneca's Rome and Shakespeare's London there was ample opportunity to exercise this philosophy.

> Our Lorde keep me continuallye true, faithfull and playne, to the contrarye whereof I beseche hym hartelye never to suffer me live. For as for long life (as I have often told thee Megge) I neyther look for, nor long for, but am well content to goe, if God call me hence to morowe.[6]

Nor, when considering the influence of Seneca, should one forget that, overdrawn as his plays are, they do concern themselves with certain abiding human realities, with emotions and catastrophes which are common stock and are intelligibly presented. Theatrically ludicrous as some of his scenes are—as, for example, when Phaedra kills herself before her husband's eyes, but is conveniently not noticed by him until the end of the play—one cannot deny the dramatic and emotional attraction of such speeches as this in which Antigone speaks to her father Oedipus.

> Undaunted Prince, most noble Syre, with humble mynde I sue
> That I your daughter may be bolde to muse some speech to you:
> And that you would with patience digest my poore advice:
> My suite is not to draw your minde to thinges, that earst in price
> You highly held, ne to the view of glittring Pallace olde,
> Ne bravery of your noble realme, scarce able to be tolde:
> But that you would these yrefull fittes, by tract of time now quallde,

With patient minde sustayne and beare: this vertue never
    faylde
In any Prince of such a spright as in your noble Grace
Appeareth bryght: it fitteth not that such should once abase
Themselves as thralles to Sorrowes checke, or once the
    conquest yeelde
To adverse hap: or courage lose lyke dastards in the fielde.
It is no prayse, syr, though perhappes you so your reckening
    cast
To make of lyfe so small accoumpt, and thus to bee agast
At every wagging of a leafe, and combersome mischaunce.[7]

It is very possible, too, on the evidence of many Elizabethan
plays, that the audiences would have been even more prepared to
accept the theatrical excesses of the Roman than we ourselves.
An audience which could take the death of Cloten in *Cymbeline*,
and the visual and verbal tautologies of the murder scene in *The
Duchess of Malfi*, would surely not cavil overmuch at Seneca. An
Elizabethan audience was not so avid for feasibility in dramatic representation as is the audience of today, which has been conditioned
in the inviolability of naturalism and realism. The Elizabethans
accepted convention with great readiness, and the plays they
admired are evidence that they made few distinctions between
what we would call dramatic modes; to them 'that's all one'. The
Elizabethans appear to have accepted a flux of conventions, and
their dramatists wrote thus because there was no compulsion to
write otherwise.

What, in fact, Shakespeare and his contemporaries found in
Seneca was the paradox of a highly formalized five-act structure
in which a near-chaotic series of conventions swirled about. A
dramatist like Shakespeare would, one suspects, have dipped his
sensibilities into Seneca and in such a scene as this would have
found the essence of vital dramatic life. (The pity is that this
vitality occurs so intermittently in Seneca.)

Andromache pleads with Ulysses on behalf of Astyanax.

Thus evil haps, the haughtiest heart at length they bring to
    naught,
If ye wil needes oppresse a wretch what thing more grievous
    were
Then on his noble neck he should the yoke of bondage bere?
To serve in life doth any man this to a King denye?

Ul.: Nor Ulisses with his death, but Calchas prophecy.

An.: O false inventor of deceipt and hainous cruelty,
By manhode of whose hand in warre no man did ever dye
But by disceipt and crafty trayne of mynde that mischiefe seekes,
Before this time ful many one dead is, yea of the Greekes,
The Prophets words and guiltles Gods saist thou my sonne require,
Nay: mischiefe of thy breast it is, thou dost his death desyre.
Thou night souldier, and stout of hart a little child to slay.
This enterprise thou takste alone and that by open day.

Ul.: Ulisses manhood wel to Greekes too much to you is knowne,
I may not spend the tyme in wordes, our Navy wil be gone.

An.: A little stay, while I my last farewel geve to my child,
And have with oft embracing him my greedy sorrowes fild.

Ul.: Thy grievous sorrowes to redresse, would God it lay in mee,
But at thy wil to take delay of tyme I graunt it thee.
Now take thy last leave of thy Sonne, and fil thy selfe with teares,
Oft tymes the weeping of the eyes, the inward griefe out weares.[8]

Such short scenes as this, hamstrung as they are by the jingling weight of the translator's rhyming couplets, cry out for dramatic representation. A woman is angrily pleading for her son, a man is grievously adamant that the son shall not be spared. Emotion and language go together, here yoked by an almost indefinable sense of dramatic correctitude. When Coriolanus's mother in Shakespeare's play appeals, not for her son, but for Rome to be spared, it is this kind of Senecan influence which is most potent. Seneca taught Shakespeare the art of writing the scene in which two opposed emotional forces do battle over a silent third. In such scenes it is language and language alone, not action, which creates the tension of the situation.

Cor.:   I beseech you, peace!
Or, if you'd ask, remember this before:
The thing I have forsworn to grant may never
Be held by your denials. Do not bid me
Dismiss my soldiers, or capitulate
Again with Rome's mechanics. Tell me not
Wherein I seem unnatural; desire not
T'allay my rages and revenges with
Your colder reasons.

Vol.:   O, no more, no more!
  You have said you will not grant us any-thing
  For we have nothing else to ask but that
  Which you deny already; yet we will ask,
  That if you fail in our request, the blame
  May hang upon your hardness; therefore hear us.
Cor.: Aufidius, and you Volsces, mark; for we'll
  Hear nought from Rome in private. Your request?
Vol.: Should we be silent and not speak, our raiment
  And state of bodies would bewray what life
  We have led since thy exile. Think with thyself
  How more unfortunate than all living women
  Are we come hither; since that thy sight, which should
  Make our eyes flow with joy, hearts dance with comforts,
  Constrains them weep and shake with fear and sorrow,
  Making the mother, wife, and child, to see
  The son, the husband, and the father, tearing
  His country's bowels out.[9]

But, on the other hand, the most characteristic vein of Seneca is shown in the long speech at the beginning of *Oedipus*.

  The Night is gon: and dredfull day begins at length t'appeere:
  And Phoebus all bedim'de with Clowdes, himselfe aloft doth reere.
  And glyding forth with deadly hue, a dolefull blase in Skies
  Doth beare: Great terror and dismay to the beholders Eyes.
  Now shall the houses voyde be seene, with Plague devoured quight:
  And slaughter that the night hath made, shall day bring forth to light.
  Doth any man in Princely throne rejoyce? O brittle Joy,
  How many ills? how fayre a Face? and yet how much annoy
  In thee doth lurke, and hidden lies? what heapes of endless strife?[10]

And so it proceeds, over its long course of 170 lines. There is much in it that militates against drama, and much that 'proves' that Seneca's plays were never subjected to the harsh demands of public theatrical performance. In the first place the speech is addressed to Jocasta, but it is impossible to guess from the speech that there is another person present. The words take their flight in the empty air. Secondly, it has not the quality of a man unburdening his mind to another, nor even to himself, but of

1. Terracotta brazier. Delos. 2nd century B.C. 'Gorgias'.

2. Terracotta mask. Heidelberg TK 98. About
300 B.C. 'Polemon'.

3. *Titus Andronicus*—Titus.

making a formalized rhetorical sermon upon a certain occasion. Thus.

> For as the Mountaynes huge and hie, the blustring windes withstand,
> And craggy Rocks, the belching fluds do bash, and drive from land:
> Though that the Seas in quiet are, and calme on every side:
> So kingdoms great all Windes and Waves of Fortune must abide.[11]

Further, as Mendell has pointed out in detail, it is not after 90 lines have passed that we have any hint of place; it is a 'colon-toned' speech which does not advance the story in any significant fashion. Finally, it is thematically, immensely repetitive. The same ideas are expressed again and again in different image-garments. In short, the speech fulfils none of the demands of dramatic speech. It does not give any sense of the reality of person, place, or theme. What is true of this speech goes also for most of the obvious scenes of violence, blood and revenge in Seneca's plays. Drama is at a premium and rhetoric rules the roost.

In *Thyestes*, one of the grosser and most central scenes is that in which the protagonist feeds upon his own sons at a banquet prepared for him by Atreus. The scene is tautologically rhetorical, being given an overt ritualism through its epigrammatic phrases:

> Whatever of thy sons is left thou hast; whatever is not left thou hast.

> The father asks naught of thee with hopes of having, but of losing it.

> The earth lies all unmoved, an insensate mass; the gods have fled away.

In the scene there is a multiplicity of question marks—always the tell-tale mark in drama of a rhetorical objectivity unrelated to psychological truth.

> Oh this it is that sham'de the Gods and day from hence did dryve
> Turn'd back to east, alas I wretch what waylings may I geve ?
> Or what complayntes? What woeful woordes may be enough for mee?
> Their heads cut of, and handes of torne, I from their bodyes see,
> And wretched feete from broken thighes I here behold agayn

Tys this that greedy father could not suffer to sustayne.
In belly roll my bowels round, and cloased cryme so great
Without a passage stryves within and seekes away to get.
Thy sword (O brother) lend to me much of my bloud alas
It hath: let us therwith make way for all my sonnes to passe.
Is yet the sword from me witheld? thy self thy bosoms teare,
And let thy brestes resound with stroakes: yet wretch thy hand
    forbeare
And spare the deade; who ever saw such mischiefe put in
    proofe?[12]

This is sensational rhetoric but, in its intermittent attempts to provide naturalistic detail of a horrific nature, it falls into that comic trap which always awaits the writer who tries to dignify and to shock at the same time.

But, in Shakespeare's *Titus Andronicus*, which has a similar scene,[13] the dramatist, for all his immaturity, displays a truer intuition for the effects of the situation.

Tit.: Welcome, my lord; welcome, dread Queen;
         Welcome, ye warlike Goths; welcome, Lucius;
         And welcome all. Although the cheer be poor,
         'Twill fill your stomachs; please you eat of it.
Sat.: Why art thou thus attir'd, Andronicus?
Tit.: Because I would be sure to have all well
         To entertain your Highness and your Empress.
Tam.: We are beholding to you, good Andronicus.
Tit.: An if your Highness knew my heart, you were.
         My lord the Emperor, resolve me this:
         Was it well done of rash Virginius
         To slay his daughter with his own right hand,
         Because she was enforc'd, stain'd and deflower'd?
Sat.: It was, Andronicus.
Tit.: Your reason, mighty lord.
Sat.: Because the girl should not survive her shame,
         And by her presence still renew his sorrows.
Tit.: A reason mighty, strong, and effectual;
         A pattern, precedent, and lively warrant
         For me, most wretched, to perform the like.
         Die, die, Lavinia, and thy shame with thee;
                              (*He kills her*)
         And with thy shame thy father's sorrow die!
Sat.: What hast thou done, unnatural and unkind?

Tit.:   Kill'd her for whom my tears have made me blind.
       I am as woeful as Virginius was,
       And have a thousand times more cause than he
       To do this outrage; and it now is done.
Sat.: What, was she ravish'd? Tell who did the deed.
Tit.:   Will't please you eat? Will't please your Highness feed?
Tam.: Why hast thou slain thine only daughter thus?
Tit.:   Not I; 'twas Chiron and Demetrius.
       They ravish'd her, and cut away her tongue;
       And they, 'twas they, that did her all this wrong.
Sat.: Go, fetch them hither to us presently.
Tit.:   Why, there they are, both baked in this pie,
       Whereof their mother daintily hath fed,
       Eating the flesh that she herself hath bred.
       'Tis true, 'tis true: witness my knife's sharp point.
                       (*He stabs the Empress*).[13]

In this version the tension is built up towards the moment when Tamora will realize what it is she has eaten. This is achieved by short sharp exchanges in the midst of which the stabbing of Lavinia is almost a detail. Her death, however, is saved from bathos by the anguished lyricism of her father's words, 'Killed her for whom my tears have made me blind'. But her death does not slacken the speed of the build-up of the tension. We are given no chance to relax into incredulity—the deeds are upon us. Furthermore, as soon as Tamora learns that she has eaten of her sons, she is despatched. The agony of realization is not prolonged, and therefore the possibility of the audience's already strained belief being increased is minimized. In Seneca we are made to suffer overtly the spectacle of a man suffering from acute indigestion after his outré meal, in Shakespeare the revenge is sharp, swift, and final.

Of all Shakespeare's plays, *Titus Andronicus* is the one most readily comparable with Seneca's mode. Though its setting is wide Rome it has, like Seneca's plays, that bunched up, walled-in, claustrophobic privacy of horror and cruelty characteristic of the classical writer. Again, like Seneca, it deals with the spectacular intricacies of the relationships of the high-born where political life is seen through the blood-tinged spectacles of private lust, pride, and ambition. Revenge, and revenge alone, in both Seneca and Shakespeare is the motivation of action, and vengeance in its most gruesome form constitutes the largest proportion of the action or implied action of the play. In one scene certainly Shakespeare shows a much shrewder grasp of theatrical feasibility, but there are occasions in his play when he is a complete captive of Seneca's world of lingering undramatic rhetoric.

The most notable example is in Act II, Sc. iv, where Lavinia appears mutilated and ravaged by Chiron and Demetrius. This ghastly appearance we witness—it tells its own story—but Shakespeare, through the mouth of Marcus, will not let it rest there. In a speech of 47 lines we are treated to a high-flown rhetorical paean while Lavinia stands there before us. In one sense the speech may be termed emotionally moving—it moves pity, and it incites feelings of revulsion; neither does it deny us the slaking of the human thirst for curiosity—Marcus spares us few details. It is poetry of a high technical and aural efficiency. Yet the total effect is one of almost complete dramatic irrelevancy, and because of this it is incredible. But its striking ritualistic movement is very noticeable. Lavinia stands like the ruined statue of a despoiled Goddess and she is, as it were, 'addressed' by an outraged worshipper. The facts of the immediate situation are rationalized and generalized by typically Senecan appeals to myth and legend—Tereus, Philomela, Cerberus. But the most striking conclusion forced upon us by the speech is that we cannot believe that this man who speaks it is an outraged, grief-wracked relative, horror-struck at the deed. He is much more the declaiming Roman actor declaiming, performing a poetic rite.

> Alas, a crimson river of warm blood,
> Like to a bubbling fountain stirr'd with wind,
> Doth rise and fall between thy rosed lips,
> Coming and going with thy honey breath.
> But sure some Tereus hath deflowered thee,
> And, lest thou should detect him, cut thy tongue.
> Ah, now thou turn'st away thy face for shame!
> And notwithstanding all this loss of blood—
> As from a conduit with three issuing spouts—
> Yet do thy cheeks look red as Titan's face
> Blushing to be encount'rd with a cloud.
> Shall I speak for thee? shall I say 'tis so?[14]

And noticeably, too, the tell-tale question marks appear.

Far more dramatically effective, and much richer in credibility to character, is the short scene immediately before Marcus's speech in which Chiron and Demetrius enter with Lavinia after her despoliation. This scene, short as it is, brings out the horror of the situation with greater sharpness. This is because the reactions of the characters to the spectacle before them are not couched in formalistic terms but in language which is as near to naturalistic speech as Shakespeare's early rhythmic verse was capable of reaching. But, more than this, what is said is, by implication, a judgment on the perpetrators of the deed. They implicitly condemn themselves out of their own mouths. The sheer horror of what we see and hear is given a validity by this implied moral self-judgment.

> *Dem.:* So, now, go tell, an if thy tongue can speak,
> Who 'twas that cut thy tongue and ravish'd thee.
> *Chi.:* Write down thy mind, bewray thy meaning so,
> An if thy stumps will let thee play the scribe.
> *Dem.:* See how with signs and tokens she can scrowl.
> *Chi.:* Go home, call for sweet water, wash thy hands.
> *Dem.:* She hath no tongue to call, nor hands to wash;
> And so let's leave her to her silent walks.
> *Chi.:* An 'twere my cause, I should go hang myself.
> *Dem.:* If thou had'st hands to help thee knit the cord.[15]

This has that double-edged quality in which truth to character and comment upon that character are in alignment—the fingerprint of Shakespeare's genius which became the firm handprint of the later tragedies.

The 'cannibalism' of *Titus Andronicus* derives from Seneca's *Thyestes*, the act of sacrifice in Act I, Sc. i, derives from *Troas*. But, in general, the parallels of mood and movement between Shakespeare's play and Seneca are too near to avoid the conclusion that, whether in translation or not, he knew his originals well. At the same time he already begins to show, in his early play, qualities which might take him beyond Seneca. Shakespeare can never be saddled with the albatross of a definitive influence. What Seneca generated in the Elizabethan period was a climate which, in many ways, suited the predisposition of both audiences and playwrights. His stoicism, his reflectiveness, his ritualized horror, suited with the time. But there is no legislation for the operations of the creative imagination and the visionary humanist—there is, in fact, nothing more wrong than to set Shakespeare too closely into the Senecan mould.

Peter Brook's production of the play in 1955 at Stratford-upon-Avon demonstrated brilliantly not only the Senecan elements in it, but also the ways in which Shakespeare had advanced from the influence. The Senecan elements were made plain in the deliberately ritualistic movement of the production whose impression was increased by the eerie and echoing 'musique concrète' which formed a background. Moreover, Brook had preserved the sense of claustrophobia with his stolid sets which were lit drably. He made no attempt to minimize the sensational scenes of cruelty, achieving a frightening verisimilitude in the spectacle of the ravished Lavinia, the chopping of Titus's hand, and the formalistic disgust of the banquet scene. But he maintained a great swiftness of pace so that the mind did not have time to dwell on the horrors and cruelties. The scenes of horror and cruelty did not occasion laughter but the emotional reactions of outrage and disgust.

Sir Laurence Olivier as Titus kneaded from the verse which, for the most part, seems intractable and undramatic, a shape and a texture which commanded the attention throughout the entire play. The cynic's reaction was that between them Brook and Olivier had 'contrived' a tragedy out of Shakespeare's base material. What such a judgment failed to realize was the extent to which both Olivier's performance and Brook's production took their form from the play itself. Thus, if Olivier's Titus emerged as a tragic figure, the ingredients were compounded of the text. Shakespeare's Titus is a man moving in cold rhythms between reason and unreason, blinding rage, and blinding grief. He does not display the torturing self-knowledge, the awareness of eternity and damnation, ironies of grandeur and weakness of the major tragic figures. His context, too—the unnatural and sensational revenge play—militates against his acceptance as a tragic figure in the highest sense. Yet the depth of grief and rage, both growing into unfathomable weariness and madness, make Titus transcend the crude theatricalities which surround him. This is the Titus which Brook and Olivier discovered in the play, and he moved against the blazing ritual of his background like a man in a nightmare from which there was no possible release.

The important quality of the plays *Henry VI* and *Richard III* is in the emergence of an individual dramatist from identifiable sources and influences. These plays, particularly the latter, display very well the lack of a clear distinction between tragedy and history in Elizabethan practice. In these plays, as indeed to a certain extent in Seneca, history is the repository of examples of behaviour whose results are often bloody and, to the Elizabethans, therefore tragic. History is the example and great men are the evidence. Seneca's plays are about 'heroes', the impact of whose actions would be no less familiar to his small public than were those of Henry VI and Richard III. History was as much a lesson in Shakespeare as in Seneca, and the lesson that both sought to teach amounted to a warning. In Shakespeare *Henry V* alone (if one excludes the doubtful *Henry VIII*) is a celebration; the rest are agonizing examples of how easy it is for wrong and sin to be committed, for blood to be spilled and cruelty let loose. Among all the commentaries on Shakespeare's history plays none has more than implied that only one of his histories is an image of the 'good kingdom'. For Shakespeare the lessons of history are sharp, not sweet.

Henry VI and *Richard III* show the canker of kingdoms in an extreme and violent form; *Henry IV* shows it in a more subtle form—without horror, and with the revenge motivation strongly mutated. In *Henry IV*, Hotspur and the anti-Henry faction are motivated less by revenge than by an indignant sense of right. There is, of course, a strong acquisitiveness in the play's dissenting nobility—the Crown Imperial makes their eyes shine with anticipation—but this is firmly latched by Shakespeare on to the concept that a usurping king in order to be removed must himself be usurped. Personal revenge is not an absolute motivation in the two parts of the play—it is largely displaced by envy and jealousy. In *Henry VI* and *Richard III*, however, the personal revenge motive, the sinister disposition of forces to expunge an actual or imagined hurt or slight, is still very much to the forefront. The fractious nobility of *Henry VI* are a squabbling mob of individuals whose greed is shown 'straight' as it were, without the matrix of political necessity which characterizes *Henry IV*.

In the midst of all this personal viciousness there crawls the supreme evil—Richard of Gloucester. But it would be wrong to assume that he is a typical Senecan revenge figure. In Seneca, and in the typical Elizabethan counterpart like *The Spanish Tragedy*, the avenging figure always has, however thin, a precise fact to work upon. The typical 'hero' is determined to do to another or others that which has been practised upon him. He has always, according to his own lights, a reason for what he does. Richard has no particular reason, and no particular fact that he works upon. He springs out of the maelstrom of the *Henry VI* plays like an elemental force come to earth to work mischief. If he can be said to be avenging anything at all then it is the idea that any human being should stand in his path. Richard's way to the throne is, in his own eyes, littered with irritants which must be swept aside. He avenges himself upon the idea of opposition, and not upon a particular deed done against him. When he does present himself in the guise of avenger, the impression he gives is of a playful and nauseating rationalizer.

> Why, love forswore me in my mother's womb;
> And, for I should not deal in her soft laws,
> She did corrupt frail nature with some bribe
> To shrink mine arm up like a wither'd shrub;
> To make an envious mountain on my back,
> Where sits deformity to mock my body;
> To shape my legs of an unequal size;
> To disproportion me in every part,
> Like to a chaos, or an unlick'd bear-whelp
> That carries no impression like the dam.[16]

Richard's malevolent playfulness is indeed another of the characteristics which marks him off from the Senecan villain. There is something dull about the Senecan avenger—a kind of stolid dedication to the mere act of revenge, a dedication which steam-rollers out of him any deviousness of character. But Richard of Gloucester makes a wit out of villainy, and the proof of this lies in many scenes of the play, most notably in the wooing of Anne. His most callous exercise of it is when he appears flanked by two clergymen allegedly reading a holy book. This is a gruesome impersonation of Herny VI, the truly devout king. But Richard always succeeds in his witty villainy, and in this lies a clue to yet another difference between him and the Senecan 'hero'. Richard's success can be largely attributed to a personality which charms (in the sense of 'bewitching'). Anne is certainly wooed in the spirit of villainous wit, but it is his 'charm' which wins her—and he knows it.

> Was ever woman in this humour woo'd?
> Was ever woman in this humour won?

Richard's charm takes us a long way in subtlety beyond the implacably stoical avenger of Seneca.

The clue lies in the short scene towards the end of *Henry VI* (3) when Richard suddenly falls upon his knees and weeps. One's first instinct is to wonder whether this man has cracked at last, his conscience having climbed on to his twisted back. But equally suddenly he looks up, perfectly dry-eyed, and asks us, and himself, 'Can I do this and cannot get a crown'?[17] The source of the power of Richard's charm is in his dissembling, and it is of that kind which is consciously practised by the actor.[18] It is the actor's task so to work upon an audience that they are completely gulled into believing in the truth of the image of what they see, although the validity of what they see is only superficial. Such is the case with Richard—he has that special kind of dissembling ability and narcissism which characterizes the actor. His first speech in the play displays this with astonishing self-knowledge.

> I—that am curtail'd of this fair proportion,
> Cheated of feature by dissembling nature,
> Deform'd, unfinish'd, sent before my time
> Into this breathing world scarce half made up,
> And that so lamely and unfashionable
> That dogs bark at me as I halt by them—
> Why I, in this weak piping time of peace,
> Have no delight to pass away the time,
> Unless to spy my shadow in the sun
> And descant on mine own deformity.[19]

Thus this Richard, having killed her husband, 'becomes' for the bemused Anne (much as the actor 'becomes' his role) a lover. Thus, too, this Richard, who is a superb actor, takes on consummately the role of sympathetic brother to the doomed Clarence. And thus, coming to the court of the dying King Edward, this man adopts with almost complete credibility the part of a man of outraged sensibilities. Now indeed he proves the truth of his earlier assertion—'I can add colours to the chameleon / Change shapes with Porteus for advantages'.[20]

How far away, in fact, is this from the villainy of the avenging hero of Seneca? Here is Atreus, the tyrant of *Thyestes*, commenting to himself upon the way he will disguise his intentions to commit the gross act of forcing the unknowing Thyestes to eat his own sons.

> Entrapt in trayne the beast is caught and in the snare doth fall:
> Both him, and eke of hated stocke with him the offspring all,
> About the fathers syde I see: and now in saufety stands
> And surest ground my wrathfull hate: nowe comes into my hands
> At length Thyestes: yea he comes and all at once to mee.
> I scant refrayne my self, and scant may anger brydled bee.
> So when the Bloudhound seekes the beast, by step and quick of sent
> Drawes in the leame, and pace by pace to wynde the wayes hee went,
> With nose to soyle doth hunt, while he the Boore aloofe hath founde
> Farre of by sent, he yet refraynes and wanders through the grounde
> With silent mouth: but when at hand he once perceives the pray,
> With all the strength he hath he strives, with voyce and calls away
> His lingring maister, and from him by force out breaketh hee
> When Ire doth hope the present bloud, it may not hydden bee.
> Yet let it hydden be, beholde with ugly hayre to sight
> How yrkesomely deform'de with filthe his fowlest face is dight,
> How lothsome lyes his Bearde unkempt: but let us friendship fayne.
> To see my brother me delights: geve now to me agayne
> Embracing long desyred for: what ever stryfe there was
> Before this time betwene us twayne, forget and let it pas.[21]

This self-conscious reflectiveness is the mark of the Senecan villain, as indeed is the melodramatic posturing which the face and words of evil indulge in. Typically Senecan, too, is the sudden and naive deception at the end of the speech. It might be suggested that these qualities are shared by Richard in a speech of similar tone and mood.

> Why, then I do but dream on sovereignty;
> Like one that stands upon a promontory
> And spies a far-off shore that he would tread,
> Wishing his foot were equal with his eye;

And chides the sea that sunders him from thence,
Saying he'll lade it dry to have his way—
So do I with the crown, being so far off;
And so I chide the means that keeps me from it;
And so I say I'll cut the causes off,
Flattering me with impossibilities.
My eye's too quick, my heart o'erweens too much,
Unless my hand and strength could equal them.
Well, say there is no kingdom then for Richard;
What other pleasure can the world afford?
I'll make my heaven in a lady's lap,
And deck my body in gay ornaments,
And witch sweet ladies with my words and looks.
O miserable thought! and more unlikely
Than to accomplish twenty golden crowns.[22]

Then there follows the monstrous condemnation of his mother quoted earlier. Accepting the melodramatic reflectiveness of both speeches, the invocations of natural imagery, the extrovertism of villainy, the differences between the speeches are greater than the similarities. Neither in the original nor in translation has Seneca's language any variation of pace; in Shakespeare, however, the pace of the verse, as it slows, almost stops, speeds up, itself embodies the workings of a mind as it proceeds upon its devious ways. In Shakespeare evil is creating itself within the cauldron of the character's imagination.

Secondly, in Seneca, the effect is more 'descriptive' than 'creative'—that is, the speech seems to be describing merely a state of mind rather than embodying that state—the images, though generally suitable to the theme (Boar, Bloodhound, Beast) lack a particular application either to the person speaking the words, or the situation which they describe. In Shakespeare, however, images, words, phrases, constantly individualize the speaker, illuminating the mind's wanderings, and making actively malevolent the theme of the speech.

'And so I say I'll cut the causes off'
'And witch sweet ladies with my words and looks'.

Richard's speech not only demonstrates that he can 'charm' because he is, knowingly, a great actor, but it shows how the

Senecan mode may be present in Shakespeare without being dominant. But the difference is essentially that between rhetorical poetry and dramatic rhetoric.

The way in which Shakespeare's developing vision and technique gradually pulled him away from Seneca may be further illustrated by Richard of Gloucester. He shows no stoicism. If many in the play are beguiled by him and attracted by him, it is because of his histrionic gifts. But, again, if we in the audience find him beguiling and magnetising it is partly because he is *not* stoical. Because he has the courage of his own villainy one finds oneself half-grudgingly looking for this man even when he is not there. In *Richard III* there is the beginning of that more typically Shakespearean conception of tragedy which reached its apotheosis in *Macbeth*. It is a conception which adds to villainy a species of courage which, misplaced though it may be, provides an intense excitement for and a grudging admiration in the beholder. When Macbeth cries out, 'Blow winds, come wrack, at least we'll die with harness on our back', our guts go out with him and to him in the fury of his hopeless defiance. There is little of this in Seneca, but there is much of it in *Richard III*. At the end this little man cries out, 'My kingdom for a horse'. In a battlefield of lost hopes, with death lurking behind every hedge, and beginning to stink in every ditch, this twisted charmer with a withered arm cries out his defiance. This is not stoicism, it is an earnest of that Shakespearean vision which sees a desperate courage even in the worst of men.

Nevertheless, it would be inaccurate to minimize the Senecan influence on *Richard III*. If the conception of the protagonist thrusts beyond the Senecan mould, there is much in the surrounds of the play which indicates the pervasiveness of the Senecan atmosphere. There is, for example, the use of prophecy and oracle. To Seneca these were serious prognostications; they were part of his world of thought and feeling.

> sonuit ecce vesano gradu
> canitque. Mundus vocibus primis tremit.[23]

At the very beginning of *Richard III*, Shakespeare makes use of a superstitious prophecy. Its import in fact becomes almost irrelevant when one realizes that Richard had no need of prophecy to promulgate his dark designs. It is, instead, skilfully used to underline his sardonic wit, and Richard's own use of the prophecy emphasizes the cynical playfulness of his evil.

Yet another strong Senecan element in *Richard III* is the frequent appearance of physically repulsive references. The most outstanding example is Queen Margaret's description of her son. But, yet again, Shakespeare achieves theatrical and psychological depth through more than one stratum of character and atmosphere.

> stay, dog,
> For thou shalt hear me.
> If heaven have any grievous plague in store
> Exceeding those that I can wish upon thee,
> O, let them keep it till thy sins be ripe,
> And then hurl down their indignation
> On thee, the troubler of the poor world's peace!
> The worm of conscience still be-gnaw thy soul.
> Thy friends suspect for traitors while thou liv'st,
> And take deep traitors for thy dearest friends!
> No sleep close up that deadly eye of thine,
> Unless it be while some tormenting dream
> Affrights thee with a hell of ugly devils!
> Thou elvish-marked, abortive, rooting, hog,
> Thou that was sealed in thy nativity
> The slave of nature and the son of hell,
> Thou slander of thy heavy mother's womb,
> Thou loathed issue of thy father's loins,
> Thou rag of honour, thou detested . . .[24]

Obliquely perhaps, but certainly, this curse restores a balance which could have tipped too much in the direction of Richard's emergence as something attractively abstract. The facts of his evil mind we already know, and some of the results of his machinations, but visually his crookback has become precisely what he wants it to become—a weapon in his armoury of beguilement. Margaret's description of him concentrates on the physical, and gives us a clear picture of the contours of evil. In Margaret's words, and most notably in the invocation of Lady Macbeth to the spirits that tend on mortal thoughts, it is noticeable that the curse or invocation couched in terms of physical repulsiveness, is rooted very firmly in a solid naturalism. Margaret uses 'hog', 'slander', 'womb', 'father's loins', which give a firm basis to the more abstract references—'slave of hell', 'rag of honour'. Lady Macbeth similarly refuses to absent herself from the hard realities of natural life in her appeal to the spirits to unsex her. Abstractions like 'murdering ministers', 'Nature's mischief', 'dunnest smoke of hell' are sharply shored up with 'woman's breasts', 'milk for gall', 'keen knife'. In marked contrast is Medea's first invocation in Seneca's play.

> O Dungeon darke, most dreadfull den of everlasting night,
> O dampned Ghosts: O kingdome set against the Gods aright:
> O Lord of sad and lowring lakes, O Lady dyre of Hell,
> (Whom though that Pluto stale by force yet did his troth excell
> With ficle fayth of Jasons love, that hee to mee doth beare,)
> With cursed throate I conjure you, O grisly Ghostes appeare.
> Come out, come out, yee hellish hagges, revenge this deede so dyre,
> Bring in your scratting paws a burning brand of deadly fyre.[25]

Here, the phrase 'scratting paws' ('cruentis manibus') alone gives an immediacy to the speech. The rest, typically Senecan, is spoken in and to a void. That Minerva, Pluto, and Prosperpina, to whom the injunction is made, would be commonplace references to Seneca's audience still does not give the speech the immediacy of direct and palpable sense data.

In Seneca, the ritual curse is often paralleled by generalized statements of presentiments of evil. In Act II, Sc. iii, of *Richard III* these occur and are put in the mouths of 'citizens'—in Seneca they are usually given to a chorus. So that, whereas in Shakespeare, we are made to feel the personal fear, the single fear, of the common man who smells death in the air, in Seneca there is a depersonalization.

> Mittit luctus signa futuri
> mens, ante sui praesaga mali;
> instat nautis fera tempestas,
> cum sine vento tranquilla tument.
> quos tibi luctus quosve tumultus
> fingis, demens? credula praesta
> pectora fratri. iam quidquid id est,
> vel sine causa vel sero times.
> nolo infelix, sed vagus intra
> terror oberrat, subitos fundunt
> oculi fletus, nec causa subest.
> dolor an metus est? an habet lacrimas
> magna voluptas?[26]

In *Richard III*, though the language still smacks of the formalization of natural imagery to give the moment a quality of frozen ritual, the voice that speaks is a human individual's.

> 1. Cit. Come, come, we fear the worst; all will be well.
> 3. Cit. When clouds are seen, wise men put on their cloaks;
> When great leaves fall, then winter is at hand;
> When the sun sets, who doth not look for night?
> Untimely storms make men expect a dearth.
> All may be well; but, if God sort it so,
> 'Tis more than we deserve or I expect.[27]

There is much else of mutated Seneca in *Richard III*, but always the direction is away from the Roman dramatist. The play is Senecan by blood, in its high-born villainy, in its evocation of violence, but it is in the long run the arass of Machiavelli rather than the pillars of Nero's Rome which form the context for what we see. The complicated figure of Richard himself, for all the elementalism which informs it, has about it a characteristically renaissance flux of human deviousness. Even at the end, when Richard turns upon himself, it is a man we hear and not a disembodied voice.

> There is no creature loves me;
> And if I die no soul will pity me:
> And wherefore should they, since that I myself
> Find in myself no pity to myself?
> Methought the souls of all that I had murder'd
> Came to my tent, and every one did threat
> Tomorrow's vengeance on the head of Richard.[28]

There is still no stoicism here—we are in another country. Ribner expresses it thus:

> In *Richard III* Shakespeare finds himself with a tragic hero who had already been cast for him in conventional Senecan terms by several generations of writers. He is not, however, satisfied with what literary tradition has bequeathed to him. Out of his deliberation emerges a Senecan villain-hero who is not entirely like his forebears, who is involved in a complex of events unlike that of *Titus Andronicus*, the play in its entirety exposing a different facet of the great problem of man's relation to the forces which may destroy him.[29]

This implies truly that the matrix of Shakespeare's tragedies is, in many of its elements, a complex of blood, violence, and revenge, but that these become of less importance as the plays proceed into the darker and richer territories of tragedy. Seneca's true Elizabethan followers, notably Kyd, remain within the areas of blood, violence, and revenge. The latest editor of *The Spanish Tragedy* writes in his introduction:

> The moral world of the play is a make-believe world; the gods are make-believe gods. In this make-believe world the private executioner may be sympathetically portrayed and Senecan gods may countenance his actions.[30]

In the long run there is no 'make believe' in *Richard III*, and no Senecan gods countenance the actions of this most public executioner. The other country into which we have entered is one in which, as Ribner says, Shakespeare is expressing 'significant truth about the relation of mankind to the forces of evil in the world'. In Seneca the relationship is secondary to the spectacular evocation of evil and violence. In Shakespeare, as he proceeds, this relationship becomes primary.

Hamlet is often studied within the reference terms of Senecan revenge tragedy, and more precisely as having been written under the shadow of the immense popularity of Kyd's *The Spanish Tragedy*. Ribner's summary of the Kydian revenge play might seem to justify the many critical attempts to place *Hamlet* squarely beneath the blood-bolter'd flag of Elizabethan Senecanism.

> The action and interest of the Kydian revenge play are sustained by the unsuccessful attempts of the hero to avenge some ghastly crime committed by a diabolical villain. The revenge finally comes as the result of a clever stratagem at the end of the play, but until it does the avenger berates himself for his failure to accomplish his purpose; he goes temporarily mad; a ghost urges him on. His self-abuse and his madness serve only to delay his revenge and heighten the suspense. He has formidable obstacles. He must convince himself of the villain's guilt, and he usually requires an inordinate amount of proof. The villain is wily and strong, and he intrigues against the avenger as fully as he is intrigued against. The final revenge is of a peculiarly bloody sort, and it usually comes after the avenger has pretended a reconciliation with the villain in order to win his confidence.

4. *Titus Andronicus*—Lavinia.

5. *Titus Andronicus*—The Kingdom of Violence.

The soul of the villain must be sent to hell, but the soul of the avenger must go there as well. The Kydian revenge play always ends with either the murder or suicide of the avenger and incidentally the deaths of all the other principal characters in the play.[31]

This could be a description of *Hamlet*, but it may be suggested that it is Hamlet without the Prince of Denmark. The details derive from Seneca via Kyd and some are worth speculation.

There is, for example, the ghost in *Hamlet*. Seneca's ghosts, like Kyd's, are dull creatures. They emerge from a void expatiating upon the hells of torture that they have suffered or have yet to suffer. They are often engaged by a third party to incite someone to revenge. Only occasionally do they emerge of their own volition to incite revenge. The ghost of Tantalus in *Thyestes* serves as an example.

> To pooles and floods of hell agayne and styll declining lake,
> And flight of tree ful frayght with fruite that from the lippes
> doth flee,
> To dungeon darke of hateful hell let leeful be for me
> To goe: or if to light be thought the paynes that there I have,
> Remove me from those lakes agayne: in midst of worser wave
> Of Phlegethon, to stand in seas of fyre beset to bee.
> Who so beneath thy poynted paynes by destenyes decree
> Dost still endure who soo thou bee that underliest alow
> The hollow denne, or ruyne who that feares and overthrow
> Of falling hyl, or cruel cryes that sound in caves of hell
> Of greedy roaryng Lyons throats or flocks of furyes fell
> Who quakes to know or who the brandes of fyre in dyrest
> payne
> Halfe burnt throwes of harke to the voyce of Tantalus: agayne
> That hastes to hel, and, whom the truth hath taught beleeve
> wel mee
> Love wel your paynes, they are but small when shall my
> hap so bee
> To flee the light?[32]

The similarity between this and the ghost of Hamlet's father is a little more than spectral skin-deep. They have the same self-pitying whine, they both come from regions unknown, they are both given to embroidery upon the gruesome state they are in, they are both guilty of advancing the dramatic movement of the play very little beyond the mere fact of verbal incitement. In short, as characters, they do not justify the amount of time they spend upon the stage. But, by implication, the ghost of Hamlet's father plays a more important role in the play than any in Seneca or Kyd. This role lies less in his own positive function than in two important ways in which Hamlet reacts to him.

Hamlet strongly suspects that the ghost may come from hellish regions, and that what it tells him may damn his soul. There is no such doubt when a ghost appears in Seneca—the ghost is simply an agent of revenge and, as such, is obeyed. In *Hamlet*, the ghost is also a source for speculation. The standard pattern of events in a Senecan play is that the ghost incites to revenge, and that he who does the avenging is *ipso facto* damned. In Shakespeare the ghost incites to revenge, Hamlet ponders, the ghost renews his incitement, Hamlet ponders further, Hamlet eventually acts, Hamlet is doomed. Whereas, in the Senecan type, a standard pattern of events is superimposed upon the characters, in *Hamlet* there is no such pattern—the protagonist holds the reins in his own hands. It is in Hamlet's pondering, in his reflective imaginings in the face of the ghost's appearance, that a subtlety peculiar to Shakespeare appears.

There is a difference, too, in the personal relationship between ghost and avenger. It is much stronger in *Hamlet* than in Seneca. The word 'father' and its associations has a positive value in the play. There is, in fact, an emotional relationship between ghost and avenger here which is absent in Seneca, and it is to a large extent the avenger's exploration of the realities of this relationship which deepens the play's texture and makes the catastrophe much more complex in its meaning than the mere exploitation of a revenge-motive.[33]

Yet another Senecan element in *Hamlet* is found in the protagonist's propensity to brood upon revenge. In Seneca this appears with the impression that words are necessary in order to cushion the preparatory stages of the actual deed. In Thyestes particularly this brooding is evident.

> I graunte the mischiefe great to bee,
> But done ere this: some greater guilt and mischiefe more, let yre
> Fynde out. The stomacke of thy sonne O father thou enspyre,
> And syster eke, like is the cause: assist me with your powre,
> And dryve my hande: let greedy parents all his babes devowre,

And glad to rent his children bee: and on their lyms to feede.
Enogh, and well it is devis'de: this pleaseth me in deede.
In mean time where is he? So long and innocent wherefore
Doth Atreus walk? before myne eyes alredy more and more
The shade of such a slaughter walks: the want of children cast,
In fathers Jawes. But why my mynde, yet dreadst thou so at
    last,
And faint'st before thou enterprise? It must bee done, let bee.[34]

What is significant here is how quickly the moral qualm is pushed
away. There is a mere breath of a gap between the 'faint'st thou
before thou enterprise' and 'It must bee done, let bee'.

All Hamlet's ponderings and speculations about the deed to be
done, however, rest within that gap. And, in his case, the gap is a
massive one. In the 'Rogue and peasant slave' soliloquy Hamlet
broods upon the act of revenge, but more of it is devoted to a
questioning than to histrionic assertions that the bloody deed
must be done. Apart from this soliloquy the other speculations
of Hamlet before the act of revenge, in the form of soliloquy, are
less concerned with the deed, than with himself and with self-
pitying concern as to why he should have been called upon to
put things right. But his inner questioning brings to light a
further complex in the character. Hamlet is put by the ghost into
a terrible dilemma. He is asked, one suspects, to avenge the wrong
deed. No Senecan villain or hero is put into such an equivocal
position. Hamlet is certainly told whom he has to kill, and he is
specifically told whom he is not to kill. But there are some grounds
for believing that it is his mother he wishes to wreak vengeance
upon, not his uncle. All his moral susceptibilities seem bound up
with the monstrous behaviour of his mother, and he comes to
identify Ophelia with this monstrousness. She must get to a
nunnery to protect herself and mankind from the disposition of
her sex to commit adultery. Hamlet's most certain hesitancy is when
he is in his mother's bedchamber. Hamlet's personality is not
simple enough to wreak the obvious revenge—to kill his uncle—
and in the final scene of the play when, in the goriest Senecan
fashion, death is dealt out with discriminating largesse, it is not a
Senecan tying-up of plot that we remember but the almost
ritualistic consummation of what has occupied a large part of
Hamlet's mind throughout the play—death for his mother, his
uncle, and for himself. At the end of the play Horatio says

> And let me speak to th' yet unknowing world
> How these things came about. So shall you hear
> Of carnal, bloody and unnatural acts.[35]

These words come with a shock of surprise, because it is impossible to accept them as a full description of our experience of the play, even though it is impossible to deny their truth to the plot of the play. One remembers the unnatural and bloody acts only as a raucous obligato to the dramatist's exploration of the relationship of one man to Life and Time and Death.

Hamlet, too, like Richard III, has the temperament of an actor, and it is his exploitation of this temperament that disguises from us the 'real' man beneath the mask. It is a truism to say that the play is full of references to the stage and the profession of acting— its very centre is a play within a play; a pivotal scene is the coming of the actors to Elsinore; the chief actor in the visiting company is given a most important task by the protagonist. But at the core of this there is the Dane with the 'antic disposition', which he himself tells us he will 'put on' as clearly as if he were a star performer informing us of his role for the evening's performance. An antic disposition is a disposition to 'feign' playfully, but one of the ironies of the play is that, as manipulated by Hamlet, the disposition is in deadly earnest. In the five years preceding the writing of *Hamlet* Shakespeare had written several plays in which one character, usually a focal one, puts on, or plays, or acts, a disposition. Prince Hal states explicitly that he is putting on a false face in order to hide his true intents. In *Twelfth Night* and *As You Like It*, immediately preceding *Hamlet*, there are two characters (so-called Fools) whose very function it is to be not what they are. From behind the mask of Fool Feste speaks wisdom, discovers, and watches. 'He wears not motley in his brain.' He is, indeed, the most conspicuous of a series of characters who put on a disposition so that they might better from behind its mask seek more surely the fruition of their purposes. Jaques teaches us not to despise the mask-wearers and the wearers of motley and antic dispositions. From behind these strange appearances, he says, the truth may be sought out—a purging truth.

> Invest me in my motley; give me leave
> To speak my mind, and I will through and through
> Cleanse the foul body of th' infected world,
> If they will patiently receive my medicine.[36]

It is but a short step from professional fooling to that state which Hamlet takes upon himself; a state in which he can speak to Polonius almost with the catechizing wit of a Fool; a state in which he can dwell on the skull of a dead jester as if it were the repository of a wry and ironic wisdom. Hamlet himself is wearing the mask of the actor. Melancholic he is by nature, suspicious he certainly is of the ghost's incitements to revenge, and his nature cries out to him to take a certain course. He hides that nature with another aspect, and from behind the mask of an 'antic disposition' seeks to cleanse the foul body of the infected world of Elsinore. In his soliloquies it is as if he is acting himself to himself. One has the disturbing sense that there are two people present— one who takes up, very often, a histrionic posture, and another who watches and comments. The question marks in a Hamlet soliloquy do not have the empty rhetorical quality of those of Seneca or Kyd, for an agonized human voice tries at least to give an answer to the questions.

One distinguishing mark of Hamlet as a dramatic agent is, quite simply, that which distinguishes any sensitive human being—he is both part of a situation and capable of speculating within himself on his relationship to that situation. It is the function of true drama to make explicit what is involved in this dual condition. But the character of Hamlet is complicated by the intervention of a puzzling third factor—that part of him which makes us question what sort of man he is. We ask the question 'Is he mad?' and 'Why does he behave thus to Ophelia?' and 'Why thus to Polonius?' Why does he seize upon the extraordinary device of the mousetrap? There is, very obviously, something in this character which defies analysis. There is nothing in any Senecan character that excites such puzzlement. His characters are firmly bound to the revenge-formula, and though we see and hear them in moments of grief and exultation, we at no point feel that we are being shown more than the examples of certain kinds of behaviour. We are never taken near enough to them to hear them question themselves and, at the nearest point to which we arrive, when they are in the moments of highest emotional tension, they seem less to be themselves than spokesmen for some external conceptual generalization.

Thematically very close to one of Hamlet's most famous soliloquies is a chorus from *Troas*.

May this be true, or doth the Fable fayne,
When corps is deade the Sprite to live as yet?
When Death our eies with heavy hand doth strain,
And fatall day our leames of light hath shet,
And in the Tombe our ashes once be set,
Hath not the soule likewyse his funerall,
But still (alas) do wretches live in thrall?

Or els doth all at once togeather die?
And may no part his fatal howre delay.
But with the breath the soul from hence doth flie?
And eke the Cloudes to vanish quite awaye,
As danky shade fleeth from the poale by day?
And may no jote escape from desteny,
When once the brand hath burned the body?

What ever then the ryse of Sunne may see,
And what the West that sets the Sunne doth know.
In all Neptunus raygne what ever bee,
That restless Seas do wash and overflow,
With purple waves stil tombling to and fro.
Age shal consume: each thing that livth shall die,
With swifter race than Pegasus doth flie.

And with what whirle, the twyse six signs do flie,
With course as swift as rector of the Spheares,
Doth guide those glistering Globes eternally.
And Hecate her chaunged hornes repeares,
So drauth on death, and life of each thing weares,
And never may the man returne to sight
That once hath felt the stroke of Parcas might.

   .   .   .   .   .

Death hurtes the Corpes and spareth not the spright,
And as for all the dennes of Taenere deepe,
With Cerberus kingdome darke that knowes no light,
And streightest gates, that he there sittes to keepe,
They fancies are that follow folke by sleepe
Such rumors vayne, but fayned lies they are,
And fables like the dreames in heavy care.[37]

The last stanza, particularly, takes us near to the bourn of Hamlet's
'To be or not to be' speculation. It is remarkable how, after the
high-flown description of the preceding stanzas with the evocation
of the vast images of eternity and space, the simple statement of
the last three lines of the final stanza which brings us to earth and
to common experience is much more affecting and human than

all the rest. But the aerial imagery of vapours, fires of hell, the rising sun, the twelve signs which fly along, and Hecate hastening, give the speech a theoretical quality. In the Hamlet soliloquy the realities of material existence are constantly used to support or deny the possible realities of eternity. In many ways the soliloquy is an argument between the temporal and the timeless. 'Slings', 'arrows,' 'arms', 'fardles', 'grunt and sweat', 'the law', 'a bare bodkin', are all set against outrageous fortune, 'sea of troubles', 'dreams', 'undiscovered country', the puzzled will. The emotional tension of the speech depends upon the contrapuntal effect of these two quite separate complexes—that of the sentient man, and that of the man in the context of a bewildering eternity. In Seneca, choric speculation is creating its own abstractions, but these, except fleetingly at the end, are neither 'proved' nor 'denied' on the pulse of a human being.

In *Hamlet* there is a very strong sense (stronger than in *Richard III*) that not only is the relationship of a man to something outside himself being explored, but that the man himself is being explored. If Richard is non-Senecan in his exciting deviousness, he remains the heir of Seneca in his unquestioning progress towards destruction. But Hamlet is non-Senecan both by the complexity of his character and by his constant questioning of his relationship not only to the proposed deed but to his status as a human being in the desert of eternity. It might indeed be said that one element of Shakespeare's humanism is this increasing concern to put man in the foreground of his plays, and to explore the often agonizing irony of potential wrecked by weakness. His recognition of this irony gives his later plays their characteristic humanity.

In the final analysis it is simply the word 'humanity' which distinguishes Shakespeare's work from that of Seneca and Seneca's Elizabethan followers. I have tried to indicate some of the ways in which this 'humanity' grows out of an early acceptance of a formalism of theme, style, and characterization which Shakespeare, no less than many of his contemporaries, was bequeathed by Seneca. What ones sees, in fact, is the growth of a complete dramatist out of the material of an incomplete dramatist.

To say this is to denigrate neither Shakespeare's own early work nor Seneca's. It is simply to underline the fact that Shakespeare's mature plays, by implication, add up to the most comprehensive definition of Drama, and that Seneca's work, in relation to

Shakespeare's, can only be regarded as the ore whose form was changed and whose substance was refined by a surer hand and eye.

NOTES

[1] The quotations in this study come from Thomas Newton's edition (1929).

[2] J. W. Cunliffe, *The Influence of Seneca on Elizabethan Tragedy* (1893).

[3] See F. L. Lucas, *Seneca and Elizabethan Tragedy*; Irving Ribner, *Patterns in Shakespearean Tragedy* (1960); Ashley Thorndike, *Tragedy*; T. S. Eliot, *Elizabethan Essays*; Fredson Bowers, *Elizabethan Revenge Tragedy*.

[4] Note that Hamlet's first reaction (I. v) is melodramatic and extrovert. But even in the midst of this he never says that he will avenge his father, only that he will 'remember' him. The next time we see him alone he has begun the agonizing process of speculating about whether it is right or wrong to do the deed (III. i).

[5] 'The sentences of the Ancients had a kind of special authority and sanctity; the epigrams and sentences of Seneca became axiomatic, and provided the play with a body of common belief fixed in particular formulae—with a liturgy as well as a creed'. M. C. Bradbrook, *Themes and Conventions of Elizabethan Tragedy*.

[6] Letter from Sir Thomas More to his wife, 1535.

[7] *Phoenissae*, 182-196.

[8] *Troas*, 745-765.

[9] *Coriolanus*, V. iii.

[10] *Oedipus*, 1-9.

[11] *Ibid.*, 9-13.

[12] *Thyestes*, 1035-1049.

[13] *Titus Andronicus*, V. iii.

[14] *Ibid.*, II. iii.

[15] *Ibid.*, II. iii.

[16] *Henry VI* (3), III. iii.

[17] *Ibid.*, III. iii.

[18] 'He is histrionic. The assertions of his innocence are always supported by elaborate acting; as much as Hamlet or Iago he has a genius for entrance and displays . . . he loves his art too well not to know its finest devices'. Mark Van Doren, *Shakespeare*.

[19] *Richard III*, I. i.

[20] *Henry VI* (3), III. iii.

[21] *Thyestes*, 491-511.

[22] *Henry VI* (3), III. iii.

[23] *Medea*, 738-739.

[24] *Richard III*, I. iii.

[25] *Medea*, 8-16.

[26] *Thyestes*, 957-969.

[27] *Richard III*, III. iii.

[28] *Ibid.*, V. iii.

[29] Irving Ribner. *Patterns in Shakesperean Tragedy*.

[30] Philip Edwards (ed.), *The Spanish Tragedy* (Revels Series).

[31] Ribner.

[32] *Thyestes*, 68-83.

[33] If my remarks about the ghost seem unduly dismissive, this is because his function in the play has been exhaustively dealt with. See Sister Miriam Joseph, *Discerning the Ghost in 'Hamlet'*—P.M.L.A. LXXVI, No. 5, Dec. 1961. This study, though it ignores Seneca, makes large claims for the theatrical importance of the ghost in *Hamlet*. It has an excellent bibliography.

[34] *Thyestes*, 273-285.

[35] *Hamlet*, V. ii.

[36] *As You Like It*, II. vii.

[37] *Troas*, 371-402.

VI

Seneca and Corneille

ANDRE STEEGMAN

In thirty years of playwriting, Corneille only quoted Seneca[1] some fifteen times. He used him as a model only in *Médée*, his first tragedy, at the beginning of his dramatic career (1635), under circumstances which it will be interesting to recall.

One finds only two allusions to the philosophical works, an extract from the *De Clementia* in *Cinna* and a sentence from the 7th letter to Lucilius, curiously inserted in a chapter of the *Imitation de Jésus Christ*.

> Un païen nous l'apprend, tout chrétiens que nous sommes
> 'Je n'ai jamais, dit-il, été parmi les hommes
> Que je n'en sois sorti moins homme et plus brutal?'
>
> (L. I, ch. 20)

When one thinks of the importance the Cordovan poet still had in the eyes of both Christian moralists and dramatists, one may wonder at Corneille's attitude, which is akin to a refusal. The question is an important one; an answer to it would provide one of the ways of drawing a clearer line between the Renaissance and classicism on the one hand, classicism and the baroque on the other hand.

It will be objected that the popularity of Seneca is so constant and so well established that Corneille's comparative silence in this respect has little significance. . . . It is therefore necessary to make a thorough study of the attitude of Corneille's immediate predecessors and of his contemporaries.

Monsieur Lebègue,[2] in an authoritative article, long ago brought into light the absolute pre-eminence of Seneca's influence in France, towards the end of the sixteenth century, on two of the best tragic writers, among others Montchrestien and Robert

Garnier, who still make a reasonable use of him. Their successors, under the reign of Henri IV, go one better, and seek after every form of Senecan horror, including rapes and incests, and Billard de Courgenay, in 1610, sets up this melodramatic pathos as a principle: '*Ou il y a effusion de sang, mort et marque de grandeur, c'est vraie matière tragique*'. Undoubtedly, between 1600 and 1630, Seneca's influence is on the wane: tragi-comedies and pastorals take the lead, before tragedies; even in the works of playwrights— some fifteen of them—there is a wider choice of subjects, less respect for the unities, and the language strays from the learned, noble, and lofty style of Seneca: playwrights seem to be tending, though with less bold freedom than in Spain, towards that free form of tragedy, defined as far back as 1600, by Lope de Vega.

Between 1580 and 1600, a few forerunners had attempted to write political tragedies on modern subjects: Du Tronchet Belyard, Bourrée, de la Porte with their *Guisiades*, Fronton du Duc with his *Pucelle d' Orléans*. That trend becomes stronger from 1600 to 1630, and Montchrestien's *l'Ecossaise* (Mary Stuart) is no isolated work. In this respect, the works of Chrestien des Croix, Billard de Courgenay, and Denis Coppée deserve a particular place.

Chrestien des Croix, a Norman poet, finds in Camerarius's historical works the source of his *Portugais Infortunes*, in the opera by Rimiccini, from Florence, that of *Le Ravissement de Céphela*— soon to be taken up by Hardy; in Cavallerino's famous *Rosemonde* (1582), that of *Alboin*, a subject also treated by Nicholas Billard in 1610. His *Grande Pastorale* (1613) is only a pastoral by its title and setting. The historical purpose of the play is stressed by fine interludes, which constitute a symbolical epitome of the history of France: Clovis, Compostella in Charlemange's power, Godefrey de Bouillon in Jerusalem, the taking of Damietta, Joan of Arc. . . .

Billard de Courgenay (1560-1618) stages *Gaston de Foix* and *La Mort de Henri IV* in the very year of the King's murder.

As for Denis Coppée, a writer from Liège, besides his *M. Curtius* he takes an interest in the historical part played by his country with St. Justine and St. Cyprian, St. Aldegonde, the patron saint of Maubeuge, St. Lambert, the patron saint of Liège, and in *La Bataille des Impériaux et Bohêmes*, a grand pageant with twenty-five characters, dedicated to Maximilian of Bavaria, Coppée broaches the delicate problem of elective monarchy, and

The Murder of Sultan Osman is part of a real cycle of historical plays on Oriental subjects.[3]

All this is relevant to a study of Corneille because almost all those tragedies were published or republished in Rouen between 1610 and 1630. It was in that atmosphere that his dramatic genius was born, it was normally along those lines that he should have directed his dramatic output.

Now Corneille turns wholly to a genre which he brings back to life, no less; to which he grants, so to speak, letters patent of nobility by expurgating it of all the truculent scurrilities of the actors of farce at the Pont Neuf, Tabarin and Gaultier-Garguille, who both died at the very moment when *Mélite*, *La Veuve*, *La Galarie du Palais*, *la Suivante*, and *La Place Royale* were meeting with triumphal success.

Admittedly, there is one exception. *Clitandre*, Corneille's second play, written between 1630 and 1632. This play, to our mind, remains an enigma.[4] Owing to its melodramatic character and the violence of the action—an attempted rape, an eye put out on the stage—one might feel inclined to see at least an indirect influence of Seneca in it; but that would be a rather hasty concession to the dangerous temptation of analogy. Corneille seems to present his work as a 'pièce a clef'. '*Si mon sujet est véritable, j'ai raison de la taire; si c'est une fiction, quelle apparence de donner un soufflet à l'histoire*'.[5] Moreover, he stresses his independence from the classics and among those, Seneca, though he is not named, seems to be the main target. The setting of the play is obviously that of a pastoral, and it may be in order to avoid the insipidity of this rather stale genre that Corneille introduced a violent action into it. Lastly, the source of *Clitandre* may well be an Italian play (the latter would be difficult to identify, since Corneille, when he copies a play, usually changes the names of the characters); or perhaps he simply wanted to beat Hardy on his own ground, as the young 'generation' of 1630, with Mairet, Scudèry, Rotrou, Du Ryer, and Corneille, was eager to get rid of the tiresome shadow of that prolific playwright. Thus *Clitandre* may be ranged with the irregular tragi-comedies, on spectacular subjects, such as the whole group writes between 1630 and 1632: Du Ryer's *Lisandre et Caliste*, Mareschal's *La généreuse Allemande*, Rotrou's *La bague de l'oubli*.

Such is not the case with *Médée*; this is a true Cornelian palinode.

In 1633, a general return to Seneca took place, which has not yet been accounted for: Rotrou, La Pinelière, and Corneille each write a tragedy drawn from Seneca; all three were performed in 1634, two of them at the *Hotel de Bourgogne*, Corneille's play at the *Marais*.

Rotrou, the 'paid poet' of the *Hotel de Bourgogne*, after having written tragi-comedies and comedies for five years, writes a very free adaptation of Hercules Oetaeus entitled *Hercule Mourant*,[6] to be published in 1636 only. A. Adam has stressed the importance of the poet's visit to Chapelain in 1632.[7] If Chapelain tried to win Rotrou over to the rules, it appears that two years were needed for his intervention to take effect. La Pinelière, an obscure Angevin, who died soon after 1640, staged a *Hippolyte* adapted from Seneca,[8] also at the *Hotel*. It seems likely that the three writers acted in full agreement. Rotrou, Corneille's perpetual rival, was also his friend, and probably an early one. At any rate, he is one of the contributors to the 26 tributes published with the edition of *La Veuve* in March 1634. To la Pinelière's *Hippolyte*, Corneille, who is usually chary of praise, gives a prefatory poem— these are the last lines he ever wrote to a fellow-writer.[9] Besides, only one year later, La Pineliere, in his *Parnasse*, will conduct an underhand campaign against his too powerful rival.

Obviously, the explanations C. Lancaster[10] gives of Corneille's return to Seneca are, to my mind, rather tame. C. Lancaster thinks it is accounted for by the success of Mairet's *Sophonisbe* (1634) and the talent of Mondory as a tragic actor. Now the success of *Sophonisbe* came probably after those three plays had been written, and there is a great difference between writing a tragedy inspired by Livy and writing a straightforward and deliberate imitation of three different Senecan plays. As to providing Mondory with a good tragic part, Corneille could have found a better one than the very unrewarding part of Jason, who falls a victim to his own political ambition and to the coquettish Créuse—Mairet had served him better with Massinissa, and Corneille will give him a better part in *Le Cid*, if indeed he did play the part of Rodrigue. In fact, his real triumphs were in the part of Torrismon in *Vion d'Alibray's* play, and in that of Herod, in Tristan's *Marianne*.

Therefore, the reasons why it was in 1634 that Corneille came to Seneca remain unknown. He had known him well from his childhood. He was commented upon, and his plays were performed in the Jesuit Colleges. Delrio, a Spaniard, had published a monumental edition of his works at the beginning of the century, with an impressive profusion of historical footnotes, which were not always apt, and which at all events were stodgy stuff for the brains of twelve-year-old boys, even if they were keen. A detail on *Médée* proves that Corneille was familiar with this edition: melodious lines which describe the sorceress:

> Quand, les cheveux flottants, le bras et le pied nu
> J'en dépouillai jadis un climat inconnu.   (983-4)

sound less like a translation of Seneca than of one of Delrio's notes: '*Solebant magae nudis pedibus et parso capillo sacra sua peragere*'.

Corneille must also have known another edition by a famous author of his time: that of Th. Farnaby, a former pupil of the Jesuits, who published all the Latin authors on the Fathers' syllabus. His edition of Seneca's works was published, oddly enough, in Paris, in 1625. In his edition, *Medea* is the first play. He discusses the question of the personality of Seneca, and distinguishes two Senecas: a philosopher and a dramatist, but he ascribes the writing of *Troades*, *Hippolytus*, and *Medea* to the philosopher—the latter plays are those chosen by La Pinelière and Corneille—Farnaby, graduate of both Oxford and Cambridge, was headmaster of a school of 300 pupils in London. When one remembers that *Melite* was performed in Whitehall as early as 1635, before the King and Queen, by Floridor, the actor, it appears that the hypothesis of a more direct influence of French-English relations (as yet not very well known) must not be rejected. This influence may have been exerted either through Dutchmen, such as Heinsius, with whom Farnaby was on writing terms, or through actors, or through a passionate lover of the theatre like Sir Kenelm Digby, to whom the *Comédie des Tuileries*, of which Corneille was a co-writer, was dedicated in 1638.

Corneille himself acknowledges the debt he owes Seneca. He even exaggerates it, if one is inclined to see, in the tragedy of the seventeenth century, a more or less straightforward imitation of the Latin poet. In fact, Corneille only uses about 200 lines from *Medea*, that is to say a fifth of the play, He cuts out the choruses, of course, curtails the soliloquies, reduces the lyrical dialogues. Corneille's first task is therefore that of schematizing Seneca's play and to make clear the essential psychological stages, which will be arranged thus:

> I, 4 : Médée's soliloquy
> II, 2 : Creon—Médée
> III, 3 : Jason—Médée
> IV, 1 : Médée—Nérine
> V, 2 : Médée's final inner struggle
> V, 6 : Médée—Jason

Corneille commented on the alterations he introduced, in the *Examen de* 1660. This is important because it reveals that Corneille was already fully won over to the great classical laws, and it appears that any attempt to define Corneille's work at large, and particular *Médée*, as a baroque production must be based on very uncertain ground. . . . Like a true classicist, Corneille obeys the newly rediscovered rules—in 1630 there was no talk about them yet—and alters Seneca's play in the name of verisimilitude and propriety.[11] It is not in the name of freedom, but in the name of verisimilitude, that he ignores the unity of place: thus Médée, the magician, is not seen preparing her drugs in the public square, of all places. In order to give a more convincing air of truth to the scene in which Créuse welcomes the poisoned robe, Corneille makes Créon's daughter a coquette: she herself asks Jason for the robe. Besides verisimilitude, Corneille explains an important feature of the alterations which he will effect in the psychology of the characters. Créuse and Jason prove futile and incredibly selfish—thus Médée wins some of the spectators' sympathy. As regards propriety, Corneille assumes a qualified but clear attitude, which will remain one of the constant rules of his dramatic production.

First, he reproaches Seneca with his melodramatic disposition to horror. Everything which '*peut soulever le coeur des dames*', 'Everything that might upset the ladies' stomachs' (according to a humorous formula which he used later, writing about *Oedipe*) must be left out. That is why he reduces the account of the children's murder to four unobtrusive lines, devoid of any violent realism, whereas Seneca dwells on the subject.

> Perfruere lento scelere, ne propera, dolor . . . (p. 1016)

Fifty lines separate the murders of the two children.

But at the same time Corneille refuses to suppress the spectacular elements altogether, against the opinion of the learned, who would like tragedy to be what it has too often been said to be, a purely intellectual spectacle. In order to stir the spectators' feelings (and this remains the chief purpose of *Médée*), he must, before all, appeal to the eyes; and Corneille makes us witness the deaths of Créuse and Créon, the paroxysm of Jason's despair, and his attempt to commit suicide; just as, twenty-five years later, he will bring back Oedipus, with his bleeding eyes, on the stage, or recall, with proper realism, Attila's well-known nose-bleeding.

Moreover, he will resist the 'learned' throughout his life on one essential point; propriety and morality must not be confused with moralism. On this point he remains true to Seneca, and Boileau, the classical theorist, will codify these views: *monsters* come within the sphere of tragedy. Moral propriety is at variance with the very nature of tragedy. Heroism implies a transcending of human nature, which consists in a transgression of natural laws. Any hero, at some time or other, utters Rodogune's '*Sors de mon coeur, Nature*'. In the delicate determination of the limits of amoralism and immoralism lies the ever open but nearly always badly put and badly solved problem of Aristotle's famous *catharsis*. Therefore Corneille openly admits that with *Médée* he shows 'Crime on her triumphal chariot', but he will do his utmost, if not to justify Médée, at any rate to make a thorough analysis of the psychology of her character, and to give an explanation of it which does not make her an exceptional being: the spectator could feel no sympathy for such a character, and he would experience nothing but horror. *Catharsis* consists, precisely, in making the spectator feel that any man has a potential hero or monster in his heart, and that the strange mechanism of Fate need only place a human being on the horns of such a dilemma that the only way out may be found through the exertion of a feat of desperate will-power, leaving him, whatever the solution, nobler but ruined, a victim, but also a man who is '*maitre de tout son sort*' (Master of his whole fate). For the spectator, at any rate, horror has disappeared, leaving only admiration and pity.

In order to achieve this purpose, which he understood long before he wrote the three *Discours* (1660),[12] Corneille alters his model noticeably.

In Seneca's play, Medea appears, from the start, as a tragical character. She is not only betrayed in her love, she is also a wife outraged in her honour, a princess who is the victim of a political plot, an enchantress determined to make use of her supernatural powers in order to take an unprecedented revenge; she is also a guilty woman, conscious of the dangerous anomaly of a love based on the double murder of her father Pelias and her brother Absyrte.

Corneille makes this fundamental duality sharper and emphasizes it. Jason fears both his wife's justified reproaches and the domineering power by which Médée has deliberately isolated him and made him a party to her crimes. But to the weak and pathetic character of this paltry hero, Corneille has added a note of tranquil cynicism,[13] and a disreputable ladies' man attitude towards his latest conquest. For Creuse is incredibly petty: a selfish lover

> Ayant Jason à moi, j'ai tout ce que je veux. (180)

and a fickle coquette: the price of the children's safety will be . . . Médée's robe! It is to this creature that Jason addresses this cynical madrigal:

> l'éclat d'un tel visage
> Du plus constant du monde attirerait l'hommage
> Et semble reprocher à ma fidélité
> D'avoir osé tenir contre tant de beauté. (173-6)

Here Corneille invents a new form of *tragic humour*, unknown to Seneca, which turns Médée's enemies into caricatures.

With Créon, the political debate assumes clearer contours than in Seneca's play. Besides the meeting in the course of which Médée easily shatters the tyrant's specious argumentation, Créon, whose part is considerably more important, appears as a Machiavellian prince, guided by profit only, but cunning when necessary (the lion and the fox of Machiavelli), and, like the Florentine, anxious to preserve an appearance of rectitude and virtue.

But Jason, *who is neither quite good nor quite bad*, has preserved the soul of a father. There lie his greatness as well as his weakness, and his vulnerable point. Corneille also adds the part of Aegée, King of Athens, but does not meet with equal success: yet, we have a likeable hero, the first old man in love in Corneille's dramatic production, which is to number so many moving ones in the later part of his career; he is there only to increase the spectator's sympathy for Médée: she it is who lets him out from the prison in which Créon had thrown him; it is in his palace that she will find refuge.

Besides the light which these four characters throw on Médée, Corneille endows the heroine herself with all the qualities likely to make her more human. In the first place Corneille leaves out all the features which put too much stress on the superhuman character of the enchantress: in Seneca's play, the betrayed Medea does not seek an exemplary vengeance: her despair urges her to wish for universal destruction:

> . . . Sola est quies
> mecum ruina cuncta si video obruta. (427)

Later, she identifies herself with the spirit of evil:

> Medea nunc sum; crevit ingenium malis. (910)

Seneca devotes nearly two hundred lines (one-fifth of the play) to showing the enchantress at work, and multiplies the eerie sights. Corneille does away with all this: Médée seems too strange, too tranquil, too powerful, and even more so after carrying out her terrible vengeance.

In Seneca's play, Medea only has short glimpses of her own guilt, and only once does she show motherly feelings:

> Cor pepulit horror . . .
>   . . . Ira discessit loco
> materque tota, conjuge expulsa, redit. (925-7)

In Corneille's play, the inner struggle is enlarged upon, and it is in this essential scene (Seneca, 895-925, and Corneille, V. 2) that Corneille's creative work can best be appreciated. He shortens, condenses and simplifies the various stages of the inner struggle, but keeps to the general outline:

> Vindicta levis est quam ferunt purae manus. (902)
> Ex paelice utinam liberos hostis meus aliquos haberet! (920)
>   liberi quondam mei. (925)
> vos pro paternis sceleribus poenas date. (930)
> Egone ut meorum liberum ac prolis meae fundam cruorem?
> Scelus est Jason genitor . . . (933)

But Corneille cuts out the image of anger compared to ocean waves, the over-precise memory of Médée's first crimes, the appearance of the Furies, and the atrocious joy of the mother when she reaches her decision, the immoderate violence which makes her wish she had not only two but fourteen children to kill! (954-5). The actual tearing off is simpler, and more moving. Above all, Corneille introduces a subtle psychological explanation of this murder, which gives it an entirely different meaning:

> *Chers fruits de mon amour* (what violence in tenderness, when their death-sentence has just been pronounced).

> . . . *si je vous ai fait naitre*
> *Ce n'est pas seulement pour caresser un traître.* (1349-50)

So she kills them not only for her own good, but also *for theirs:* to spare them the *degradation* which living with their father and stepmother would mean. This bears much resemblance to the murder of Camille by Horace, her brother; it is an act of justice, in the name of the glory of Rome, to punish his sister's blasphemous curses, but also an act of reason and *love*, since death is her dearest desire:

> Va dedans les enfers *joindre*[14] ton Curiace.

At the end of this quick, breathless inner struggle, in the light of a passional logic, Médée is on the horns of this tragic dilemma, which constitutes an excellent definition of Corneillian situations:

> Je n'exécute rien, et mon âme *eperdue*
> Entre deux *passions* demeure suspendue. (1353-4)

Either Médée will save her children's lives, thus acting with the legitimate selfishness of a mother, or Jason will remain unpunished. The murder of the rival is but a commonplace revenge, which does not sting the faithless husband to the quick, in his own flesh, once and for all: the murder of the children is the *only* possible revenge; or Médée resigns herself, at the cost of a severance which will grieve her as much as it will grieve Jason, to the supreme sacrifice, beyond the law of nature: amoralism, but not immoralism. What the tragic catharsis affords the spectator is not an invitation to kill her children—it is the *extreme case* of the sacrifice of an egoism (to be legitimate), it is an invitation to the greatness one attains by foregoing personal happiness, when a higher law—in this case the permanence of the couple—is involved.

Thus one may see what Seneca gave Corneille: the discovery of the nature of tragedy, the art of building the dramatic development around a few essential, properly distributed scenes, and a few essential features of the tragic style—of which more later—though in 1660 Corneille, severely criticizing his own work, finds the style of Médée uneven, whereas he praises that of *La Mort de Pompée* without restrictions.[15]

Only once, with *Rodogune*, will he again attempt to present a great criminal. Another offer of mad infanticide (but only in thought) will be found in *Pertharite* (1652), in which Queen Rodelinde asks the usurper who wants to marry her to act as a cynical tyrant, by first uniting with her through a murder.

Corneille will search in other directions for more legitimate examples of the wrench or heroic sacrifice, and he will find them, in a theatre which will successively present all forms of civic and political problems.

The starting-point of this evolution is also *Médée*. We have already seen how Corneille—copying Italian intricate tragedies—added to the individual moral subject treated by Euripides and Seneca a political tragedy. From the very first scene, Jason announces that he is acting '*par maxime d'état*': this is the formula currently used by all the writers of the long Machiavellian lineage, and of the dozens of '*Raisons d'État*' which are still in the forefront of French libraries in 1635.[16] The scene between Créon and Médée (II. 2), longer and more methodical than in Seneca's play, is a regular legal debate. Médée's presence on Corinthian ground is undesirable for political reasons. Her banishment has already been ordered. Médée wants to know the reason for this decision; Créon attempts to evade the question by an ironical answer:

Ah! l'innocence même, et la même candeur!   (384)

then attempts to answer in terms of international politics:

J'ai racheté la paix à ces conditions.   (396)

This is what Médée was waiting for: the *compromises* of any peace-treaty are made at the expense of a powerless third party, whose voice is not heeded (396-405). Créon has to fall back on Médée's supernatural powers. Is she a criminal? She is; but whom did she murder, and to what purpose? The victim, her father Pelias, behaved like a tyrant towards Jason. The reward for the murder was the Golden Fleece, and the saftey of the Argonauts, '*fleur de la Grèce*', '*tous vos heros enfin . . .*' (405-51). Créon avoids justifying himself: it is from Colchos, not from Corinth, that Médée must ask for her retribution. Certainly, Médée answers, but together with the purpose of the murder and of the glory, Jason, for whom Créon finds excuses, whilst charging Médée (451-8).

The tyrant retorts:

> Son crime, s'il en a, c'est de t'avoir pour femme.   (465)

Médée can answer that easily, by quoting the manly saying: '*Est criminel, celui a qui profite le crime*', and she adds this irrefutable argument:

> Mais vous les saviez vous m'avez reçue (*les* = my crimes)
> Quand votre coeur, sensible à la compassion,
> Malgré tous mes forfaits, prit ma protection.   (477-84)

and she concludes:

> Je suis coupable ailleurs, mais innocente ici.   (688)

The only possible reply for Créon is a blunt reminder of the initial order:

> Va, dis-je, en d'autres lieux
> Par tes cris importune solliciter les Dieux.   (492)

adding to it the still more cruel (and unexplained) order to leave her children behind. Two scenes later, Aegée, Créuse's legitimate fiancée, is surprised at this sudden, unexpected disgrace, and at Créuse's new suitor. To which Créuse answers by alleging the blindness of love, and also the '*raison d'État*':

> Je perdrais ma couronne en acceptant la vôtre.   (666)

Aegée leaves, after declaring war (II. 5). The betrothal of Créuse and Aegée which constitutes an aggravating circumstance for Jason, could now serve as a good pretext for him to free himself of any obligation to the King of Corinth, and, if not to go back to Médée, at all events to give up his political ambition. On the contrary, he himself will take Aegée prisoner. The latter, in his jail, laments (IV. 4):

> Malheureux prince, on te méprise
> Quand tu t'arrêtes a servir.   (1177-8)

Jason makes a very cynical use of this loving submission of the old king: the greatest token of his love that Aegée can give her, is to give her up: a strange reversal of courtly love!

> Il doit vous témoigner par son obéissance
> Combien sur son esprit vous avez de puissance.   (529-30)

In her meeting with Jason, which does not occur until the middle of the third act, Médée, calm and dignified, sadly opens her soul, which is guilty because it is in love. Jason, who is embarrassed, cuts a poor figure, and once more alleges political reasons:

> Tes discours, dont Créon de plus en plus s'offense,
> Le forceraient enfin à quelque violence.   (840-1)

which Médée, once more, can easily see through:

> A travers tes conseils je vois assez ta ruse.   (845)

Jason, cowardly, accuses Fate, and asserts that he goes on living only for the sake of his children; and he dares to mention the children whom Créuse will give him (877). He endeavours to use as an argument the Machiavellian 'Cédons à la force' which draws a new cry from Médée:

> Ah, coeur rempli de feinte,
> Tu masques tes désirs d'un faux titre de crainte.   (887)

and Jason, mercilessly hunted down in the poor reasons he gives, retreats prudently, with a great solemn—ridiculous—promise to remain true to the memory of Médée!

We have only dwelt on the political web of the play in order to emphasize to what extent (apart from the direct alterations made by Corneille as regards the psychology of the characters) this political web influences the general purpose of the play.

A few remarks must be added, concerning the respective attitudes of Corneille and Seneca towards the religious problem.

The stoic hero rises up in protest against a blind and unfair destiny, unlike the average man, whose attitude, in front of the vicissitudes of fate, which are considered as providential, is one of acceptance. The first chorus in *Medea* is a ritual bridal song, in honour of Créuse (56, 115) which affords a striking contrast with Médée's pathetic appeal to the gods of marriage and to Lucine (1, 55).

Medea, now trusting only to her own power, stands up to fate freely:

> Fortuna, opes auferre, non animum potest.   (177)

and, in her rage, she hurls defiance at the gods:

> . . . invadam deos
> et cuncta quatiam.   (423-4)

In the same way, Jason appears, with a curse in his mouth:

> O dura fata semper et sortem asperam
> cum saevit et cum parcit ex aequo malam.   (431-2)

He distinguishes between destiny and divine justice, with a serious restriction—if the latter exists.

> . . . Sancta si caelum incolis
> Justitia, numen invoco ac testor tuum.   (440-1)

Medea also calls upon it, as an agent of punishment:

> Nunc summe toto Jupiter caelo tona . . .
> . . . quisquis e nobis cadet
> Nocens peribit. . . .   (321-535)

The chorus, on the other hand, appeals to its clemency (595-6), but man, that proud conqueror, has provoked the divinity of the sea. As for the nurse, she is frightened by the pact her mistress has concluded with the infernal powers, and indeed the magical evocation of Medea makes this alliance a formidable weapon of destruction. The chorus's only hope is in the help of Phoebus, who may hurl down the sun. But Medea now sees the Erinyes. She is ready for expiation. With frightful joy she consummates her first murder, and thinks that the divinity is propitious, and the play ends on Jason's well-known blasphemy:

> Per alta vade spatia sublimis aetheris
> testare nullos esse, qua veheris, deos.   (1026-7)

Corneille could not possibly agree with such views. In the first place, he eliminates Seneca's last two lines and the apparition of the Furies. He preserves the whole of Médée's beautiful prayer to the 'Souverains protecteurs des lois de l'hyménée' (I. 4) and does not pit the celestial gods against the infernal powers.

Although he does not do away with Médée's supernatural power (whereas later on he will not tolerate any element of wonder in his dramatic works),[17] although Médée still wishes for the alliance of the sun to destroy Corinth, he shows the magician less in her relations with the divinities of this world than in the chemical origin of her philtres. The few curses against fate have no particular value in the mouth of imprisoned Aegée:

> Destin qui punis mon audace,
> Tu n'as que de justes rigueurs.   (1185-6)

or of Jason before the bodies of Créon and Créuse:

> Quel malheureux destin vous avait réservés
> A porter le trépas a qui vous a sauvés.   (1531-2)

But instead of Jason's well-known final blasphemy, Corneille introduces a line which suggests that Médée's triumph will be short-lived:

> Ma reine, ta belle âme, en partant de ces lieux
> M'a laissé la vengeance et je la laisse aux Dieux.   (1623-4)

On one point only does Corneille follow Seneca's stoicism. Jason approves Créon's suicide, seeing it in the last course open to a generous courage 'pour braver le destin qui l'outrage' (1489-90).

Thus, Corneille's attitude is utterly negative; he is content with expurgating Seneca, without as yet setting forth the mystique of heroism which will define the action of Providence clearly, and will establish a definite hierarchy between the words Heaven, Destiny, and individual fate. This action appears, though rather confusedly, in *Le Cid*, begins to take shape in *Horace* and is already completely formulated in *Cinna*.

To the first edition of the latter play (January 1643)—but it was probably staged in the 1640-41 season—Corneille joins a page of the *De Clementia* (book 1, ch. 9); he makes an accurate adaptation of it in the scene between Auguste and Livie (IV. 3). It would be an exaggeration to say that the whole play is based on this page. Corneille owes much more to the numerous writers on political philosophy (most of them Italian) who, in his time, opposed Machiavelli and commented upon the famous episode of Augustus's clemency, particularly L. Settala (1627), Father Sartonio (1628), and Gabriel Maudé's political considerations on *coups d'état* (1629) with which Corneille did not at all agree.

Let us merely point out that Corneille does not agree with the self-interested arguments which Seneca does not scruple, humanly enough, to put forward (ch. 6). To the end, even after Livie's intervention, Auguste believes in the duties of his righteousness, and is reconciled to clemency only when he discovers the importance of the disaster, and Corneille is careful to make him discover this gradually: Cinna, then Emilie, then Maxime. Heaven, which is the cause of everything, finally grants Livie a prophetic vision:

> . . . une céleste flamme
> D'un rayon prophétique illumine mon âme.
> Oyez ce que les Dieux vous font savoir par moi.   (1753-5)

Finally, let us add that Seneca, in *De Beneficiis* (IV. ch. 30, §2), ranges Cinna among the 'infamous men who, thanks to their noble origin, passed before industrious men in the pursuit of honours'; this man is very different from the tormented but heroical character who is, as much as Auguste, the soul of Corneille's tragedy.

Immediately after Cinna, in the series of Roman plays, comes *Le Mort de Pompée* (printed in February 1644); Seneca associates Pompey with Cinna in *De Beneficiis*; he recalls in *De Clementia* that Cinna is Cn. Pompeius's great-grandson. It is quite possible— though Corneille says nothing about this —that this relationship induced the playwright to compare these two destinies. But Corneille is directly indebted to a Latin play written on the subject by a Jesuit, and to a recent tragedy (1638) by one of his countrymen, Chaulmer.

If Corneille did read Seneca, it was to oppose his views. The Latin writer ranges Pompeius among the great criminals who, in their vengeance, wished for the ruin of their motherland (book 5, ch. 16, §4), whereas Corneille presents in his dedication to Mazarin *'le plus grand personnage de l'ancienne Rome . . . un héros qui dans sa bonne fortune fut le protecteur de beaucoup de rois et qui dans sa mauvais eut encore des rois pour ses ministres'*, and in fact, Pompée, who does not appear in the play, is cleared by Corneille of all his political blunders and of his human weaknesses, and is presented as the innocent victim of a Machiavellian Council of State, under a weak Egyptian prince. Admittedly, in *De tranquillitate animi*,

Seneca ranks Pompeius, with Socrates, Rutilius, Cicero, and Cato among the honourable men who come to a bad end (ch. 16, §1). These brief remarks cannot have influenced Corneille.

For one more of his plays, Corneille may have used Seneca. In *Sertorius* (1662) Corneille opposes the noble exile to the tyrannical Sulla. But does one carry away one's fatherland with the dust on one's shoes? The senate, which has been re-assembled at Nertobriga, in Spain, is a noble but short-lived institution. The senate in Rome, though servile and degenerate, has an age-old tradition behind it. Corneille offers one solution to the problem he sets. Assuredly, Sertorius is presented as a fine heroic figure. But what would happen if he were not murdered?

Seneca calls Sulla a tyrant; none more than he ever *'drank human blood so greedily'* (De Clementia, X. 1); he is unfair and depraved (Ad. marc. 17, 5). Corneille never applies such severe terms to him, and he presents Sulla's envoy, Pompée, as a moderate, almost likeable ambassador, who is able to oppose Sertorius with some solid political reasoning, and to stir his feelings by mentioning the fatherland.

Il est doux de revoir les murs de la patrie.   (925)

At any rate, there is a far cry from Seneca's brief remarks to the beautiful, moving political play of Corneille's late period.

After a silence of seven years, in 1659, Corneille comes back to play-writing, urged by a new Maecenas, who was to fall into disgrace soon after, Procureur Fouquet, who suggested three subjects to the poet: *Oedipus*, *Camma*, which was to be treated by his brother Thomas. The third is unknown—one does not know how the poet reacted to having a set subject. Never since *Médée* had he treated a subject already made famous by a predecessor. Four years later, he was to write his version of *Sophonisbe* which, after some Italian versions, had proved a success for Mairet in 1634. Corneille himself has said in the *Avis au lecteur* how, after first being convinced that such a subject would gain the support of the learned, he had later trembled when he had examined it *'de pres et un peu plus a loisir qu'il ne l'avait fait en le choisissant'*. Everything tends to show that there is no reason for establishing a parallel between him and his two predecessors, Sophocles and Seneca, since his purpose was different. His contemporaries seem to have understood this, for they greeted the play very favourably,

whereas modern critics cannot but draw a parallel which has always
been to Corneille's disadvantage; his play throws into the background what seems to us the main interest of this theme, namely
the horrible grip of Fate and the frightful tragedy of incest.
Corneille, in the first three acts, presents an original treatment of
the theme; then his subject forces him to relate the traditional
episodes in the last two acts. The two actions are rather badly
knitted together, and contradictory judgments have been passed
on this play.[18]

Undoubtedly Corneille, as in *Médée*, reduces the element of
horror of his subject, and avoids bloodthirsty pathos—Oedipe,
after his punishment, does not come back on the stage, and he is
described very briefly, with a realism which is tempered by
poetry:

> Là, ses yeux arrachés par ses barbares mains,
> Font distiller un sang qui rend l'âme aux Thébains.
> Ce sang si précieux touche à peine la terre,
> Que le courroux du ciel ne leur fait plus la guerre. (1995-9)

The French *Oedipe* is primarily a political play. Corneille invents
the character of Dircé, and gives her a prominent part: she is
Jocaste's daughter and the rightful heir to the throne: the first
three acts are taken up by her obstinate and proud fight against the
usurper—she is helped by Thésée, prince of Athens, and a
generous lover.[19] These two put one in mind of Laodice and
Nicomède in the play which bears the latter's name (1651).
Oedipe, a vain, despotic man, is therefore transformed from a
victim into a guilty man, and the first meeting between Jocaste
and Oedipe (I. 4) turns into a bitter-sweet quarrel about Dircé,
whom Jocaste defends as a mother. Besides, the latter is far from
the sympathetic stoic attitude of Seneca's character:

> Quid juvat, conjunx, mala
> Gravare questu?   Regium hoc ipsum reor
> Adversa capere. (80-3)

In Corneille's play, she borrows from La Rochefoucauld a few
forcible maxims on the power of *self-love:*

> Parlons-en comme il faut: nous nous aimons plus qu'elle. (330)

Yet Oedipe moves our feelings when, with characteristic unconscious imprudence, he points to himself as to the future victim of a fair revenge of the Gods against Laius and Jocaste who disobeyed them:

> Les Dieux, qui tôt ou tard savent se ressentir,
> Dédaignent de répondre à qui les fait mentir.
> Ce fils dont ils avaient prédit les aventures,
> Exposé par votre ordre, a trompé leurs augures,
> Et ce sang innocent, et ces Dieux irrités,
> Se vengent maintenant de vos impiétés. (371-7)

In fact, Oedipe is not a hero according to Aristotle's definition: '*Neither quite good nor quite bad*', if one means thereby that he should be now the one now the other, or that his virtues should be mingled with weaknesses. Oedipe is an ambiguous hero. His actions can be interpreted in two ways. Corneille is also indebted to La Rochefoucauld for this new way of looking at things. The moralist, who at that time used to read his maxims in the Paris *salons*, criticizes even the most dangerous actions, which he attributes to consciously or unconsciously selfish motives. This ambiguity appears most clearly in the dialogue between Dircé and Mégare, her maid of honour (II. 2). The latter defends Oedipe who has always behaved like a father towards Dircé. '*Par politique*', replies Dircé. But he defended Aemon, Dircé's lover? '*Politique partout . . .?*' (lines 520-30). So that Oedipe's true personality remains a mystery: is he a truly generous heart or a clever politician? If the action, in the first three acts, owes nothing to Seneca, the presentation of the protagonist, at the moment when Corneille takes up the traditional subject, has had a great influence on the impression he makes. Every word Oedipe utters makes us both suspicious and compassionate. Corneille alters the legend noticeably and casts a doubt on the identity of that '*sang de Laius*' which the oracle claims on three characters in turn: Dircé believes she has been chosen and accepts death generously (III. 2 and 3), though not without a piteous look towards love and life:

> J'en fais gloire, mais je me cache
> Un comble affreux de déplaisirs,
> Je fais taire tous mes désirs,
> Mon coeur à soi-même s'arrache. (819-23)

But Oedipe prudently interrupts the sacrifice that was to take place

. . . Vous pourriez mourir et perdre votre mort. (964)

and no one knows, according to Dircé's own words, whether Oedipe behaves so out of an excess of generosity (927) or whether this is a clever trap set for her vitue.

Oedipe begins his enquiry (III. 4) when Thésée, who believes he is the chosen victim, appears. Phaedime, who was the only survivor among his retinue, has just revealed it to him before dying, though without giving him any clear proof (1083-5). He complains, not of his coming death, but of losing Dircé, since it appears that he is her brother. Corneille harps on this ambiguous theme for a while (IV. 1): he only suggests an innocent 'amour inceste' between brother and sister in order to prepare the discovery of the other one, between Oedipe and Jocaste. Thenceforth Dircé endeavours to love Thésée as a brother, but she hopes the truth is different.

Ah! Prince, s'il se peut, ne soyez point mon frère. (1261)

Meanwhile Phorbas has given some further details concerning the murder of Laius. Thus Thésée is nearly undeceived. Phorbas is ordered to name the murderer—Oedipe appears and as the two men recognize each other, Phorbas has no need to accuse Oedipe —he himself owns he is Laius's murderer—Thésée, who keeps thinking he is Jocaste's son, then appears as an avenger . . . and challenges Oedipe to a duel (IV. 4). The people revolt, and Oedipe fears the loss of his throne (V. 1), which both Thésée and Dircé may claim. Thus the political plot, which was rather in the background in Act IV, devoted to the enquiry, on the blood of Laius and the resulting *quid pro quo*, comes to the fore again a few scenes before the dénouement. Corneille cannot invent any new development and he hastens towards the traditional catastrophe. A messenger arrives from Corinth. King Polybe, on his death-bed, has revealed that Oedipe was not his son, but an exposed child. Oedipe still hesitates, and, in his pride, reacts once more: since he is of lowly birth, he is a *self-made* man:

Je ne dois plus qu'à moi tout ce que j'eus de rang. (1720)

Corneille certainly goes too far here. The messenger adds that he is a Theban and that he was exposed on Mt. Cithaeron. That clinches it. Oedipe can deceive himself no longer. But he is not over-whelmed: as he has already said in Act I, the three guilty ones are gathered there—Phorbas, Iphicrate, Jocaste—who have been the tools of Destiny; not blind tools, but tools actuated by a kind of *misleading prudence* (1758-1771). Phorbas does not attempt to deny his guilt; he will punish himself for it; Iphicrate still attempts to find an excuse (V. 4), but Dircé appears: she now is her enemy's sister. To the very end, Corneille does his utmost to attract our attention on the true tragedy of Oedipe: his patient enquiry and tragic solitude—Dircé, although she does not utterly disavow her past attitude, forgives everything:

> Quel crime avez-vous fait que d'etre malheureux? (1819)

and Oedipe, who suddenly appears greater, utters a bitter and solemn protest:

> Mon souvenir n'est plein que d'explits généreux,
> Cependant je me trouve inceste et parricide . . .
> Aux crimes malgré moi l'ordre du ciel m'attache . . . (1820-6)

Thus Oedipe must die for the general good. Dircé tries, generously, to take his place (40-55). Oedipe refuses; but Thésée appears (V. 6); he also feels nothing but pity. Oedipe protests once more:

> Vous voyez où des Dieux nous a reduits la haine. (1876)

All of them admire the prince's tranquil firmness, and Thésée describes him in Senecan lines:

> . . . cette âme innocente,
> Qui brave impunément la fortune impuissants,
> Regarde avec dédain ce qu'elle a combattu,
> Et se rend tout entiere à toute sa vertu. (1893-7)

After the relation of Jocaste's suicide, and that of Oedipe's self-inflicted punishment—but the gods are content with the blood fallen from his eyes—the dénouement is brightened up by the joy of the people of Thebes, who come to life again, and Corneille replaces the bitter protests of an innocent by the double submission of Thésée and Dircé to the mysterious order of the gods in this matter, which wipes out the injustice of it:

Thésée: . . . le ciel fait assez voir
Que le sang de Laius a rempli son devoir:
Son ombre est satisfaite . . .

and Dircé: . . . remettons aux Dieux a disposer du reste
(last line).

We have given a rather long summary of Corneille's play, which is not as well known as Seneca's, in order not to attempt to draw an impossible parallel between the two plays. Corneille, in this case, did not alter the Latin play, as when he wrote *Médée:* he wrote an entirely different play. This was probably a mistake: he should not have chosen Oedipus for the purpose of treating an interesting political problem on the twofold theme of usurpation and marriages of convenience. And Oedipus cannot be turned into a detective story.

Having made those serious restrictions, we must observe that they do not suffice to make a bad play of Corneille's *Oedipe*. It is very characteristic of his manner, and, as regards our subject, it throws a light on the difference between Corneille and Seneca, in spite of the dénouement, which is apparently so stoic, at any rate as regards Oedipe's reactions, on which, it will be noticed, Corneille does not close his play. Apparently stoic, because in fact the whole play is based not on a liberation of the individual from unfair or blind gods, but on an effort to grant him a free will, in front of a Providence whose intentions are mysterious. It has been noted that it was in the very midst of a Jansenistic controversy that Corneille added, at the end of Act III, in Thésée's mouth, a long protest against any form of predestination, whether it be astral or not.

> Et pour remplir un nom dont vous êtes avide,
> Acceptez ceux d'inceste et de fils parricide.
> J'en croirai ces témoins que le ciel m'a prescrits,
> Et ne vous puis donner mon aveu qu'à ce prix.

And to Jocaste, Thésée replies:

> Quoi la nécessité des vertus et des vices
> D'un astre impérieux doit suivre les caprices,
> Et Delphes, malgre nous, conduit nos actions
> Au plus bizarre effet de ses prédictions?
> L'âme est donc toute esclave . . . (1145-53)

D'un tel aveuglement daignez me dispenser.
Le ciel, juste à punir, juste à récompenser,
Pour rendre aux actions leur peine ou leur salaire,
Doit nous offrir son aide, et puis nous laisser faire.
N'enfoncons toutefois ni votre oeil ni le mien
Dans ce profond abîme où nous ne voyons rien.   (1167-72)

Nothing is more alien, if not opposed, to Sophocles and Seneca. This passage was not superadded: it should be backed up by a complete record of the use of such words as *ciel, sort, dieux, destin* in order to make clear the cohesion of Corneille's views: in this respect *Oedipe* is no exception: the whole of Corneille's theatre has the same metaphysical background: man faces fate, but in so doing he obeys a higher intelligence which demands a sacrifice the purpose of which he does not understand at first. These lines from *Horace* can be applied to every play.

> Et comme il voit en nous des âmes peu communes
> Hors de l'ordre commun il nous fait des fortunes.

It would therefore be an exaggeration to submit that Corneille, in 1660, uses Seneca's glory only to protest against stoic ethics. In fact, like all seventeenth-century Christians, he admires the Latin author too much to attack him systematically. Of stoic asceticism he preserves what raises man to an heroical level; he does away with what offends or embarrasses him, without emphasizing it or being indignant about it.

Although a comparison between the two plays taken as a whole is impossible, it is interesting to note a series of differences in the details. From the first, Seneca's stoic Oedipus considers power a burden.

> Quisquamne regno gaudet? O fallax bonum.   (I. 6)

In Corneille's play, we have seen that Oedipe was prepared to fight against Dircé, then against Thésée or the people's will, in order to keep a sceptre of which he is proud.

While Seneca's Oedipus scorned power, his royal relative Créon relishes the privileges it affords, with the flat realism of a parasite.

> . . . cultus, opulentae dapes
> donata multis gratia nostra salus.   (691-2)

This ludicrous caricature is true to the stoic spirit, but it clashes with tragic majesty. Corneille does not share these views, and avoids this clashing of two tones.

Oedipus, in Seneca's play, is both pious and modest (lines 23-5), but he fears the snares of Destiny.

> Jam jam aliquid in nos fata moliri parant.   (29)

There is nothing of the kind in Corneille's play. From the moment he appears (I. 2) Oedipe shows great self-confidence, waits for the oracle of Delphi optimistically, and immediately comes to his main preoccupation—a matrimonial policy, which would strengthen his position as king of Thebes—Thésée may have either Antigone or Ismene: the prince of Athens is no ordinary son-in-law.

In Seneca's play, Oedipus promises Créon—who is surprised to see that there has been no punishment yet for Laius's murder—that justice will be done soon, with the help of the gods, to whom he addresses a fervent prayer (250-8). In Corneille's play, Oedipe, although he displays a somewhat pharisaical religious zeal, always acts as a kingly judge, anxious to bring back discipline and activity among his subjects. When the truth is known, and when Thésée offers to leave it to the Gods to decide, by fighting a duel, Oedipe's only thought still is of the throne.

> Prince, je vous entends, il faut venger ce père,
> Et ma perte à l'État semble être necessaire.   (1489-90)

and he adds, by no means resigned:

> Peut-être aurez-vous peine à reprendre son rang,
> Qu'il ne vous ait coûte quelque peu de ce sang.   (1504-5)

Corneille cuts out the famous meeting with Tirésias, whom Oedipus accuses, and through him the whole clergy. It was probably impossible to write such a scene in the seventeenth century in France. But it seems that Corneille did so, not out of prudence, but of his own accord; neither his life, nor his work, induced him to such violent anticlericalism. Yet, he does not completely dismiss it.

> L'argent put inspirer la voix qui les prononce,
> Cet organe des Dieux put se laisser gagner
> A ceux que ma naissance éloignait de régner,
> Et par tous les climats on n'a que trop d'exemples
> Qu'il est ainsi qu'ailleurs des méchants dans les temples.
> (1174-8)

Those bold lines, which Voltaire used to read with glee, did not give rise to any protest in 1659. France was more liberal under Louis XIV's reign than the prohibition of Tartuffe might lead one to believe.

Let us add that these lines are not uttered by Oedipe, but by Thésée, immediately after the defence of human freewill.

Corneille also does away with one of the guilty men: in Seneca's play, Phorbas has known everything for a long time and he confesses only when threatened with torture.

Corneille's Phorbas only knows that he gave a child to a Corinthian and that he was present at the murder of Laius: he has never put two and two together. To the very end, he will not believe it; when Iphicrate tells him that the child is there before his very eyes, he still answers:

> . . . Je ne vois que le Roi . . .   (1752)

The news of his suicide follows soon after this.

> Pour venger sur son sang un ordre mal suivi.   (1916)

Corneille also cuts out Seneca's ingenious invention to explain why Oedipus does not kill himself:

> Mors innocentem sola Fortunae eripit . . .   (934)
> . . . Utere ingenio, miser
> Quod saepe fieri non potest fiat diu
> Mors eligatur longa.

Finally, we have already seen, in the course of our study of *Médée*, how Corneille opposed the fatalistic views expressed in the final chorus of Seneca's play: a man who was led by his destiny, a blind Fate whose course even the gods cannot change, give place in Corneille's play, to a man who is free to collaborate, by his deliberate acceptance, with a destiny which is the tool of a mysterious higher Providence. This general conception, which Corneille has been defending ever since *Horace*, cannot easily fit in with the traditional *Oedipus*; Corneille stumbles upon Oedipus's fundamental innocence, and he solves this problem only by bringing into play the subtle notion of an original sin which he does not call by its proper name. Oedipe is paying for the trespass of Jocaste, who disobeyed the oracles. He pretends not to realize that he is merely shifting his ground. In the name of what justice could gods doom man to parricide and incest? Corneille is interested only in his character's heroical decision:

> . . . cette âme innocente,
> Qui brave impunément la fortune impuissante,
> Regarde avec dédain ce qu'elle a combattu,
> Et se rend tout entière à toute sa vertu.   (1893-6)

When he puts out his eyes, Oedipe is not trying to fulfil the oracle but to forestall an unfair punishment *as a free man:*

> Prévenons, a-t-il dit, l'injustice des Dieux,
> Commençons à mourir avant qu'ils nous l'ordonnent.
>   (1988-1989)

There is no reason for dwelling on the basic differences between the two authors' intentions as regards the manner: we should only be repeating our remarks about *Médée*. Corneille cuts out all the weird elements: in the present case the ritual conjuring up of the oracles, and all the elements of terror resulting from a horrible realism, which are given much more importance in *Oedipe* than in *Médée*.[20]

Lastly, it seems to us that a study of *Médée* and *Oedipe* spares us an answer to the more general question: is Corneille a *stoic*?

He has often been called one; never after due reflection, in our opinion. This assertion is usually brought forward without being proved. Whenever attempts to prove it have been made, they have always been made indirectly, in the course of a history of literature, and on the strength of the importance, not of a genuine stoicism, which perhaps could be found among some '*libertines*',[21] but of a Neo-stoicism, or Christian stoicism. The reasoning is syllogistic: Neo-stoicism is the main philosophical attitude under Louis XIII, particularly among writers who belong to the Church.[22] Now Corneille is a Christian and his success is a reflection of the tastes of his period: therefore he is a neo-stoic. A few quotations chosen at random substantiate this hypothesis, and once more the demon of analogy triumphs.

It is very likely that Seneca was one of the most widely read writers in France at the beginning of the seventeenth century, that Corneille had read him, as well as Du Vair and J. Lipse and their successors.

But we are struck by the fact that Corneille very seldom refers to this author, who held a privileged place among his contemporaries; it is impossible to find, in collected works amounting to 60,000 lines (his dramatic production), any Senecan *sentences*, in spite of his well-known partiality to maxims.

Médée and *Oedipe* only show us how he stands apart from the Latin philosopher, not only in the field of metaphysics, but also in the field of ethics.

In order to have a general idea of how different they are, one need but think of the constant and surprising relations[23] between Descartes and Corneille. This being known, it is enough to say that Corneille is a stoic in so far as Descartes is a stoic.

It remains that Corneille, as a playwright, not being a stoic, may have followed Seneca only in the field of dramatic technique. He does so, but, like all his contemporaries, unconsciously, taking into account the technical and psychological alterations introduced in Italy, then in France, by Lodovico Dolce's adaptations. Seneca's theatre was still on the syllabus of every school. But to any good pupil endowed with a critical mind, this lyrical outline interrupted by tedious choruses must have seemed both boring and slender. The dramatist who was looking for a model was hard put to it to find five acts in a few beautiful scenes: the sacrosanct division, invented by the theorists of the Renaissance, could only be found in a very sketchy state in those plays.

One thing, at all events, is certain: Corneille, as a theorist of tragedy in the *Three Discourses* (1660) studies Aristotle, praises Horace, but quotes Seneca only three times, the first time[24] in order to criticize the plot of *Thyestes* and praise a *Médée* 'qui se fait elle-même justice de ceux qui l'oppriment'—his own character, and not that of his Latin model; the second time[25] in order to criticize the old man in *Oedipus* who 'semble tomber des nues par miracles'; the third time[26] in order to criticize the dual action in *Troades*. Judging from these remarks, it would seem that Seneca inspired Corneille with nothing but criticism and scorn. This would be a mistake—Corneille, whom the '*doctes*' pestered throughout his career, preserves a critical attitude towards the ancients and accumulates the examples he finds in ancient plays of 'faults' which according to the 'doctes' can be found only in the plays of their contemporaries. This is a polemic attitude, which does not represent everything Corneille thinks about Sophocles,

Euripides, or Seneca. . . . The fact remains that, on the point
of the difficult art of writing tragedies, Corneille strictly abides
by Aristotle's technical views, which he tries to make clearer, and
to free from all the narrow-minded comments made upon them.
As for the subjects and their ideological content, it is a matter for
the particular genius of each writer. On this point Corneille praises
Seneca only in the preface to *Médée*—we have seen that it was on
that occasion that his own temperament was formed: it is to
Seneca that he is indebted for his discovery of the nature of tragedy.

He owes even more to him: enough has been made of their
difference in tastes—what Corneille cuts out was perhaps what
Seneca most sought after. Yet Seneca gave to Corneille the best
devices of his style: the lofty but not bombastic style, the
antithetic reply, the irony, the simple images, the use of sentences,
certain unusual associations of words which give new freshness to
a term. This influence, which, to my knowledge, has never been
analysed, would deserve a better study than the few following
remarks.

In 1660, Corneille always joins, to the *Examens* of his plays,
some remarks on their style. He passes some surprising
condemnations, on *Médée* for example, and generally praises
clarity and compactness but also *'pomp'*, by which he means a
majesty free from bombast, and *art*, a rather difficult term to
define, probably a kind of elegance due to the propriety of the
words used, and to harmony.

The main traits of this lofty style are, in Seneca's works, the
varied use of short sentences or on the contrary of a simple,
clearly upward movement.

Short sentences: passionate questions by which the character
analyses himself, or by which suddenly, in the midst of an inner
struggle, he breaks the movement of auto-suggestion which
tends to justify his first inner impulse.

> Occidimus! Aures pepulit hymenaeus meas . . .
> Utinam esset illi frater! Est conjunx: in hanc ferrum
>   exigatur . . . (115-25)

> Bene est, tenetur, vulneri patuit locus. (550)

The character changes his mind:

> Egone ut recedam? . . .
> Quid anime, cessas? Sequere felicem impetum. (893-6)

and, after a continuous movement of 30 lines, which ends with a clear decision:

> Vos pro paternis sceleribus poenas date. (925)

an effective change of mind which leads to the opposite decisions:

> Cor pepulit horror . . .
> Egone ut meorum liberum ac prolis meae fundam cruorem?
> (925-30)

The movement of passion is often expressed by a succession of vocatives interrupted by appositions, or causal-conditional clauses with a main clause in the imperative mood:

> Si vivis, anime, si quid antiqui tibi remanet vigoris, pelle
> femineos metus. (41-2)

It is also expressed by a brief accumulation of words, between which full play is given to the emotional reverberation of language which is—silence.

> Incerta, / vaecors, / mente vaesana / feror. (123)
> Tibi patria cessit, tibi pater, / frater, / pudor. (488)

The well-known Senecan 'sententiae' do not yet assume that petrified form which they have in the ancient or mediaeval educational selections. They crop up naturally in a psychological context which is determined by the situation of the character. To take them out of their context, as we have to do here, is to betray them:

> Quae scelere parta est, scelere linquenda est domus. (55)
>
> Levis est dolor qui capere consilium potest. (155)
>
> Fortuna fortes metuit, ignavos premit. (159)
>
> Qui nil potest sperare, desperet nihil. (164)

It will be noticed that with the most common vocabulary, an artistic effect is achieved by tenseness and the interplay of antitheses, which leads us to the famous:

> Nihil superest—Medea superest. (165)

which Corneille has rendered forcibly:

> Que vous reste-t-il? Moi, dis-je, et c'est assez.

We have analysed the Latin lines faithfully adapted by Corneille·
The reasons of his choice are clear. In his other plays, deprived,
but also freed from his models he will go on using the same devices·

Let us emphasize the most typical device, because it is related to
the very nature of tragedy: irony. A powerful dialectical instrument,
it is used as a weapon for exposing the ignoble, as an insult against
an enemy upon whom one means to inflict one's scorn once and
for all, as a catalyst to rouse the dormant generosity of a character.
It is mostly in Nicomède, Pertharite, Attila, and Agésilas that
Corneille makes a deliberate use of it. But he finds it in Seneca's
Medea, and does not fail to use it whenever his predecessor does.
We have seen some instances of it in the meeting between Médée
and Créon. The enchantress is even keener with Jason:

> . . . Eatur. Regius jussit gener. (450)
>
> Poenam putabam: munus, ut video, est fuga. (492)
>
> —Ingrata vita est cujus acceptae pudet
> —Retinenda non est cujus acceptae pudet. (504-5)

And in the final scene, Medea reaches the height of tragical
paradox, laughter, the atrocious laughter of the irreparable:

> . . . Poeniteat licet,
> feci; —voluptas magna me invitam subit
> et ecce crescit.   Deerat hoc unum mihi,
> spectator iste. (990-4)

Medea slashes at this 'spectator' with overwhelming irony:

> I nunc, superbe, virginum thalamos pete. (1007)

which Corneille changes into macabre humour. Créuse has just
died on the stage before Jason's eyes—Médée utters these
atrocious lines:

> Heureux père et mari, ma fuite et leur tombeau
> Laissent la place vide à ton hymen nouveau.
> Réjouis-t'en, Jason, *va posséder Créuse*. (1543-6)

For this verbal efficiency of irony, Corneille is indebted to Seneca.
Later, it will always preserve him, even within the narrow
conventions of regular tragedy, from conventional language.

Such is Corneille's debt to Seneca. In order to appreciate it,
one need only compare *Clitandre* with *Médée*. Only three years

elapsed between the writing of these two plays. One of them is a melodrama which may be striking on the stage, but makes very poor reading. The other is a moving, well-balanced, and already quite classical tragedy. The debt he owes Seneca is no small one, but Seneca's play has been filtered, rewritten, and completed, so that *Médée* is a peculiarly Cornelian play. From this mere exercise of virtuosity of the unities of time and place—that is what Corneille himself calls *Clitandre*.[27] he turned to a reflection on the nature of tragedy, the psychological working of the hero and the pathetic resources of language, and, in so doing, at once he found his manner. Seneca, as he often did, but in Corneille's case more successfully, has played the part of a touchstone. Between Garnier, an overfaithful and clumsy disciple, and Crébillon, who preserves only Seneca's exaggerations, Corneille represents the intelligent choice—Garnier, Corneille, Crébillon, three moments of Seneca's influence: the Renaissance, classicism and the baroque.[28]

NOTES

Unless otherwise stated, quotations from Corneille are taken from the text of the *Oeuvres Completes*, Paris, Editions du Seuil, 1963 (Abbr.: Seuil).

[1] Whether Seneca the playwright and Seneca the philosopher were one and the same man was still disputed. But most people inclined to believe that there was only one Seneca, as we do now.

[2] Revue des Cours et Conférences. XXXII.

[3] Soliman is the subject of an anonymous tragedy published in 1592. Pr. Bonarelli made him famous in 1619. Mairet and Scudéry will both write a play on the subject, in 1635 and 1637.

[4] Cf. my article on *Médée* in '*Sénèque et la tragedie de la Renaissance*'. (Recueil collectif, sous la direction de J. Jacquot, Paris, 1963).

[5] Marty-Laveaux, I, 263

[6] Cf. Jacques Morel, 'L'Hercule mourant' in *Sénèque et la tragedie de la Renaissance*, quoted in note 4.

[7] A. Adam, *Hist. de la Litterature Française* (Tome I, p. 452).

[8] Cf. R. E. Pike, *Revue de littérature comparee*, 1935 (496-519).

[9] My edition (Seuil, 1963), p. 871.

[10] *History of French Dramatic Theatre* (Pt. II, vol. I, p. 30).

[11] For a longer analysis of this, see my article on *Médée* (cf. note 4).

[12] He announces them several times in his prefaces, particularly in 1644. But he defined the law of tragic emotion as early as 1631, in his preface to *Clitandre*, his first published work (cf. Corneille, Seuil, p. 53).

[13] That is why Corneille's play does not begin with beautiful curses, as in Seneca's play, but with a dialogue between Pollux and Jason, in which the latter candidly asserts that he prefers the useful to the honest (lines 133-135).

[14] Later, Corneille was ill-inspired when he replaced their *joindre* by *plaindre*.

[15] Examen de *Médée* (in fine), Seuil, p. 175.

[16] There is a long list of them in the otherwise poor and biased compilation by G. Ferrari: *Histoire de la Raison d'État* (Paris, 1872).

[17] In *Polyeucte*, divine grace has an inner influence on the characters' souls, whereas in Italian, Spanish, and even French plays on religious subjects, angels and devils are still brought into play.

[18] Cf. Couton, *La vieillesse de Corneille*, pp. 65-69; A. Adam, *Histoire de la littérature française* (Paris, Domat, 1951, Tome IV); Lancaster, *History of French Dramatic* . . . , 3rd part, Tome II.

[19] Very different, therefore, from *Thésée* in Oedipus Coloneus.

[20] Cf. 590 and following, 625 and following, 640 . . . , 860 . . . , 955 . . . .

[21] Cf. R. Pintard, *Le libertinage érudit dans la première moitié du Siècle* (Paris, 1943). But, usually these disguised atheists rather tend towards epicureanism.

[22] Father Julien-Eymar, a Franciscan friar, has made a portrait study of this in Balzac and Camus, and in some ten members of his fraternity, also in Caussin, a Jesuit father whose works Corneille probably used as a source.

[23] Because it does not seem that Descartes may have had a direct influence on Corneille. The resemblance is probably due to a similar education of the two men by the Jesuits, followed by a similar meditation, which may have been supported, in Corneille's case, between 1642 and 1650, by his reading the Elzevir editions of the *Meditations metaphysiques* and of the *Traité des passions*.

[24] Seuil, p. 823.

[25] *Ibid.*, p. 828.

[26] *Ibid.*, p. 842.

[27] Cf. Preface, Seuil, p. 53.

[28] I am fully conscious that this conception is unorthodox. But I am inclined, personally, instead of inserting a baroque *period* between the Renaissance and classicism to see, at least as far as France is concerned, a baroque *movement* in literature which, after originating, perhaps, in the beginning of the seventeenth century, developed fully in the age of Louis XIV. The *baroque* churches in France were built between 1660 and 1720—in the field of literature, Father Ménestrier, the Jesuits' emblems and ballets, as regards prose-works, Fontanelle, Fénelon, Lesage, and perhaps even La Bruyère, as regards the theatre, Th. Corneille in his late period, Reynard and Dufresny, but chiefly La Fosse and Crébillon, seem to introduce, *consciously*, in a classical frame, a tension of ornamental detail which is determined to ignore the limits of good taste; this, to my mind, is the very spirit of the *baroque*.

VII

Five Westminster Latin Plays

T. L. ZINN

I. THE LATIN PLAY

THE Westminster Latin Play was instituted by Queen Elizabeth I almost immediately after her re-foundation of the School in A.D. 1560. She was clearly interested in the play not only as an academic exercise but as a source of entertainment. She herself is known to have been present at more than one performance and there is extant a copy of the *Mostellaria* which was presented to her when she saw the play acted at Westminster.

The Play has continued to this day. There have of course been changes since the time of Queen Elizabeth and there have been interruptions in continuity, especially during the Civil War, Commonwealth, and Protectorate, but the Play has survived them all. The most serious recent break in its production came during the Second World War and the years immediately after. Till then there had grown up a cycle of four plays in which Terence's *Adelphi*, *Andria*, and *Phormio* had featured regularly since the beginning of the eighteenth century; the fourth play, in recent years, had been Plautus's *Rudens*. The Play had for a long time been a great social event, at which members of the royal family, foreign ambassadors, and people of distinction socially and politically were regularly present.

By 1938 the Prologue and Epilogue had become almost as important as the play itself. The Prologue, written by the Head Master in iambic senarians, dealt with topical events in the life of the Country and the School. The Epilogue was cast in a modern setting; it was based on the play itself, and was composed in elegiacs by a distinguished Old Westminster; one of its main characteristics was a rich fund of puns. Both Prologue and Epilogue were printed in full in *The Times*. There were many passages in the traditional plays which were ceremonially clapped, and Monitors were accordingly given the task of raising a stick when applause was required. The Play had evolved many of the characteristics of an impressive ritual.

After the war, however, the situation had radically altered. It was felt that there was no longer the need or opportunity for the same sort of occasion. There were a great number of practical difficulties in connexion with the revival of the Play, and above all it was doubted whether a Latin Play bereft of all the pomp and circumstance of the traditional productions could possibly justify itself. This was the position in 1950 when I came to teach at Westminster. As a young master I was naturally intrigued by the thought of the Play, but bitterly regretted that a Latin Play was involved, and not a Greek tragedy. If only it had been a Greek tragedy, I thought, how I would have clamoured for a revival. But a Latin Play!

II. LATIN COMEDY

The truth of the matter is that, like so many classical scholars, I hardly knew when I had last read a Latin play. I did, however, 'know' that Latin plays were dull, derivative, badly constructed, lacking in imagination, artificial, banal, and humourless; and what is more that if you knew one you knew them all.

How have Latin plays acquired this reputation? It is difficult to explain. Primarily, no doubt, because they are so rarely acted. But there are other reasons. Latin Comedy has suffered in this age through having been praised in the past for reasons uncongenial to us. Proverbial moralizations which meant much to a nineteenth-century reader tend to leave many of us cold; subtleties of plot, long rhetorical soliloquies, puns, alliteration, and similar stylistic devices are not *nostri saeculi*. But in fact the Latin plays, as we at Westminster discovered for ourselves, abound in characteristics which are astonishingly in tune with modern values.

Before discussing Latin Comedy, and in particular the five plays which have been produced at Westminster over the last nine years, I should like at this stage to put in a plea for a 'new look' on the following lines in our approach to classical studies.

It must be that certain authors and certain works are more creatively relevant to one age than to another. If education is a dynamic force and not simply the imparting of uncoordinated facts, its purpose could be interpreted as an attempt to discover with what movements of thought, what lines, what trends, what evaluations in the past we wish to identify ourselves—where we stand in our time, at what point in what tradition, leading where; according to this interpretation, each age must give particular emphasis to those lines of thought and emotional awareness, which its own circumstances peculiarly equip it to understand. It must come in, as it were, upon these particular trends of development and must carry them further in the direction dictated by its own creative instinct. For this to happen, there must be constant re-appraisal of the past and re-orientation of emphasis involving constant vital literary criticism, capable of influencing and re-shaping the syllabus of authors and works read at schools and universities. I am not suggesting that we should exclude all authors and works which fall, as far as we are concerned, on comparatively deaf ears. The effort of imagination required in order to make something of them is a valuable experience, but if education is to encourage creativity as well as understanding, and if it is concerned with an increase of self-awareness, then the need for an effective literary criticism is paramount.

What can Latin Comedy mean to our age? After producing three plays by Terence and two by Plautus, I was struck most by the fact that though both playwrights drew upon similar originals, they were so very different from each other. Even if Latin plays are in some respects similar to each other, there could hardly be two more different comic writers than Plautus and Terence. This fact alone throws into high relief the extraordinary originality which Latin authors brought to their re-creation of Greek prototypes.

Plautus is writing in the early days of Latin literature. The dew of the dawn is on his pen. He writes in an age when the language of prose is not yet too clearly distinguished from that of poetry. In his verse, high poetic genius rubs shoulders with prosaic colloquialism: glorious diction is squandered on everyday utterances. In the *Miles Gloriosus*, Periplectomenus, the *lepidus senex*, gives the following account of his *venustas*:

> Pe.: Tute me ut fateare faciam esse adulescentem moribus,
> ita apud omnis comparebo tibi res benefactis frequens.
> opu'ne erit tibi advocato tristi, iracundo? ecce me!

opu'ne leni? leniorem dices quam mutum est mare
liquidiusculusque ero quam ventus est favonius. (III. i.
65-9)

How different this is from the wit and sophistication of Attic
comedy. How much richer and more generous. Is there anything
more poetic in Latin itself than the last line?

In another place in the same play Philocomasium, a young lady,
is pretending to have arrived in Ephesus from a sea voyage; she
goes through a ceremonial thank-offering to Diana in the
following words addressed to an attendant:

> *Ph.:* Inde ignem in aram, ut Ephesiae Dianae laeta laudes
> gratisque agam eique ut Arabico fumificem odore amoene,
> quom me in locis Neptuniis templisque turbulentis
> servavit, saevis fluctibus ubi sum adflictata multum.
> (II. v. 1-4)

No one has ever questioned Plautus's *vis comica*. The two plays
of his which we have performed, the *Mostellaria* and the *Miles
Gloriosus*, reveal it in full—and how much more so when they are
acted as well as read. The superb plot of the *Mostellaria* seems to
tail away in the reading; but on the stage the finale was arresting
and touching as well as comic. The *Miles Gloriosus* is uproarious
throughout. It abounds in comic situations. The *Mostellaria* centres
round one vastly funny situation. The best moments in 'A Funny
Thing happened on the way to the Forum' are due to Plautus!

Both Plautus and Terence are dealing with a social background
not dissimilar from our own: their older generation, for the most
part, is living in a past which is exaggeratedly out of touch with
the present. Their young men belong to a 'beat' generation:
they are superficially feckless and irresponsible, but how long will
it be before they are like their fathers? They fall in love with
unsuitable girls, they waste money, they borrow, they entrust
their future to unscrupulous slaves—but deep down they are
introspective and aware of their 'fall from grace'. They are 'mixed
up'. Luckily for them the very circumstances of the play hardly
ever go too far in the direction of awkwardness or embarrassment.
There is nearly always a 'happy ending': fate itself makes sure that
the girl turns out to be 'all right' after all, the money-lender is
coped with, even the slave is not punished for his misdoings.
The whole *mise-en-scène* is in the last resort comfortably insulated

from any real misfortune—by father's bank balance. Is this setting so very dissimilar from that of our own middle classes?

Terence is and has always been our favourite at Westminster. He is not so poetical as Plautus, but his diction is perfect throughout, and totally natural. He reminded me from the start of Mozart: he is uncannily exquisite and strong, fluent and profound. Above all, he is a master of characterization. Of course his plays are full of *senes*, *adulescentes*, *meretrices*, and *lenones*: so are Shakespeare's historical plays full of kings and queens and noblemen. They are not for this reason all the same. The *senes* in the *Phormio*, the *Adelphi*, and the *Heauton Timorumenos* (the three plays we have performed since the war) are all quite different from each other; even Demea in the *Adelphi* is only superficially similar to Demipho in the *Phormio*. They all speak a similar idiom, of course; on paper they look the same, but on the stage they instantly come into their own.

III. THE *PHORMIO*

Mention of the *Phormio* brings me back to the Westminster scene in 1953. The *Phormio* was one of the 'A' Level set books that year, and we felt a kind of duty to read it. We started off with small enthusiasm and continued in the same vein till well into the play. Then suddenly we got excited. We found ourselves repeating Terentian words and expressions: we fell in love with his language, and we fell in love with the play.

After this the form naturally wished to do something about it. The most we thought of at first was an informal rendering of one or two of the funniest scenes in the play. The *Phormio* was the last play acted before the war, in 1938. Anything we did might at least draw attention forcibly to the dormant question of the Latin Play. I myself was not over-optimistic. The problems involved seemed overwhelming. Still, the Election Dinner, a traditional event abandoned during the war, was revived that summer. At this, Latin and Greek epigrams were—and are—regularly recited, and we contented ourselves, for the time being, with supplying the following:

> Qui fuerat quondam, periit Convictus, adestque;
> Qui fuit at periit cur, cedo, Soccus abest?

It was a member of a younger classical form who had the idea which revolutionized everyone's approach to the whole question of the Play's revival. The idea was simple and brilliant. The Play had regularly been acted in College Dormitory, a great room which had been bombed during the war and rebuilt as a number of smaller rooms: it was no longer suitable, therefore, and the problem of where to act the Play if it were revived was in itself enough to damp one's ardour. One possible place was not really large enough, another was not special enough. These arguments were truly valid and no solution seemed acceptable until this boy suggested that the Play be acted in Yard—that is, Little Dean's Yard, the quadrangle on to which the houses and classrooms of the School converge. It is not like a garden or a cloister or somewhere apart, the kind of place where many open-air productions occur; it is the centre and be-all of the School: in it and round it the life of the School vibrates. In the context of school-life it was not the place that would naturally suggest itself for an entertainment. Yet, as the setting for a Latin Play it was—and is—ideal. There are walls for asides, doors interconnected from within, even an old cobbled street, exits and entries on a wide front, everything in short that is required by the action of nearly every Latin play (see Plate 7). Once suggested, the idea was irresistible. And it was agreed that a performance of the *Phormio* should be given in Yard, in 1954.

There still remained, however, a large number of subsidiary problems. The choice of Yard itself necessitated a performance in the Summer Term. Yet the Play had always been acted in the late autumn. In fact the Autumn Term is still called the Play Term in honour of it. However, the Election (the closed Scholarship to Christ Church and Trinity, Cambridge) had originally been in the Summer, and the Summer Term was and is called the Election Term, though the examination has now been held for many years in November. If the Election could take place in the Play Term, why should not the Play be performed in the Election Term? It was decided to put on the *Phormio* on the Ides of July, St. Swithin's Day!

After the two great decisions of time and place were made, other problems seemed to solve themselves. It was still necessary to decide what kind of occasion the Play was to be. An eminent Old Westminster, hearing that it was to be revived, asked our present Head Master—he was then Under Master—one question

6. Plautus *Mostellaria* at Westminster, 1958.

Tranio: Eho, an tetigisti has aedis?

Theoropides: Qur non tangerem?

(II. ii. 24)

7. Plautus' *Mostellaria* at Westminster, 1958.

Tranio: Iuppiter supremus summis opibus atque industriis
me periise et Philolachetem cupit erilem filium.

(II. i. 1-2)

only. 'Is it white ties or black?' It was to be neither. There was no attempt to continue the Play as a Social Occasion: apart from masters, boys, parents, and Old Westminsters, people were invited from universities and other schools; the Prologue and the Epilogue were severely reduced in size: the play was to be the thing, and it was hoped that a large part of the audience would follow it for its own sake.

There were also problems of dress and pronunciation. The very beautiful costumes of the old Play had been carefully preserved throughout the war years: so had the splendid back-cloth, dating from the nineteenth century, which depicts Athens, with the Acropolis in the distance. The costumes were 'ancient dress', and matched the back-cloth ideally. But now the 'back-cloth' was Ashburnham House, one of the School buildings, and ancient dress seemed less appropriate. Moreover, if Latin Plays were, as we felt they were, relevant to modern times, and if their themes and characters were readily approachable, there could be no good purpose served in putting the barrier of dress between the audience and the Play. We decided—at the risk of offending Old Westminsters—to use modern dress, and by so doing were actually following the earliest traditions of the Play: in its first productions, the dress worn was Elizabethan, and classical costumes were not introduced until 1829.

The Play had always been performed in the Westminster pronunciation of Latin: this is an English pronunciation with certain variations of its own; it is still used at Latin Prayers and for the recitation of Latin epigrams at the Election Dinner. Here again it was feared that Old Westminsters would disapprove of the new foreign pronunciation: but it was also evident that any chance of the Play's being understood, except by Old Westminsters, would be reduced to nil by the adoption of the English pronunciation. The School itself has for a long time now used the new pronunciation in the classroom. It was decided that as there were so many departures anyway from the old Play, an additional one would have to be risked and the new pronunciation used.

Finally, who was to act the Play? Traditionally, it was always performed by the Scholars alone, but there seemed no good reason for excluding the many gifted Town Boys who were classical specialists. Common sense suggested that the new Play should be acted by members of the classical forms, and this decision was also taken.

Phormio himself spoke the Prologue of the Play. It was written by the Classical VIIth (Scholarship form) in the traditional metre: I myself wrote the short Epilogue in elegiacs. And this arrangement has continued to the present. To our surprise we have found that puns—so much despised by modern purists—have crept back gradually in full force into Prologue and Epilogue. The following is part of the Prologue written for the *Phormio*. It is spoken by Phormio himself and sums up most of the problems I have mentioned:

> Dicunt duellum fulguribus flagrantibus
> demolivisse pristinum collegium:
> sed me non omne fulgur explosit quod est
> neque umquam explodet donec lectitabitur
> a pueris lingua Westmonasteriensibus
> nostra: at nunc dicam quot modis mutatu' sim:
> primo Scholares cum Oppidanorum grege
> agent me—eorum scilicet qui una student
> utrique linguae; dein pronuntiatio
> quae iam usurpatur, sane sit recentior,
> at eadem, quod solet fieri, antiquissima est;
> haec vestimenta tertio quae cernitis
> maiorum more sunt contemporanea;
> postremo, a Marte pulsos recipit Iuppiter. . . .
> sed ecce Davos: exeundum est; enico.

This part of the Prologue was translated in the programme as follows:

> Oh, I remember now: a bomb, they say
> Burnt College down on an unhappy day.
> But no amount of bombs that ever were
> Can ever kill me while at Westminster
> Boys learn the Classics: all the same you'll see
> How many ways the years have altered me.
> First, not just Scholars will be here on view;
> There are Town Boy Classics in this too;
> Next, we pronounce it modern—as you know,
> The ancient Romans used to speak it so;
> Again, these clothes—as always used to be
> The usual custom—are contemp'rary;
> Lastly, since Mars has bombed us out of home,
> Jove takes us in beneath his aerial dome.

The programme of the *Phormio* was typed and duplicated. There was an atmosphere of informality about the new Play: over the years, this has slightly altered: recent programmes have been printed. A long synopsis is, however, still duplicated. The preparation of it is a great labour, but it seems to justify itself. It is true that a long synopsis may either remain unread or may draw the audience's attention away from the 'stage'. But a short synopsis, particularly of Terence's plays, is useless.

The Epilogue of the *Phormio* was modelled on the most famous scene in the play, where Demipho, *senex*, asks the advice of his friends—three *advocati*—as to how he should proceed in the matter of his son's unwelcome marriage. The first two give directly opposite advice and the third reserves judgment—after which Demipho is worse off than ever.

Demipho: Qualis nunc fuerit comoedia nostra videtis:
    debeat haec iterum fabula necne dari,
  Hegio, dic.
Hegio: Ego? Si visumst, prior ille Cratinus
  censeat.
Demipho: At dictum redde, Cratine, mihi.
Cratinus: Mene vocas?
Demipho: Te.
Cratinus: Sic visumst mihi: talia debent,
  quae prosint, fieri. Si qua solebat agi
  fabula prisca olim, quam non intellegit ullus,
  cur non iure bono desinet illa? Tene.
Demipho: Hegio, nunc dicas.
Hegio: Ego rite hunc dicere credo;
  at populus variis moribus esse solet:
  nam quot sunt homines, sua fit sententia cuique.
  Non mihi reginae traditione piae
  quod sanctum fuerit rescindi posse videtur,
  et turpe inceptu est.
Demipho: Dic, Crito.
Crito: Plura mihi
  consilia exquiras: res magna est.
Hegio: Iam licet ire?
Demipho: Fecistis probius. (*Aside*) Si tamen ante fui
  incertus, multo sum nunc incertior. (*To audience*) Ecce,
  quid dubito? Vobis res agitanda manet.

This was translated as follows:

Demipho: You've seen our comedy and how it went.
　　　　Should we again, my Hegio, present
　　　　A Latin play, or not?
Hegio: 　　　　　　　　If you agree,
　　　　Let's ask Cratinus first.
Demipho: 　　　　　　　　Then answer me,
　　　　Cratinus.
Cratinus: 　　　I?
Demipho: 　　　　　　Yes, you.
Cratinus: 　　　　　　　　Then I suggest
　　　　That one should always do that which is best.
　　　　A dead old play which none can understand,
　　　　Though once performed, should now, mark you, be
　　　　　banned.
Demipho: Hegio, please.
Hegio: 　　　　　　　　I'm sure our friend means well,
　　　　But since we're all so different, who can tell
　　　　Another man's opinion? To my mind
　　　　That which our pious foundress has designed
　　　　As one of our traditions, cannot be,
　　　　Without disgrace, rescinded legally.
Demipho: Well, Crito?
Crito: 　　　　　　　I should say this needs more thought.
　　　　It's knotty.
Hegio: 　　　　May we go now?
Demipho: 　　　　　　　You have brought
　　　　Most excellent advice. Farewell. (*Aside*) Yet if before
　　　　I was in doubt, I still am—and much more!
　　　　(*To audience*) But heavens! Why should I make all this
　　　　　fuss?
　　　　It's up to you to work it out, not us.

The audience was for the new Play: it had come to stay.

Though we have done four plays since the *Phormio*—the Play is now biennial—I still remember whole lines of the Phormio more clearly than those of the later plays. There is something so final and unalterable about its most ordinary statements. The opening lines spoken by Davos, a slave, remain fixed in my mind, perhaps because I now see them as unfolding the whole sequence of play and plays that were to follow them:

　　Da.: Amicu' summu' meus et popularis Geta
　　　　heri ad me venit. erat ei de ratiuncula

iampridem apud me relicuom pauxillulum
nummorum: id ut conficerem. confeci: adfero.   (I. i. 1-4)

Who could forget the tongue-twisting soliloquy of Geta when
he runs back in horror from the harbour with the news that his
master Demipho has unexpectedly returned?

Ge.: Nullus es, Geta, nisi iam aliquod tibi consilium celere reperis,
ita nunc imparatum subito tanta te impendent mala! (I. iv. 1-2)

For sheer mastery of word order, could anything be more
memorable than Demipho's opening speech, as he comes stumping
on to the stage? He has just heard of his son's marriage:

De.: Itane tandem uxorem duxit Antipho—iniussu meo?
nec meum imperium—ac mitto imperium—non simultatem
meam
revereri saltem! non pudere! facinus audax! O Geta
monitor!
Ge.: (*popping up from behind the wall*): Vix tandem!   (II. i. 1-4)

The famous scenes with the *advocati* start with Demipho again,
enunciating the most onomatopoeic of Latin lines imaginable:

De.: Enumquam quoiquam contumeliosius
audisti' factam iniuriam quam haec est mihi?
adeste quaeso.   (II. iii. 1-3)

Compare the first line with the undoubted τί ποτ'οὖν's of the
Greek original, and the full genius of the Latin language stands
revealed.

The scene where Demipho asks the advice of the *advocati*
abounds in famous quotations. Cratinus speaks first. He says that
Antipho's marriage can be decently annulled. Hegio comes next.
Apologetically he tells us that:

He.: Quot homines, tot sententiae: suo' quoique mos.

(II. iv. 14)

He thinks that the marriage cannot decently be annulled. Demipho
turns to Crito—traditionally played by the smallest scholar—who
throws light on the situation with the words:

Cri.: Ego amplius deliberandum censeo:
res magnast.   (*Ibid.*, 17-18)

These famous lines were regularly clapped at old performances of the Play, and there were many other lines in the *Phormio* which were formally clapped, some for obvious reasons, others through usage. This pleasant custom has not grown up with the new Play, as we do not stick to the cycle any more. I dare say it would, if we performed any play again in the presence of Old Westminsters who remembered an earlier performance.

Demipho thanks his friends courteously for their advice:

De.:   fecistis probe: (*Ibid.*, 18)

but in the next line he turns to the audience, at his wits' end:

De.: Incertior sum multo quam dudum fui.

The part of Demipho is particularly exacting. He is hardly ever off the stage. I can never understand how boys can remember parts running into many hundreds of lines. There is an apocryphal story that the boy who was prompting the *Phormio* lost his place during the first speech and never found it again. Fortunately this did not matter. Demipho not only knew his own part impeccably but on occasions prompted his interlocutors *sotto voce*.

We have always aimed above all at a natural, colloquial style of diction combined with clarity. The most complimentary remarks that I have heard after plays have been to the effect that Latin has been made to sound like a living language, and that the actors seemed totally at home in it.

To return to the *Phormio*. I remember with delight the scene where Phormio, the parasite, unmasks Chremes, Demipho's brother, who has kept hidden from his formidable wife Nausistrata the fact that he had long ago married a second wife—since dead—in Lemnos.

Ph.: Hic quandam noram quoius vir uxorem
Ch.:   hem.
De.:   quid est?
Ph.: Lemni habuit aliam,
Ch.:   nullu' sum.
Ph.:   ex qua filiam
   suscepit; et eam clam educat.
Ch.:   sepultu' sum.
             (V. viii. 48-50)

In the next and final scene, Phormio tells all to Nausistrata:

Ch.: Non opus est dicto.
Ph.: tibi quidem; at scito huic opust.
in Lemno
De.: hem quid ais?
Ch.: non taces?
Ph.: clam te
Ch.: ei mihi!
Ph.: uxorem duxit.
Na.: mi homo, di melius duint!

(V. ix. 14-16)

Luckily Chremes comes out of it slightly better than he had expected. The old Play traditionally gave him lines 58-9 of this last scene:

Ch.: immo vero pulchre discedo et probe
et praeter spem.

These lines were traditionally clapped; and a little later the play ends with the familiar 'vos valete et plaudite!'

Throughout the play, on July 15th, 1954, rain threatened but kept off; it was a cold evening; there was no marquee for the audience; the actors used a minimum of make-up; the lights were largely lent by a recent Old Westminster, the clothes were borrowed, the props were more or less non-existent. I believe the whole production cost less than £5. There was one performance only. Now there is a marquee, there are four performances, and further elaboration in make-up, costumes and props. But I hope that the essential spirit of spontaneity and exuberance is still as much to the fore as it was throughout the performance of the *Phormio* ten years ago.

IV. THE *MILES GLORIOSUS*

The *Phormio* was one of the Westminster cycle, and was performed in the abbreviated Westminster version. In the *Miles Gloriosus* we departed from the cycle, and performed the play with comparatively few cuts. It was, in fact, one of the very first plays ever performed at Westminster, and we were glad to revive it in 1956. For the Epilogue we were particularly lucky to have two boys who were identical twins: their name was Bland, and as the twin *motif* comes into the play, it was easy to work them in. To make things unbelievably better still, their initials were E and R respectively, and they were known as Bland E and Bland R. Thus the following lines in the Epilogue were possible:

> ille, puto,
> ingeniist blandi, caret hic tamen indole blanda.

The first night of the *Miles Gloriosus* came after what was, I believe, the wettest day in this country for eighty years. Throughout the afternoon armies of boys swept puddles away from the acting area in Yard. The rain continued remorselessly till two minutes before the play was due to start, and began again immediately after it: and the same thing happened on the second night.

The opening scene of the play was a great opportunity for a motley corps-parade. The soldier comes in at the head of a band of recruits, to whom he cries out the following order:

Py.: Curate ut splendor meo sit clupeo clarior
quam solis radii esse olim quom sudumst solent.

(I. i. 1-2)

It is tempting to quote the whole scene, where Pyrgopolynices, the soldier, boasts away at his parasite Artotrogus, who loads him with gross flattery:

Ar.:   Mars haud ausit dicere
neque aequiperare suas virtutes ad tuas.
Py.: quemne ego servavi in campis Curculionieis,
ubi Bumbomachides Clutomestoridysarchides
erat imperator summus, Neptuni nepos?
Ar.: memini. nempe illum dicis cum armis aureis
quoius tu legiones difflavisti spiritu
quasi ventus folia aut peniculum tectorium.
Py.: istuc quidem edepol nihil est.
Ar.:   nihil hercle hoc quidemst
praeut alia dicam—(*to audience*) quae tu numquam feceris.

(I. i. 11-20)

Later in the scene Artotrogus mentions the elephant in India whose 'arm' the soldier broke with his fist.

Py.: quid 'bracchium'?
Ar.:   illud dicere volui, 'femur.'
Py.: at indiligenter iceram.

(*Ibid.*, 27-8)

Later still, Artotrogus tots up the number of men killed by
Pyrgopolynices in one day: this speech is very reminiscent of
Leporello's famous geographical account of Don Giovanni's
conquests in love:

> *Ar.:*   memini centum in Cilicia
> et quinquaginta, centum in Scytholatronia,
> triginta Sardos, sexaginta Macedones—
> sunt homines quos tu—occidisti uno die.
> *Py.:* quanta istaec hominum summast?
> *Ar.:*   septem milia.
> *Py.:* tantum esse oportet. recte rationem tenes.
>
> *(Ibid., 42-7)*

Artotrogus goes on to say how all the women in the town are
in love with the soldier, taking him for Achilles. Pyrgopolynices
finds their worship rather a bore:

> *Py.:* Nimiast miseria nimi' pulchrum esse hominem.
>
> *(Ibid., 68)*

The scene ends with the soldier marching off his recruits in true
military style:

> *Py.:*   Sequimini, satellites!
>
> *(Ibid., 78)*

Perhaps this is the best scene in the play: the soldier is off the
stage for too long after it. There is plenty of interest, though,
in the other characters. Periplectomenus gives a most revealing
account of himself: he has many reasons for his avoidance of
marriage: he wants no children, since:

> *Pe.:* Pol si habuissem, sati' cepissem miseriarum e liberis:
> continuo excruciarer animi: si ei fort' fuisset febris,
> censerem emori; cecidissetve ebrius aut de equo uspiam,
> metuerem ne ibi diffregisset crura aut cervices sibi.
>
> *(III. i. 122-5)*

Sceledrus, the stupid slave, is a most pathetic character. He
knows full well how his days will end:

> *Sc.:* Noli minitari: scio crucem futuram mihi sepulcrum;
> ibi mei maiores sunt siti, pater, avos, proavos, abavos.
>
> *(II. iv. 19-20)*

The *Miles Gloriosus* abounds in comic situations. In one scene
the soldier is being fooled into believing that the non-existent
wife of his neighbour Periplectomenus is madly in love with him.
Palaestrio, his slave, is telling him the 'good news':

Pa.: ad tuam formam illa una dignast.
Py.:   hercle pulchram praedicas.
    sed quis east?
Pa.:   senis huius uxor Periplectomeni e proxumo.
    ea demoritur te atque ab illo cupit abire: odit senem.

(IV. i. 21-3)

A little later, Pyrgopolynices remembers his current mistress,
Philocomasium. (The whole of Palaestrio's pretence is in fact
aimed at inducing his master to set her free: the soldier falls for it,
hook line and sinker.) Pyrgopolynices asks with characteristic
indelicacy:

Py.:   quid illa faciemus concubina quae domist?
Pa.: quin tu illam iube aps te abire quo lubet. . . .

(*Ibid.*, 26-7)

He is persuaded to let Philocomasium go and to give her plenty of
valuable presents so that the thing can be done decently. He is
still a little worried though. What if he finds himself off with the
one love and not on with the other? Palaestrio reassures him:

Py.: placet ut dicis; sed ne istanc amittam et haec mutet fidem
    vide modo.
Pa.:   vah! delicatu's, quae te tamquam oculos amet.
Py.: Venu' me amat.

(*Ibid.*, 36-8)

In the next scene Palaestrio praises Pyrgopolynices to
Milphidippa, whose mistress Acroteleutium is cast, for the plot's
sake, in the role of Periplectomenus's wife. Milphidippa is, of
course, in the plot, and plays up to Palaestrio, while the soldier
adds his own comments:

Pa.: Meri bellatores gignuntur, quas hic praegnatis fecit,
    et pueri annos octingentos vivont.
Mi.:   vae tibi, nugator!
Py.: quin mille annorum perpetuo vivont ab saeclo ad saeclum.
Pa.: eo minu' dixi ne haec censeret me advorsum se mentiri.
Mi.: perii! quot hic ipse annos vivet, quoius filii tam diu vivont?
Py.: postriduo natus sum ego, mulier, quam Iuppiter ex Ope natust.

(IV. ii. 89-94)

In Scene vi of the same act, Acroteleutium appears and pretends not to notice the soldier, who speaks aside (in our production crouching behind a wall, his horse-guard's helmet remaining well in view) to Palaestrio. Acroteleutium is 'confessing' her 'love' for the soldier to Milphidippa in a suitably carrying voice:

Ac.:	opsecro, tute ipsum convenisti?
	(*Aside to Milphidippa*) Ne parce vocem, ut audiat.
Mi.:	cum ipso pol sum locuta,
	placide, ipsae dum lubitum est mihi, otiose, meo arbitratu.
Py.:	audin quae loquitur?
Pa.:	audio. quam laeta est quia ted adiit!
Ac.:	O fortunata mulier es!
Py.:	ut amari videor!
Pa.:	dignu's.

(IV. vi. 4-8)

Acroteleutium lays it on thick. She suddenly pretends that though she cannot see the soldier, she has caught a scent of him. Then she sees him; it is too much for her:

Ac.:	tene me opsecro.
Mi.:	qur?
Ac.:	ne cadam.
Mi.:	quid ita?
Ac.:	quia stare nequeo,
	ita animus per oculos meos meu' defit.
Mi.:	militem pol
	tu aspexisti.
Ac.:	ita.
Mi.:	non video. ubi est?
Ac.:	videres pol, si amares.

(*Ibid.*, 45-7)

At this height of tension, Pyrgopolynices suddenly feels it necessary to impart the following information to Palaestrio:

Py.:	nescio tu ex me hoc audiveris an non: nepos sum Veneris.

(*Ibid.*, 50)

'Stop me if you've heard this one. . . . !'

The next scene but one is equally full of delicious fun. The soldier is sending Philocomasium away. In fact, she is delighted, as she is going straight off to her lover Pleusicles. But she pretends to be desolate with grief:

Ph.: istuc crucior, a viro tali abalienarier . . .

(IV. viii. 11)

A little later the soldier consoles her:

Py.:   a! ne fle.
Ph.:   non queo,
quom te video.

(*Ibid.*, 14-15)

She is inconsolable:

Ph.: opsecro licet complecti priu' quam proficisco?
Py.:   licet.
Ph.: o mi ocule, o mi anime.
Pa.:   opsecro, tene mulierem,
ne adfligatur.
Py.:   quid istuc quaesost?
Pa.:   quia aps te abit, animo male
factum est huic repente miserae.
Py.:   curre intro atque ecferto aquam.

(*Ibid.*, 19-22)

The departure of Philocomasium with all her luggage was a great opportunity for slapstick of every kind throughout this tumultuous scene.

In the end the soldier is caught by Periplectomenus and his *lorarii*, and comes within an ace of losing his manhood. His heroism is found distinctly wanting; he learns that he has been fooled by Palaestrio; for a moment his morale is totally lost:

Py.:   vae misero mihi!
verba mihi data esse video. scelu' viri Palaestrio
is me in hanc inlexit fraudem.

(V. i. 40-2)

Then suddenly with a magic touch the last lines of the play introduce us to a new Pyrgopolynices—no longer an adulterer but a pillar of the establishment, a writer to *The Times*, a deplorer of modern decadence; we are left with this glimpse into his future life, which pleases us no more than what we have seen of him to date:

Py.:   iure factum iudico;
si sic aliis moechis fiat, minus hic moechorum siet.
magi' metuant, minus has res studeant.

(Ibid., 42-4)

In our production he had been dishevelled, his helmet removed, during this last scene: but as he spoke these final words he tidied himself and replaced his helmet; then, fully master of himself again, he invites the whole cast to his house, and as he marches off the stage, turns to the audience and barks his final instructions at them:

Py.:   eamus ad me—plaudite.

V. THE *MOSTELLARIA*

The *Mostellaria* (1958) was performed without any cuts, and this has been the case with the two subsequent plays also. Its plot is uniquely ingenious and flows with wonderful inevitability from one situation to another. As a result, I think it was followed more closely by the audience than any other play. It had a number of picturesque props, suggested by the plot. Philolaches, one of the young men, held his party at white garden tables with umbrellas. These, incidentally, were blown over at the dress rehearsal; fortunately, as it turned out, since otherwise we might not have thought of weighing them down with heavy stones during the performances: even so, they nearly gave way more than once. And then, at Callidamates' entrance, we replaced his litter with a bright red bubble-car which was driven into Yard from the Abbey Cloisters and which gave me endless cause for alarm. Even at the dress rehearsal it had to be pushed on to the 'stage', and my relief each night as its engine revved up at the crucial moment was great.

The plot of the *Mostellaria* raised one big problem. At the end of the play Tranio, the slave, seeks refuge at an *'ara'*. What was the modern equivalent of an *'ara'*—a place so sacred that one could not decently be torn away from it? It may be an equivocal comment on our age that only one really convincing parallel suggested itself—the *'viri'*. We therefore adopted this solution, and in true Plautine style asked in the Prologue if any of the audience wished to visit our *'ara'* before the play started.

The plot of the *Mostellaria* revolves round the character of Tranio. He is the rascally slave *par excellence:* with incredible skill he steers his way from one crisis to another. He is not the frightened minion: he is a lord of scheme and intrigue, and he revels in it:

> *Tr.:* Alexandrum magnum atque Agathoclem aiunt maxumas
> duo res gessisse: quid mihi fiet tertio,
> qui solus facio facinora immortalia?

> (III. ii. 85-7)

Earlier, he had not been quite so confident, it is true. One of my happiest memories of this play is of Tranio returning from a shopping expedition—absent-mindedly waving around the fish he has bought and bewailing the return of his master Theoropides from abroad:

> *Tr.:* Iuppiter supremus summis opibus atque industriis
> me periisse et Philolachetem cupit erilem filium.

> (II. i. 1-2; see Plate VII)

But as his plot thickens, and as his control of the situation becomes increasingly effective, he enjoys every moment of it. Even at the end, when he is finally unmasked, he refuses to utter a syllable of remorse, thus winning willy-nilly our respect and admiration.

In the *Mostellaria* we made a lot of the silent parts who are implied by the text. Once, before the revival of the Latin Play, I had produced a performance of Theocritus's Fifteenth Idyll. It was a lesson to me to see how important on the stage was the part of the girl Eunoe, who does not say anything, and whom one hardly thinks of as a person in the reading. She emerges not merely as a chance for 'business', but as a real character in her own right, a classic day dreamer (Εὐνόα, οὐ φευξῇ;—she is just saved from being run over: ἀπρὶξ ἔχευ, Εὐνόα ἁμῶν—where is she now? φλίβεται Εὐνόα ἄμμιν—she is getting crushed. 'Push, you silly girl!'). In the *Mostellaria* we had to get our garden tables, plates and drinks, let alone one drunken guest, into the house in double quick time. It is all in the text, of course:

> *Philol.:* quid ego nunc faciam?
> *Tr.:*　　　　　　　iube haec hinc omnia amolirier.

> (II. i. 24)

Whom is Philolaches (Theoropides' young son) to give these orders to? We made use of four young *pueri*—one is mentioned in I. iii. 151—who presided over the party and its rapid removal, wearing our formal College dress. They nearly stole the show.

The whole question of 'business' is a very important one indeed for any producer, and particularly for the producer of a play in which the language-barrier is constantly to the fore. In Greek tragedy there is of course the same problem superficially, but it is a very different one in points of detail. In the earlier tragedies particularly, audiences do not expect the same kind of constant vital action and interplay that they expect in Comedy; they come prepared for long, stately soliloquies, and provided the right atmosphere of dignity is produced, they are content. The problem of 'business' arises more with the chorus, where the heightened tension of the language calls for some corresponding excitement in the performance. Far and away the most successful portrayal of a Greek chorus that I have seen was in the Bradfield production of the *Oedipus Coloneus*, where the choreography closely followed the lyric metres of the Greek. If you stick to the original you cannot go far wrong.

Spurious 'business' is anathema to me in the production of any play, even one in a foreign language where the temptation to throw a sop to the audience in this way is very high. It is an insult to the audience and to the author. I hate the implication that 'we must do a bit of pepping up here: someone must fall over; something must be broken; someone must make a vulgar noise.' If we stick to the text there is endless opportunity for legitimate 'business'. For example, in the *Miles Gloriosus*, in the scene where the soldier and Palaestrio are eavesdropping the conversation between Acroteleutium and Milphidippa, at one place Palaestrio says '*tace, ne audiat*'. It is legitimate to assume that the soldier has just made a noise. We had some milk bottles available which he knocked over and broke (incidentally, I am sure that many a producer has discovered, like myself, how much rehearsing it takes to break a bottle successfully). I borrowed here from a scene in a Laurel and Hardy film, where the two are trying to burgle a house and Hardy falls into a greenhouse: after many minutes of shattering noise, Laurel peers into the débris anxiously saying 'Sh! Sh!' So we tried to create as much noise as possible with these milk-bottles in order to make '*tace ne audiat*' all the funnier. It was interesting to me that one audience laughed loudly at the noise and hardly at all at the words following, the other only politely at the noise, but uproariously at the words.

Similarly, in the *Mostellaria* we made full use of '*pueri*' and also of our '*ara*'. There are places where Theoropides' presence is undesired, yet he could not go away for long. He tells us in his first speech that he is scarcely alive after his long sea voyage. What more plausible or convenient excuse could there be for a brief absence than a visit to the '*ara*'?

I have mentioned Philolaches, Theoropides' son. He is an interesting and unusual character. The first *canticum*, in which he deplores his decline into low ways, is far from funny. The language is profound and, in places, reminiscent of the Bible. The whole *canticum* should be read as a single poem (I. ii). The same Philolaches changes instantly, however, the minute he ceases to be alone and sees his delightful girl Philematium. There is a wonderful little character-vignette here in this metamorphosis, so very life-like and convincing.

The most memorable scene to me in the *Mostellaria* is the one where Tranio is showing Theoropides round the house of Simo, his old neighbour, having persuaded Theoropides—untruly of course—that Philolaches, his son, has bought it for him off Simo for a song, and having told Simo that Theoropides admires his house and wants to look round it in order to copy some of its features. There is good reason for all these inventions, of course, and every minute the cat is nearly out of the bag: each time, Tranio, who is totally at his ease, saves the situation at the eleventh hour:

Si.:   salvom te advenisse peregre gaudeo, Theoropides.
Th.:   di te ament.
Si.:   inspicere te aedis has velle aiebat mihi.
Th.:   nisi tibi est incommodum.
Si.:   immo commodum. i intro atque inspice.
Th.:   at enim mulieres—
Si.:   cave tu ullam flocci faxis mulierem.
         qualubet perambula aedis oppido tamquam tuas.
Th.:   'tamquam'?

(It is almost impossible not to say this '*tamquam*' in a Lady Bracknell voice.)

8. *A Funny Thing* . . . 'Death by Evisceration'.

9. *A Funny Thing* . . . 'Courtesans . . . The finest assortment in Rome . . .'

Tr.: ah, cave tu illi obiectes nunc in aegritudine
te has emisse. non tu vides hunc voltu uti tristi est senex ?

(III. ii. 115-21)

Theoropides is most impressed by Tranio's '*humanitas*'—poor
Simo is so upset at having let the house go cheap—he will tactfully
keep quiet about it: we breathe again, since, needless to say, we
have thoroughly identified ourselves by now with Tranio.

The last scene is also memorable. Tranio is at the '*ara*' surrounded
by vicious *lorarii*. Callidamates, a young 'blood', who was
delightfully and stutteringly drunk at the beginning of the play:

(*Cal.:* ecquid tibi videor ma-ma-madere? (I. iv. 7))

emerges sober now and begs Theoropides to let Tranio off.
Theoropides is loth to agree, until finally Tranio himself gives him
a valid reason for doing so:

Tr.: quid gravaris? quasi non cras iam commeream aliam noxiam:
ibi utrumque, et hoc et illud, poteris ulcisci probe.
Ca.: Sine te exorem.
Th.: age abi, abi impune. em huic habeto gratiam.

(V. ii. 56-8)

By the last scene, Little Dean's Yard has grown quite dark.
Ashburnham House—the 'backcloth'—has a mellow light all over
it, and in the *Mostallria* the three main characters were spotlighted
in different parts of the foreground. It is a beautiful visual memory,
and I can see it in my mind's eye now as Theoropides addressed
the next and last line to the audience. These last lines never fail to
send a thrill down my back. Could relief have anything to do with it?

Th.: Spectatores, fabula haec est acta, vos plausum date.

A distinguished Old Westminster gave me great pleasure by
comparing our production of the Latin Play in the new style with
the old pictures that had recently been cleaned in the National
Gallery. I cannot remember whether this was after the *Miles
Gloriosus* or the *Mostellaria*, but I have never forgotten the
comparison.

VI. THE *ADELPHI*

'Fabula est acta', 'Vivat Fabula'. More than once I have consoled
myself for the empty feeling with which I was left as the last

performance of a play drew to its close, by rehearsing inwardly the first scene of the next play. The *Adelphi* was an obvious choice for 1960. It was the year of our Quatercentenary, comparable with the year 1937, when King George VI had been to the Play. In that year the *Adelphi* was the play, and it seemed appropriate to return for the occasion to the cycle.

Yet, though it was a joy to come back to Terence, there were disadvantages involved in this return. Old Westminsters who remembered the old performances tended to be put off by departure from traditional interpretations. Our chief departure was perhaps concerned with the character of Micio. He is an elderly bachelor, living in town, who has adopted one of his brother Demea's sons. Demea lives in the country and is a strict and intolerant father to his other son. Micio is gentle and forbearing, more concerned with receiving the love of his adopted son Aeschinus than with punishing him for his faults. It had apparently been traditional to portray Micio as a self-indulgent, pampered old man, fat and comfortable. But I could not find this in the text. On the contrary, he seemed a pathetic figure, so obviously unsuccessful in his attempt to win love through permissive kindliness, forced in the end to marry his unattractive neighbour, Sostrata, full of *Angst*, as the first scene amply reveals. Our Micio had a most sad and wistful voice. It pleased me greatly to hear of a message sent to him by an old gentleman in the audience, over eighty years of age. I cannot remember the exact words, but the gist of it was that Micio had the most beautiful voice that the old gentleman had ever heard and had given him more pleasure than he had received for very many years or had ever hoped to receive again. I felt justified by this alone for our casting—perhaps not quite rationally. It gave me greater pleasure still when an eminent professor, who was present at the play, came behind the scene afterwards and answered my anxious question, 'Did you agree with our interpretation of Micio?' by saying that he *did*, since the play, great comedy that it was, was indeed akin to tragedy.

A great compliment was paid to me indirectly by one of our Modern Languages staff after the *Adelphi*. 'You know, Zinn', he said to me, 'this Terence is really quite good'. This made me very happy because I consider the producer's main task to be the furtherance of his author's cause. For this reason, I feel that it is of the utmost importance to render the beautiful Latin of Plautus and Terence with the greatest accuracy of quantity and metrical sensitivity. I have frequently wished that we could have had the author in the audience, and have imagined him watching us—I hope with approval—from another world.

Is Micio's first speech suggestive of a fat, smug debauchee?

Mi.: Storax!—non rediit hac nocte a cena Aeschinus
neque servolorum quisquam qui advorsum ierant. . . .
ego quia non rediit filius quae cogito et
quibus nunc sollicitor rebu'! ne aut ille alserit
aut uspiam ceciderit aut praefregerit
aliquid. vah quemquamne hominem in animo instituere aut
parare quod sit carius quam ipsest sibi!

(I. i. 1-2 and 10-14)

A little later he criticizes his brother, Demea:

Mi.: nimium ipse durust praeter aequomque et bonum,
et errat longe mea quidem sententia
qui imperium credat gravius esse aut stabilius
vi quod fit quam illud quod amicitia adiungitur.

(I. i. 39-42)

Demea is convinced that his harsh methods of upbringing are correct. Micio, one feels, is trying to persuade himself that his own opposite views are sound. Both are wrong. And the final unfolding of their wrongness is so full of pathos and delicacy, so moving and so true to life, that I consider the *Adelphi* the greatest of the five plays we have acted, though the character of Chremes in the *Heauton Timorumenos* seems to me the greatest single achievement in these plays.

As the *Adelphi* was performed in our Quatercentenary year, it had a relevant prologue. An Old Westminster, of 16th century vintage, has turned up to the Play, four hundred years late,

cum Transportatione sim Britannica
advectus huc.

He is most indignant at being stopped by a monitor on duty and asked for a ticket, but is at last pacified and led off to a seat.

quin per saecla quattuor (says the monitor)
in bello, in pace, per vicissitudines
omnes fortunae perduravit fabula
Latina, durat, semper obduret, precor.

The Old Westminster returns in the Epilogue and rebukes the two old men and the two sons for not rushing off to the Bursar and entering Aeschinus's new-born baby for Westminster.

The play starts with 'Storax!' Is this an interjection? Or a slave? The commentators are divided. We made it a slave, who entered with such a deadpan expression on his face, suggesting that he had been sent on so many similar missions in the past, to look for Aeschinus, and knew so well what to expect, that he was utterly cynical of Micio's fuss and bother, yet perforce tolerant of it; Storax brought the house down in the first line, and told us with one facial expression what half the play was about.

The most famous scene in the *Adelphi* is Demea's soliloquy in Act V. He starts off with bitter resentment of his lot. He compares his own strictness and austerity with his brother's leniency and—as he sees it—indulgence. And what has he got out of it all? Nothing.

> *De.:* ill' suam semper egit vitam in otio, in conviviis,
> clemens placidu', nulli laedere os, adridere omnibus;
> sibi vixit, sibi sumptum fecit: omnes bene dicunt, amant.
> ego ille agresti' saevo' tristi' parcu' truculentus tenax
> duxi uxorem: quam ibi miseriam vidi! . . .
>
> (V. iv. 9-13)

He continues, a little later:

> *De.:* nunc exacta aetate hoc fructi pro labore ab eis fero,
> odium; ille alter sine labore patria potitur commoda.
> illum amant, me fugitant; illi credunt consilia omnia. . . .
>
> (*Ibid.*, 16-18)

He greatly overestimates Micio's success with the young men' and in his misery sees nothing but his own comparative failure with the son whom he has brought up. Suddenly, he has a wonderful idea. Why should he continue to suffer like this? Why should not he become like his brother? Why should not he too be *clemens* and *placidus*? He has just said:

> *De.:* miseriam omnem ego capio, hic potitur gaudia.

And then comes the sudden change. Our Demea had been sitting on a street-bench facing the audience, his head in his hands, the picture of dejection. Then, after a pause, he looked up excitedly, and his soul was transformed before us:

De.: age age, nunc iam experiamur contra ecquid ego possiem
blande dicere aut benigne facere, quando hoc provocat.
ego quoque a meis me amari et magni pendi postulo: . . .

(Ibid., 22-5)

He tries out, with immediate success, his 'new look' on Syrus,
Micio's rascally slave, and on Geta, the slave of Sostrata, Micio's
neighbour. And he continues to shed light all around him, much
to the embarrassment of Micio. It is a wonderful *dénouement*, though
we are all relieved when at the very end he returns to his former
self, a little chastened. Even Aeschinus, his son, seems relieved by
this decision. Before it is reached, however, Demea has caused
the wall between Micio's and Sostrata's houses to be destroyed.
This is an exaggerated expression of his sudden acceptance of the
fact that Aeschinus has seduced Sostrata's daughter Pamphila. He
has had to acquiesce in, nay rather to insist on, Aeschinus'
marrying the girl. Now, he positively revels in it, and goes on to
make Micio marry the widow Sostrata.

The demolition of the wall was no easy problem. I shall never
cease to recall gratefully the member of our School staff who built
up day after day, not only for the performances but also for many
rehearsals a very sizeable brick wall for us to destroy. It is no
easier, incidentally, to demolish a wall (however lightly built) than
to break a bottle—certainly not to do so convincingly.

There is an uproarious scene near the beginning of the play
where Sannio, the pimp, pursues Aeschinus, who has stolen
Bacchis from him, to give her to Ctesipho, his country brother.
Till this point, all has been dignified: then Aeschinus, with his
slave Parmeno, appears—in our production from the street
outside—ushering Bacchis in before him. Sannio rushes after
them wildly:

Sa.: Obsecro, populares, ferte misero atque innocenti auxilium,
subvenite inopi. . . .

(II. i. 1-2)

But perhaps the most exquisite scene is the one where Demea
meets his old friend Hegio—one of the old school. In the midst
of his distress about Aeschinus he is greatly relieved to see him:

De.: sed quis illic est procul quem video? estne Hegio
tribuli' noster? si sati' cerno is est hercle. vah,
homo amicu' nobis iam inde a puero! di boni!

219

ne illi modi iam magna nobis civium
penuriast antiqua virtute ac fide.
haud cito mali quid ortum ex hoc sit publice.
quam gaudeo! ubi etiam huiu' generi' reliquias
restare video, vivere etiam nunc lubet.

(III. iii. 84-91)

But Hegio is no consolation to Demea: he is utterly shocked,
not so much at Aeschinus's seduction of Pamphila, but because he
has heard that Aeschinus is trying to back out of marrying her.
He condones the seduction itself as follows:

He.:   nam hoc quidem ferundum aliquo modost:
persuasit nox amor vinum adulescentia:
humanumst.

(III. iv. 23-5)

As the conversation progresses, poor Demea becomes more and
more embarrassed; he turns to the audience:

De.: pudet: nec quid agam nec quid huic respondeam
scio.

(*Ibid.*, 39-40)

The scene so far is fully masculine, concerned above all with
social forms and obligations: suddenly the air is pierced with
shrieks from inside the house. Pamphila is in the throes of
childbirth:

Pa.:   miseram me, differor doloribus!
Iuno Lucina, fer opem! serva me obsecro!

For a moment the male world is at a total loss, confronted with
this event. Hegio's response to the situation is unforgettable
(particularly the '*quaeso*'):

He.:   hem!
numnam illa quaeso parturit?

I could not bear to depart from Terence, and was already
rehearsing to myself the opening scene of the *Heauton Timorumenos*,
having fallen in love with its first line, before the last performance
of the *Adelphi* was over.

VII. THE *HEAUTON TIMORUMENOS*

The plot of the *Heauton Timorumenos* is immensely complicated,
involving many a double and treble bluff, yet the character of

Chremes holds the whole play together; and we were very lucky with our Chremes.

Terence himself, in his own prologue to the play, states his definite policy of avoiding all the 'gimmicks' and vulgarities of his rivals: this is to be a *stataria fabula*. There is not much action in the play, but the beauty of the soliloquies and dialogue is unsurpassed, and the Latinity of it was a sheer joy even, I think, to those who could only follow in part.

The first scene is perhaps the most memorable. It is evening: Chremes, a comfortable old man, is giving a *Dionysia*-party, sounds of which emerge each time the door of his house is opened. He comes out for a breath of air, and sees his new neighbour Menedemus working hard in his garden. He cannot at once make up his mind whether to speak to him or not, but being an inveterate busybody he decides to do so: he goes over to Menedemus, and starts up a little apologetically with many a construction, parenthesis, and awkwardly placed word:

Ch.: Quamquam haec inter nos nuper notitia admodumst
        (inde adeo quod agrum in proxumo hic mercatus es)
        nec rei fere sane amplius quicquam fuit,
        tamen vel virtus tua me vel vicinitas,
        (quod ego in propinqua parte amicitiae puto)
        facit ut te audacter moneam et familiariter,
        quod mihi videre praeter aetatem tuam
        facere et praeter quam res te adhortatur tua.

                                            (I. i. 1-8)

He cannot bear to see Menedemus working so unnecessarily hard at his age, and though he receives no encouragement, he warms to his task:

Ch.: nam pro deum atque hominum fidem quid vis tibi aut
        quid quaeris? annos sexaginta natus es
        aut plus eo, ut conicio. . . .

                                            (*Ibid.*, 9-11)

He continues in this vein for over ten more lines. At last Menedemus can take no more: he is surprised that Chremes has so much spare time to worry about other people's affairs. Chremes retorts with possibly the most famous line in Latin literature:

Ch.: homo sum: humani nil a me alienum puto.

                                            (I. i. 25)

Eventually he persuades Menedemus to tell him why he is tormenting himself—and the plot is well under way. This is not the place to enter into its complexities: suffice it to say that at the beginning of the play Chremes is shown as a kindly but very smug self-made old man: he is celebrating the *Dionysia:* all is well with him, and he knows it: in fact, as Menedemus has said, he has plenty of time and energy at his disposal for the running of other people's lives—always, of course, with the very best intentions possible, and with never a doubt of his own full control of the situation. Menedemus, at the start, is very different: he is clearly a 'gentleman'; far more introspective than Chremes and far more sensitive. He is punishing himself for his harshness to his son Clinia, by which he has forced him to run away from home and become a soldier. He is in utter misery, in the absence of his son, about whom he worries all the time: he will not even celebrate the *Dionysia.* We tried to bring out the contrast between the two old men's affairs by having Chremes' house fully decorated with fairy lights, balloons and paper decorations, while Menedemus's remained bare and empty.

Throughout the play, we all know only too well how Chremes is being thoroughly fooled by his clever slave, Syrus, a deep-dyed rogue. He is sympathizing with Menedemus for the bad behaviour of his son and the financial loss incurred by it, sublimely unaware of the fact—well-known to all eventually before himself—that his own son Clitipho has behaved much worse than Clinia and has involved him in a far worse plight. In this wonderful blindness of Chremes lies the genius of the play; it is frighteningly convincing: one could hardly imagine a more universal comic character than Chremes. Through maze after maze of plot and counter-plot he is led, thinking all along that he is leading, till at last he discovers the truth: here for a moment the play is almost tragic: Menedemus is gently teasing Chremes, upon whom it dawns that Bacchis, the expensive courtesan, is his own son Clitipho's mistress and not Clinia's, as he had been induced to think:

Ch.: quid postquam hoc est factum?
Me.:   dictum factum huc abiit Clitipho.
Ch.: solu'?
Me.:   solu'.
Ch.:   timeo.
Me.:   Bacchi' consecutast ilico.

Ch.: sola?
Me.:   sola.
Ch.:   perii.
Me.:   ubi abiere intro, operuere ostium.
Ch.:   hem
        Clinia haec fieri videbat?
Me.:   quidni? mecum una simul.
Ch.: fili est amica Bacchi': Menedeme, occidi.

                                        (V. i. 31-5)

But Chremes has not the stuff of tragedy in him; in the next line we see that his first concern is for his bank balance:

Me.: quam ob rem?
Ch.:   decem dierum vix mi est familia.

In the earlier scenes of the play, Chremes had deplored Menedemus' lack of balance and wisdom. He blames both Menedemus and Clinia for an unfortunate misunderstanding; his first comment upon Menedemus' heart-rending confidences is:

Ch.: ambo accusandi. . . . (I. i. 67)

Later he sums up Menedemus's situation as follows, while Menedemus listens humbly:

Ch.:   verum nec tu illum sati' noveras
        nec te ille; hoc qui fit? ubi non vere vivitur.
        tu illum numquam ostendisti quanti penderes
        nec tibi illest credere ausu' quae est aequom patri.
        quod si esset factum, haec numquam evenissent tibi.
Me.: ita res est, fateor: peccatum a me maxumest.

                                        (I. i. 101-6)

How fully now are the tables turned. In Act V Chremes is far more unbalanced than ever Menedemus was before:

Ch.: at ne illud haud inultum, si vivo, ferent!
        nam iam . . .
Me.:   non tu te cohibes? non te respicis?
        non tibi ego exempli sati' sum?
Ch.:   prae iracundia,
        Menedeme, non sum apud me.
Me.:   tene istuc loqui!
        nonne id flagitiumst te aliis consilium dare,
        foris sapere, tibi non posse te auxiliarier?

                                        (V. i. 45-50)

                        223

During this last act, Menedemus is celebrating the marriage of his son, Clinia. Now his house is decorated, the lights are shining and there is dignified music inside, while Chremes' decorations look faded and his lights are no longer on.

I should perhaps mention one big problem in connexion with this play, and its solution. At the beginning of Act II, Sc. iii, Syrus and Dromo arrive well in advance of Bacchis and her *ancillae*, whom they are apparently escorting. Syrus is worried at having outstripped these women. In fact Bacchis and the *ancillae* do not appear till line 135 of this scene; they are known to be bringing great loads of luggage with them, far more than any modern *ancillae* could have plausibly carried: yet if they were travelling in a motor-vehicle, why would Syrus be so worried about their welfare? Besides, what manageable motor-vehicle could have housed the great numbers implied by the '*ancillarum grex*' referred to in line 4 of the scene? After much thought we decided to have the *ancillae* on foot and the luggage brought in on a horse and cart. It was the text which made this necessary, and not the desire to produce a 'gimmick'. Nevertheless, I need hardly say that the horse, which came with its owner to two dress-rehearsals and four performances, was a great favourite with cast and audience alike.

Another smaller problem was that the action of the play starts in the evening, while Act III starts with Chremes busily furthering his schemes the next morning: yet our performance starts while it is still light, but by Act III artificial lights are in operation. How could we bring home the fact that it was morning? We decided to make Chremes speak the opening lines of the act ('luciscit hoc iam . . .') from his bedroom-window, passing an electric razor over his face.

Yet again, in Act III, Sc. i, line 89, Chremes says he will postpone an appointment with Simus and Crito over a boundary dispute, in order to deal with Menedemus's affairs. He does not go off till line 93, and by line 99 he has returned. What were we to do about this? We solved it by having a public telephone, most courteously lent by the General Post Office, in the acting area. Even so it must have been a very brief conversation!

The *Heauton Timorumenos* was the first play during which it rained heavily; the large marquee which we now have for most of the audience fully justified itself. The actors continued gallantly, and the play went on to its end, where Chremes, more or less fully recovered, forces poor Clitipho to make a sensible marriage.

We took this play in August to a Delphiade or festival of ancient plays performed by student-companies from many countries and held that year in Mainz as part of the city's bimillennial celebrations. The Prologue and Epilogue of the Westminster production dealt largely with the coming Delphiade, and we wrote a special prologue for the Mainz performance itself dealing with the bimillennium. Our whole production had to be geared to a normal stage in one day, but we managed to do this largely through the magnificent support of the theatre staff, who had—*inter alia*—prepared some beautiful scenery for us. In spite of the many drastic changes which a conventional stage imposed upon us, the essence of the performance remained unchanged.

VIII. CONCLUSION

What is the essence of our performances? It is hard for me to speak of this myself. I can only say what I hope is it. Before doing so, however, I must express my gratitude to the host of helpers, professional and non-professional, boys and adults, whose attention to dress, make-up, props, lights, and innumerable details is essential to the success of a play. I have always been amazed by the unselfishness with which people have contributed to the production without any hope of achieving any limelight or even of being acknowledged at all; and herein lie some of the pleasantest and happiest memories I have of our plays.

We read the play in the forms from which the cast is to be chosen a term before the performance, and start rehearsals about eleven weeks or so before it. This gives us time to concentrate on correctness and clarity of diction, but not so much time that we become stale or stereotyped. Above all, none of us would ever dream of thinking of the play as a 'piece of literature', a relic of academic interest, a revival of something dead: to us, the language is alive and the play is alive. People have said to me after performances that the boys seem to speak Latin as if it were a living language, and this is—in my experience—what impresses the audience most.

How is this achieved? I can well see that the producer of one of the earlier Greek tragedies must have a complete vision of the effect he wishes to create before he starts, and that his actors must submit themselves entirely to his direction: the result at its best is a wonderful stylized fresco, dignified and monolithic. Latin Comedy is in itself, I submit, a more vital and universal achievement: it depends on no particular religious or patriotic background against which it is to be appreciated: it portrays all mankind at all times: it is far closer to the heart, far nearer the core of all of us. And how should the producer of such a Comedy approach his task? By making his actors realize from the start that he is not creating the play alone but that they are all part of a living organism: thus, the performance slowly matures into shape and acquires its own character *ambulando*. Above all, the producer must let Plautus and Terence speak to his cast themselves and breathe their abundant life into every voice and every gesture. Perhaps our 'secret' can best be expressed as the sure knowledge that Latin *is* a living language.

Index